BEHAVIOURAL SKILLS FOR EFFECTIVE POLICING

The Service Speaks

The editors and authors have kindly opted to donate all their royalties from this book to Police Care UK.

Police Care UK is a charity that has been supporting the police family, including officers, staff and volunteers, throughout the United Kingdom for over 90 years. We understand modern policing and the impact this has on those who protect our communities and aim to ensure both serving and former colleagues who suffer harm, and their families, have someone to turn to when things get tough. We identify and help fill gaps in care, provide support for those in need, and act as a lifeline for those who carry the physical and psychological scars of public service.

Our work wouldn't be possible without the generous support of fundraisers and donors and we thank all the authors of this book for donating to Police Care UK. Together we are building a future where no one suffering harm is left without help.

More information on our work is available at www.policecare.org.uk.

To order, or for details of our bulk discounts, please go to our website www.criticalpublishing.com or contact our distributor, Ingram Publisher Services (IPS UK), 10 Thornbury Road, Plymouth PL6 7PP, telephone 01752 202301 or email IPSUK.orders@ingramcontent.com.

BEHAVIOURAL SKILLS FOR EFFECTIVE POLICING

The Service Speaks

Edited by Mark Kilgallon and Martin Wright

First published in 2022 by Critical Publishing Ltd

All rights reserved. No part of this publication may be reproduced, stored in a retrieval system, or transmitted in any form or by any means, electronic, mechanical, photocopying, recording or otherwise, without prior permission in writing from the publisher.

The authors and editors have made every effort to ensure the accuracy of information contained in this publication, but assume no responsibility for any errors, inaccuracies, inconsistencies and omissions. Likewise, every effort has been made to contact copyright holders. If any copyright material has been reproduced unwittingly and without permission the Publisher will gladly receive information enabling them to rectify any error or omission in subsequent editions.

Copyright © 2022 Mike Barton, Julie Brierley, Dee Collins, Suzette Davenport, Peter Fahy, Judith Gillespie, Dave Hartley, Serena Kennedy, Will Kerr, Ashley Kilgallon, Mark Kilgallon, Brian Langston, Jim McAllister, Kate Moss, Peter Nicholas, Ken Pease, Cameron Thomson and Martin Wright

British Library Cataloguing in Publication Data
A CIP record for this book is available from the British Library

ISBN: 9781914171383
This book is also available in the following e-book formats:

EPUB ISBN: 9781914171390
Adobe e-book ISBN: 9781914171406

The rights of Mike Barton, Julie Brierley, Dee Collins, Suzette Davenport, Peter Fahy, Judith Gillespie, Dave Hartley, Serena Kennedy, Will Kerr, Ashley Kilgallon, Mark Kilgallon, Brian Langston, Jim McAllister, Kate Moss, Peter Nicholas, Ken Pease, Cameron Thomson and Martin Wright to be identified as the Authors of this work have been asserted by them in accordance with the Copyright, Design and Patents Act 1988.

Cover design by Out of House Limited
Text design by Greensplash Limited
Project Management by Deanta Global Publishing Services, Dublin, Ireland
Typeset by Deanta Global Publishing Services, Chennai, India
Printed and bound in Great Britain by 4edge, Essex

Critical Publishing
3 Connaught Road
St Albans
AL3 5RX

www.criticalpublishing.com

Paper from responsible sources

Contents

Meet the editors and authors — viii

Introduction — 1

PART 1 POLICING WITH AUTHORITY — 5

1. Inclusive UK policing: a personal perspective — 7
   Brian Langston

2. Building rapport — 27
   Peter Nicholas

PART 2 ORGANISATIONAL CULTURES — 45

3. Building emotional buy-in — 47
   Will Kerr

4. A culture of coaching to support the next big leaps in policing — 59
   Serena Kennedy and Cameron Thomson

5. Leading effective teams — 81
   Dee Collins

6. Challenging conversations — 99
   Suzette Davenport

PART 3 OPERATIONAL LEARNING — 121

7. Firearms: emotional management — 123
   David Hartley

8	Wise policing: soft skills and strong principles *Kate Moss and Ken Pease*	141
9	Public order: conflict resolution *Jim McAllister and Ashley Kilgallon*	161

PART 4   LEADING THE STRATEGIC NARRATIVE 183

10	Personal and organisational transformation *Mike Barton*	185
11	Creating the climate *Peter Fahy*	207
12	Ethics, values and standards *Judith K Gillespie*	221
13	Developing a learning culture and environment *Julie Brierley*	235

Index 255

Dedication

This book is dedicated to the memory of Professor P A J (Tank) Waddington, a critical friend of the police. He strongly believed police officers and staff should study and write about their professional practice, skills and knowledge. It is hoped he will be pleased with this book and the work of the authors.

Meet the editors and authors

Meet the editors

Mark Kilgallon

Mark Kilgallon has spent the last 25 years helping to develop leaders in the public and private sectors. He has substantial experience in creating testing executive development events that confront the challenges facing leaders within their environments. His unique work with the UK police service is recognised as world class. He works with individuals, teams, organisations and strategic partnerships to help them deliver their core purpose. He regularly writes and delivers programmes to senior leaders across the United Kingdom. Mark is an Honorary Professor at Nottingham Trent University with academic interests in formal and informal leadership, organisational cultures and power dynamics within teams. He is a regular leadership blogger.

Martin Wright

Martin Wright served in the police for 30 years and is the only police officer ever to be awarded a Doctoral Studentship by the Association of British Insurers. He is the creator of the community safety initiative, 'Retail Radio Links'. He is a visiting senior research fellow at the Canterbury Centre for Policing Research at Canterbury Christ Church University. He is currently the Managing Editor of the Oxford University Press journal *Policing: A Journal of Policy and Practice*.

Meet the authors

Mike Barton

Mike was a police officer within the Lancashire Constabulary, rising from Police Constable to Chief Superintendent. As Head of Crime in Lancashire he introduced Restorative Justice and led the training and introduction of Problem Oriented Policing (POP). He joined Durham Constabulary as ACC, was Deputy Chief Constable and, from 2012, Chief Constable. He led the successful implementation of Nimrod operations to close open drug markets, the investigation into a right-wing extremist plot and the regional development of serious crime investigation with a particular interest in prison intelligence. He is a regular contributor to BBC Breakfast as a reviewer of national newspapers and contributor on policing issues, and also works with the Durham University Leadership mentoring programme.

Julie Brierley

Julie is the senior lead for the learning and development service in North Wales Police with additional responsibility for leading a range of corporate workforce transformation projects and organisational development workstreams including resource management, performance and development, HR system development and improvement and implementation of the new entry routes within the Police Education Qualification Framework. Julie also spent time in learning and development for the East Midlands Police collaboration, working across Leicestershire, Nottinghamshire, Derbyshire and Northamptonshire Police Services to develop the collaborative service model. She is a Member of the Chartered Institute of Professional Development, an LGBT+ Ally and Co-Chair of the Welsh Police LGBT+ Network (North Wales Police Branch). As an ambassador for inclusivity and equality, Julie advocates for organisational and cultural development in the police service.

Dee Collins

Dee Collins was the Chief Constable of West Yorkshire Police between 2014 and 2019. Her career involved working within four different forces and latterly as the regional lead for forensics and counter-terrorism. Dee is passionate about inclusion and was the president of the British Association of Women in Policing, and also the NPCC lead for Gender. Dee's commitment to developing leaders of the future led her to her last policing role as the Policing Director of the Strategic Command Course in 2019. She is currently involved in a number of supporting policing roles including the Strategic Review of Policing Advisory Board with the Police Foundation.

Suzette Davenport

Suzette retired from policing in May 2017 after 31 years of service in five different forces. She worked at an executive level as a Chief Officer for 12 years and her last role was as Chief Constable of Gloucestershire Police. There she led the transformation of the policing model and the development of an open and engaged leadership approach, with a real focus on service to the public.

Peter Fahy

Sir Peter Fahy served as a police officer for 34 years in five police forces rising through the ranks to spend eight years as Chief Constable of Cheshire and five years as Chief Constable of Greater Manchester. He held a number of national responsibilities on counterterrorism, race and diversity and workforce development, and was elected Vice President of the Association of Chief Police Officers. He was Director of the Strategic Command Course at the Police Staff College for eight years and is a life member of the US Police Executives Research Forum. He has been involved in training police leaders in Uganda, Ethiopia, Malawi and India. On leaving policing he became chief executive of the street children charity Retrak, later merging the charity with Hope for Justice to address issues of child trafficking and modern slavery. He served on the Irish Government Commission on the Future of Policing and as advisor to the Home Affairs Select Committee.

Judith Gillespie

Judith served across a range of uniformed and detective disciplines within the Royal Ulster Constabulary. She presented *Crimecall*, the RUC's first weekly television crime prevention and detection programme, served as co-ordinator of child abuse and rape enquiry units, headed the drugs squad and participated in drafting the PSNI Code of Ethics. Judith made history as the first female in Northern Ireland policing to reach the rank of Assistant Chief Constable in 2004 and led on numerous initiatives and strategies. She Left PSNI in March 2014 having served for 32 years, 10 of which were as a Chief Officer. Post RUC/PSNI she became a Visiting Professor at the Ulster University Business School and has been appointed to a range of organisations and boards including the Equality Commission for Northern Ireland, the Probation Board for Northern Ireland, the Garda Policing Authority's Performance and Strategy Committee. She has been awarded the CBE for services to policing.

David Hartley

David Hartley is a serving Assistant Chief Constable with South Yorkshire Police. He is a Specialist Strategic Firearms Commander (SFC), and has been since 2015. He assesses SFC candidates on the College of Policing national Specialist Firearms Command Course. He is also a Gold Public Order Commander, Level 3 Critical Incident Commander and was a hostage negotiator and coordinator for 18 years. David has commanded 482 preplanned firearms operations to date, notably including the hunt for Raoul Moat and Dale Cregan. David has been the Independent Office for Police Conduct specialist advisor for a fatal police shooting. David has a passion for the psychology of command and performance under pressure.

Serena Kennedy

Serena started her career in policing in 1993 with Greater Manchester Police. Since then she has had a varied career across three forces. She started her service working in response, neighbourhood policing, intelligence and some time as a Detective up to the rank of Inspector. In 2008 she was promoted to Detective Chief Inspector with the Major Incident Team where she led teams of detectives investigating some of the most serious crimes including murders. In 2010 she became Superintendent in charge of partnerships and local policing in Moss Side and Longsight in Manchester. Two years later she returned to the Serious Crime Division as Detective Superintendent until she transferred Cheshire Constabulary as Chief Superintendent, Head of Public Protection. In 2017 Serena joined Merseyside Police as Assistant Chief Constable, Investigation and Intelligence, in 2018 she was promoted to Deputy Chief Constable, and in April 2021 became the first female Chief Constable to lead Merseyside Police. Serena is passionate about leadership and invests time coaching and mentoring people both regionally and nationally.

Will Kerr

Will Kerr has over 30 years of policing experience and, having started his policing career in Northern Ireland straight from university, has served as a Chief Officer in three national policing agencies across the UK. In the Police Service of Northern Ireland, Will was latterly the ACC responsible for counter-terrorism and serious crime. As a Director in the NCA he was responsible for coordinating the United Kingdom's international and domestic response to CSAE, modern slavery and human trafficking as well as organised immigration crime. Will is currently a DCC with Police Scotland, the second largest police service in the United Kingdom. As well as his primary degree, Will has master's degrees in human rights law, criminology and policing and community safety, as well as a number of other postgraduate qualifications. He has lectured on human rights law both domestically and internationally.

Ashley Kilgallon

Ashley Kilgallon completed her PhD at the University of Leeds. Her thesis, 'Performance and Dialogue', was an ethnographic study into police liaison teams (PLTs) and was fundamentally concerned with understanding how dialogue impacts social order within a public order setting. Since completing her thesis, Ashley has worked as the project manager of the MPS's deferred prosecution scheme, Turning Point.

Brian Langston

Brian is a retired Assistant Chief Constable from Thames Valley Police and rose through the ranks to become one of the most senior ethnic minority officers in British Policing. He was the founder and President of the Thames Valley Black Police Association and the only officer to have served on the National Executive of both the BPA and the Superintendents' Association. He was awarded the Queen's Police Medal in 2007 for his services to community policing. He currently runs a consultancy specialising in leadership and diversity.

Jim McAllister

Jim McAllister is a nationally recognised expert in public order policing, with extensive experience in crisis management, training design and consultancy. Jim has provided much guidance on a national and international platform in policing public order, public safety and event dynamics, alongside delivering training and operational consultancy in Sierra Leon, Bahrain, Trinidad, Lebanon and Uzbekistan.

Kate Moss

Kate is Professor of Applied Criminology at the University of Derby. She specialises in applied research, project management and income generation. She has led on research for numerous police forces, local authorities and charitable organisations throughout England. Working with the police she has provided policy inputs to the Home Office crime reduction unit both regionally and nationally and for the Policing and Reducing Crime Unit at the Home Office and National Police Training Units. She has provided crime and disorder training for Nottinghamshire, Hampshire, Greater Manchester and Sussex police forces. In 2002 Kate led a project for Nottinghamshire police identifying location and victim risk factors in relation to domestic burglary to produce an overall risk-based index, the first of its kind and in 2020 she carried out research into protracted disciplinary proceedings against police officers which has fed into the Police Federation's call for time limits on such cases.

Peter Nicholas

Peter is Director of PNA training: www.pnatraining.com. His background is in psychology, and people and business transformation. For over 25 years he has delivered impactful and innovative leadership programmes and one-to-one executive coaching to businesses around the world. He still retains his fascination for discovering what makes people tick, with a passion for seeing people and teams flourish and thrive. He believes real change only happens when people become the best coach they can be for themselves, full of self-awareness and compassion.

Ken Pease

Ken is a chartered forensic psychologist, still holding a licence to practise. Ken is currently Professor of Policing at Derby University and Visiting Professor at UCL, Loughborough and Manchester. He held chairs at the Universities of Manchester and Saskatchewan where he worked in the maximum security Regional Psychiatric Centre (Prairies). He has acted as Head of the Police Research Group at the Home Office and has been a member of the Parole Board for England and Wales. He was awarded the R V Clarke Prize by the Environmental Criminology Association in 2014 and has an Honorary Doctorate from Nottingham Trent University.

Cameron Thomson

Cameron is experienced in supporting organisations develop their culture, and works across several sectors including finance, health care, education, tourism, professional services and policing. He is an Institute of Leadership Management accredited coach, and he supports the personal development of leaders and their teams. Cameron is father of three boys and enjoys football, golf, running and reading. He credits his two retrievers with teaching him about the importance of creating an environment of psychological safety.

Introduction

Thanks

The editors wish to thank, most sincerely, the chapter authors for their contributions to this book. For many this has been the first time they have written such a chapter, while for others it forms part of a distinguished list of publications. It is important to note that the editors and authors have chosen to donate their royalties to a police charity and in so doing they thank you, the reader, for your kind support and contribution.

What is this book about?

When thinking about the many roles and responsibilities within the police it soon becomes apparent that to be effective when discharging their duties an officer or staff member needs to be a 'people person'. The officer will logically have to interact with individuals, families, groups and communities when they are experiencing some trauma or stress in their lives, such as being a victim of crime, offending when under the influence of alcohol or drugs or experiencing discrimination. The primary intention of this book is therefore to define and understand what these people skills (we call them behavioural skills) are that the police need to both possess and deploy to be truly effective. As a number of the authors note, there is a dearth of study and literature regarding such skills and this text therefore also seeks to promote enquiry into these behavioural or soft skills among both the service and academia. The importance of recognising and understanding these behavioural skills must be contrasted with the seemingly incessant focus upon the quantitative measurement of police performance. While it is accepted that any measurement of impact, for example of an officer engaging empathetically with a victim, will invariably be difficult to achieve, this does not and should not prove to be a barrier to the recognition and promotion of such core policing skills. The attention given by policy makers to the statistical measurement of such a people-based profession as policing is, we argue, at odds with those qualitative outcomes most desired by the police and those they serve.

The second key intention is to encourage the police service to both reflect upon but also write about its own professional practice. As the late P A J (Tank) Waddington once sadly reflected, *'Cops don't write'*. To that end the many contributions within this book, written by both serving and recently retired police officers and staff, highlight the importance of publishing the often self-critical reflections of those who have served. Finally, it is clear to the editors that for the police to truly transition to becoming and being recognised as a profession then its members should routinely undertake research into its own skills, practice and knowledge and thereafter publish the findings for wider scrutiny and assimilation. The inclusion of chapters authored by officers and staff from all four nations of the United Kingdom as well as those from constable to chief constable rank is therefore welcomed. As such, this text seeks to be a catalyst for redressing the imbalance between the wider enquiry and publication of police knowledge and skills by academics and policy makers rather than those serving. It is hoped, this will promote the professionalisation of the police. In summary, the book aims to be a core text that centres upon the more transformational aspects of effective policing – the so-called soft skills!

Book structure and content

This book comprises a number of discreet chapters written by notable academics, coaches and police leaders who have experienced the challenges of operating within highly complex environments. The chapter authors have been specifically asked to express their views on their chosen topic matter; to recount or create some scenarios that encourage you to think your way through a problem; give practical examples of where they have dealt with issues in the past; and summarise the key points they want to impart. At the conclusion of each chapter some of the authors have offered suggestions as to further reading that will hopefully encourage you to move from thinking about behavioural skills to practically engaging with them in policing.

The textbook is divided into four parts that reflect the policing career journey.

1. Policing with authenticity.
2. Organisational cultures.
3. Operational learning.
4. Leading the strategic narrative.

It is hoped that this organisation will allow all readers, acknowledging that you come from a range of backgrounds and interests, to engage with the varying nature and application of policing behavioural skills.

- Part 1, Policing with authenticity, is more universal in application and should be of particular interest to undergraduate policing degree students, pre-join as well as newly appointed police officers and staff. They are also vital components to the success of policing and as such are fundamental in shaping the future of the service.

- Part 2, Organisational cultures, is intended to be of maximum utility and impact for first- and second-line leaders and managers. The chapters in this section also give a sound foundation for leaders as they progress in their leadership journey and can be applied at all levels.

- Part 3, Operational learning, is suggested to be primarily of interest to command level police leaders.

- Part 4, Leading the strategic narrative, is primarily targeted at those involved in strategic leadership.

However, every section of this book has something to offer any police officer or member of police staff regardless of rank and role including those with a wider interest in the study of policing and its place in society.

Conclusion

This text is purposefully focused on bridging the gap between theory and practice – between strategy and action – and therefore has a highly practical approach, clearly contextualising the range of behavioural skills. It is hopefully the beginning of a more informed debate around the 'truth' of the essence of professional practice and human interaction, a book written by the service for the service. In conclusion, it is sincerely hoped that it will promote a number of professional and academic reflections that may in time become the subject of further research and publications.

Mark Kilgallon and Martin Wright

Part 1
Policing with authority

1 Inclusive UK policing: a personal perspective

Brian Langston

CHAPTER OBJECTIVES

This chapter will help you:

- explore the relationship between UK policing and local communities particularly those communities from black and minority ethnic (BAME) backgrounds;
- examine and evaluate the various strategies adopted by UK policing to increase the diversity of the service;
- consider different approaches to embedding diversity and difference as a critical success factor within policing;
- explore strategies for moving from co-operation to co-production with local communities, with particular reference to black and minority ethnic communities.

Introduction

The death of George Floyd in 2020 in Minneapolis, United States, was far more than simply the latest in the line of fatal encounters between black men and the police; the Floyd case is differentiated from its predecessors by a number of factors. Taking place as it did in a nation led by arguably the most inflammatory president in its history, the speed with which the shock waves crossed the Atlantic via the power of social media led to unprecedented unrest in the United Kingdom, a country still divided after its own acrimonious split with Europe. Add to this mix, the context of a global pandemic which itself has created tensions between the police and the community and the police service once again finds itself at a crossroads about its future role in society.

Should the British police service, unique in its tradition of policing by consent, continue to strive towards regaining the trust and confidence of the *whole* of society or abandon its community policing ambitions in favour of a purely reactive enforcement role?

This chapter argues strongly in favour of the former but challenges the fiercely held assumptions upon which the service has based its community relations and recruitment strategy for decades. By examining the problematic relationship between the police and the citizen, particularly those from BAME backgrounds, the author argues that a fundamental rethink is required of its relationship with the community. Furthermore, the way in which the service approaches the subject of Equality, Diversity and Inclusivity (EDI) is in need of a radical overhaul if the concept of a community-based police service is to survive into future generations.

The futile quest

Although there are many positive aspects to the police culture such as the can-do attitude which still permeates the service and the bond of the 'Thin Blue Line' which is readily in evidence particularly when an officer is injured or killed, the media perception of the police culture is portrayed as overwhelmingly negative. Much of this has been fuelled by its reluctance to depart from the traditional image of policing. Originally recruited more for brawn than brain, the police service has clung for too long to an outdated authoritarian and paternalistic image which has often been at odds with more contemporary ideas on inclusivity. It took until the late twentieth century for the police service to finally abandon the archaic notions of height limits and age requirements and come to terms with the fact that female officers were quite capable of patrolling alone.

Other aspects of diversity and inclusivity, however, remain a challenge. Despite its ambition to reflect the community it serves, the police service still seems to have difficulty accepting people who do not conform to the idealistic and wholly fictional image of the 'Bobby on the Beat'. Therefore, people with alternative lifestyles, unusual appearance or those who simply shun convention will find it very difficult indeed to get through their doors, let alone make progress within the service.

Far from being typically representative of the general public, the selection criteria for police officers actively weeds out the unconventional and unorthodox, insisting on strict standards of appearance covering hairstyles, make-up, piercings, jewellery and tattoos. Furthermore, factors such as disability, mental and physical health, drug and alcohol use, financial solvency and criminal history are scrutinised in forensic detail together with those of close family and associates.

This recruitment funnel creates a very narrow field for selection indeed and the attrition rate is very high even before we have considered the latest requirement to hold or obtain a university degree. It should not therefore be surprising that those who survive the intensive and intrusive triage are *not* representative of the average citizen. To expect them also to be ethnically diverse in the same proportion as the local population is both unrealistic and unnecessary.

Therefore, even before we begin to consider ethnicity, we have already filtered out a great deal of the 'representative' population. If we also factor-in a pattern of working rotating shifts, in all weathers, unarmed and often alone in the most violent and life-threatening of situations, under the scrutiny of everyone with a mobile phone, while wearing a funny hat, we begin to understand why the police service is not the career choice of everyone. Indeed, it takes a very special person indeed to become a good police officer. Few who satisfy the qualifying requirements have an *aptitude* for the work. Fewer still have the right *attitude* for the job. We are fortunate in the UK, despite what the media would have us believe, to have the best police service in the world bar none.

Few would argue against the Peelian principle that the police service should aspire to represent the community it serves. Indeed, the goal of creating an ethnically representative police force has been at the heart of government policy for almost 50 years. Despite an unprecedented number of initiatives, targets and public inquiries, the impact has been underwhelming.

Although the situation has improved since the landmark Stephen Lawrence Inquiry in 1999 (Macpherson, Sir William (1999) The Stephen Lawrence Inquiry) when 2 per cent of the service was BAME compared to 6.5 per cent of the population, the current position of 7.3 per cent, compared with the UK population as a whole of 14 per cent, does not represent a particularly impressive return on investment. No other agency has made such strenuous efforts to become 'representative', and yet hitting this moving target becomes increasingly difficult as society becomes increasingly diverse.

REFLECTIVE PRACTICE

- Consider why the collective efforts of one of the greatest 'can-do' cultures in public service have failed to solve this intractable problem.

An emotional connection

Perhaps one of the reasons may be because the premise upon which it is based is fundamentally flawed. The police do not have to mirror the community they serve – at least not in terms of 'identity' diversity. As a convenient proxy for 'diversity' the government has determined that anyone with black or brown skin will suffice and has set targets for local recruitment accordingly, ranging from 40 per cent for London to less than 1 per cent in the North of England.

The concept of having a 'rainbow' police service perfectly reflecting the community is unrealistic, unachievable and misguided. This approach is a throwback to an archaic view that the way to tackle discrimination and thereby change attitudes is simply to co-opt minorities into organisations. This, however, fails to recognise the power of the underlying culture and the weight of the dead hand of the status quo. To continue to pursue, this futile quest, in today's complex multi-layered society, will continue to result in disappointment. A more radical approach to equality, diversity and inclusivity (EDI) is called for which is less about counting heads and more about making heads count.

I know from first-hand experience that there have been incidents when being from a visible ethnic minority has undoubtedly given me an advantage with minority communities. (I include a couple of examples in the case studies later in this chapter.) Usually this has been because the 'novelty value' has piqued their curiosity and given me a valuable but brief window of opportunity to shatter the stereotypical views they might hold about the police. It may have been my *appearance* that allowed me to get a foot in the door, but it was my *attitude* that made the sale. It was my character and not my colour that capitalised on that opportunity to build rapport, change perceptions and dislodge prejudice.

The police cannot physically represent every facet of society within its ranks, but they should be able to provide an equitable and responsive service to everyone, providing those within its ranks have the necessary emotional intelligence (EQ) to be able to empathise with those in need. It is a shocking omission that EQ forms no part in the selection of police officers. Instead, the current policy simply assumes that skin colour carries with it an automatic empathy towards minority communities and will thereby transmit a warm glow of trust and confidence by simply being present within an organisation.

Defining the issues: hire for attitude

In order to change the monolithic culture, the service needs to begin with a much broader interpretation of diversity than the one currently employed by the Home Office in its superficial obsession with an increased BAME head count. EDI extends far beyond the narrow reach of the nine 'protected characteristics' of the Equality Act (Equality Act 2010) and encompasses the much-neglected diversity of thought.

Cognitive diversity explains why there are thousands of white police officers held in the highest regard by minority communities. These are the people who have high levels of emotional intelligence, self-awareness and empathy. They are able to quickly build a rapport with the person in front of them, regardless of their background, and develop a level of trust which transcends the suspicion with which they may initially be viewed. They feel the pain of the people before them and act accordingly. These qualities do not automatically come with skin colour. Surprisingly, given its potential for building positive relationships, emotional intelligence has never been an explicit pre-requisite for a police officer and is a competency which remains to a large extent, unmeasured in police recruiting and promotion processes. This significant omission helps to explain the drift away from a people-centred serviced towards one which is task-focused and process-driven.

Cognitive diversity, also referred to as neuro-diversity, is often overlooked in EDI debates and yet it allows people who *think* differently and break away from the mould and shape their service in a way which will enhance people's lives. Professor Scott Page in his landmark book *The Difference 2007* argues in favour of a greater recognition of the value of cognitive diversity, encouraging as it does multiple perspectives stemming from the cultural differences between group or organisational members resulting in creative problem solving and innovation. It is the polar opposite to the command-and-control culture which has dominated the police service for the past century and a half. These are the 'Wicked Thinkers' who are not bound by standard operating procedures but think laterally, creatively and flexibly and tailor a bespoke resolution for specific problems rather than look for a one-size-fits-all solution.

In order to inject much-needed innovation, the service needs to adopt the policy of hiring for attitude and training for skill, but it does not need to start from scratch. The British police service is a world-class organisation in terms of its commitment and dedication to the public. Contrary to popular belief, police officers are not all the same. Within their ranks lies a rich seam of great diversity of thought which is all too often constrained by policy, politics and the press. Ironically their cognitive diversity is frequently inhibited by the spectre of political correctness leaving them fearful of being accused of the latest 'ism'.

Even at senior levels, officers are so weary of being under the diversity cosh that they keep their heads down, noses clean and hope by not mentioning the 'D' word they won't make a career-limiting gaffe. In fact, the opposite is true, equality, diversity and inclusivity should be openly discussed in the streets, workplaces and locker rooms and not driven underground. It should be recognised for the valuable resource it is, far wider than the dusty and outdated view of diversity espoused by the Home Office. It is a source of infinite innovation and creativity and the antidote to the all-too-common monolithic aspects of the police culture where the status quo rarely yields to originality.

Belongingness and uniqueness: a model for consideration

Amy E Randel et al (2018) argue that inclusivity is achieved when *uniqueness* is truly valued, and a sense of genuine *belongingness* is brought together within an organisational framework. Applying their four-box model to the police service (see below), it is possible to chart the different approaches taken to EDI over the past generation and suggest how uniqueness and belongingness could be harnessed to create a sustainable culture of inclusivity for the next generation.

In examining each approach, I will take the liberty of overlaying my personal experiences of living through these phases as a BAME police officer in a busy provincial force during a period of unprecedented change and turbulence for the service from 1980 to 2010.

Exclusion

During my formative years the prevailing culture of the police was very machismo, and overt racism, sexism and homophobia were endemic. There was no appetite for changing the profile of recruits because the system worked perfectly well as it was. There was little meaningful oversight and very limited accountability. The role of women was starting to expand in the wake of the 1975 Sex Discrimination Act, although it remained tokenistic and paternalistic for many years afterwards. A height limit for recruits remained in force, a throwback to its Victorian heritage of recruiting brawn rather than brain where 'looking the part' was the most important attribute. Although the Race Relations Act had been passed in 1976, it was almost a decade before it began to make its presence felt in the police service. Ethnic minorities like me in the police were few and far between and certainly none existed in senior ranks.

For me joining as a newly married 18½ year-old with a teenage stepdaughter, the two-year probationary period was a sword of Damocles hanging over my head. I had spent the previous year on the dole living hand to mouth on a notorious crime-ridden council estate in the Black Country unable to find work. The local force, who had a regular presence on the estate arresting our neighbours, seemed less than keen to have me join them. I stuck a pin in a map and ended up in a force a hundred miles south who were fortunately desperate to recruit all-comers. Failing my probation was not an option. It would mean homelessness, unemployment and return to poverty for me and my family. Putting up with overt and outrageous racism and smiling sweetly through gritted teeth at racist jibes even from supervisors seemed therefore a small price to pay until I secured my position.

Arriving in such a totally alien environment, I felt very much an outsider. When joining an authoritarian and hierarchical organisation with such a strong culture like the police, the overwhelming desire is to fit in as soon as possible and demonstrate your worth to your team.

This was exacerbated by the knowledge that when you called for urgent assistance, you could not afford for your colleagues to take 'the scenic route'. This was an issue of survival in every sense of the word. My feeling of belonging was very low and anyone displaying difference from the 'norm' was treated with suspicion and certainly not valued by either the team or the organisation. This was a culture of *Exclusion* (see Figure 1.1) specifically designed to weed out those who lacked the necessary resilience to do the job.

'If you haven't got a sense of humour, you shouldn't have joined the job' was a common refrain and was used to justify all manner of outrageous treatment to those who were not valued.

In common with all of my peer group of probationers, the majority of whom were white, it was considered part of the suitability testing process to endure what we would now recognise as bullying. Although mine often took on a racist element, all kinds of abuse were justified on the basis that it was character building, and I would get worse out on the streets. I never did.

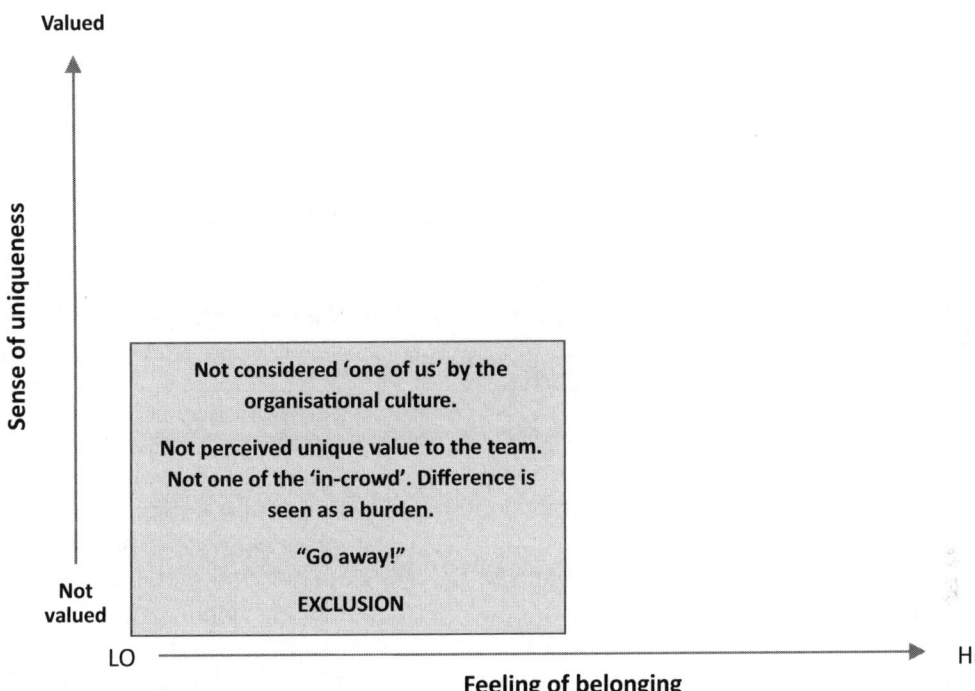

Figure 1.1 Exclusion

I remained like a fish out of water in the bottom left-hand corner of the model and survived because I knuckled down and didn't make a fuss. I played the game, rolled with the punches and went along with the exclusionary banter and became accepted within the culture. Over a period of two years, I became accepted and slowly moved across to the bottom right of the model to become assimilated.

Assimilation

In the wake of the Brixton Riots in 1985, community and race relations began to feature more strongly in the policing lexicon. The Scarman Report had castigated the service for poor engagement with minority communities and pushed the service to be more representative of the community it serves. The Home Office interpretation was to set targets to increase ethnic minority recruits.

Although purporting to embrace diversity, the practical application within the service was that you would be accepted providing you downplayed your differences and conformed to the dominant culture. During this period, the service saw hundreds of recruits enthusiastically ushered in through the front door only to leave disaffected within a very short period of time through the back door.

14 • *Behavioural Skills for Effective Policing*

To a greater or lesser extent this situation of 'conditional diversity' remains the case in many places around the country. Difference is recognised at the recruiting stage but should remain in the locker room when the corporate mantle of uniformity is donned while on duty. People will feel they belong providing they behave and conform. However, their sense of uniqueness is given a low value. The mantra here is very much 'You're one of us now!'

I found it easier than many in my position to become assimilated. Although I was mixed race I had been brought up by a single white parent. Assimilation was more difficult for those whose 'difference' was more evident either because of their darker skin, foreign name or strong Asian accent. I saw Black and Asian officers fall by the wayside either driven out through an inability to cope with the hostile culture or kicked out as having a 'chip on their shoulder' for trying to resist it.

In the years that followed I established myself as an operationally capable and competent officer and became more confident in returning to my core values and challenging what I considered to be unacceptable behaviour. After I embarked upon my promotion journey, I occasionally encountered it at senior levels. One example being a Chief Superintendent who six times blocked my application for promotion to Inspector despite being strongly recommended by my line management chain. When he moved on, I was finally successful on the seventh attempt. It was not until 20 years later when personal files were opened up, did I discover the line in the confidential feedback that had scuppered my aspirations.

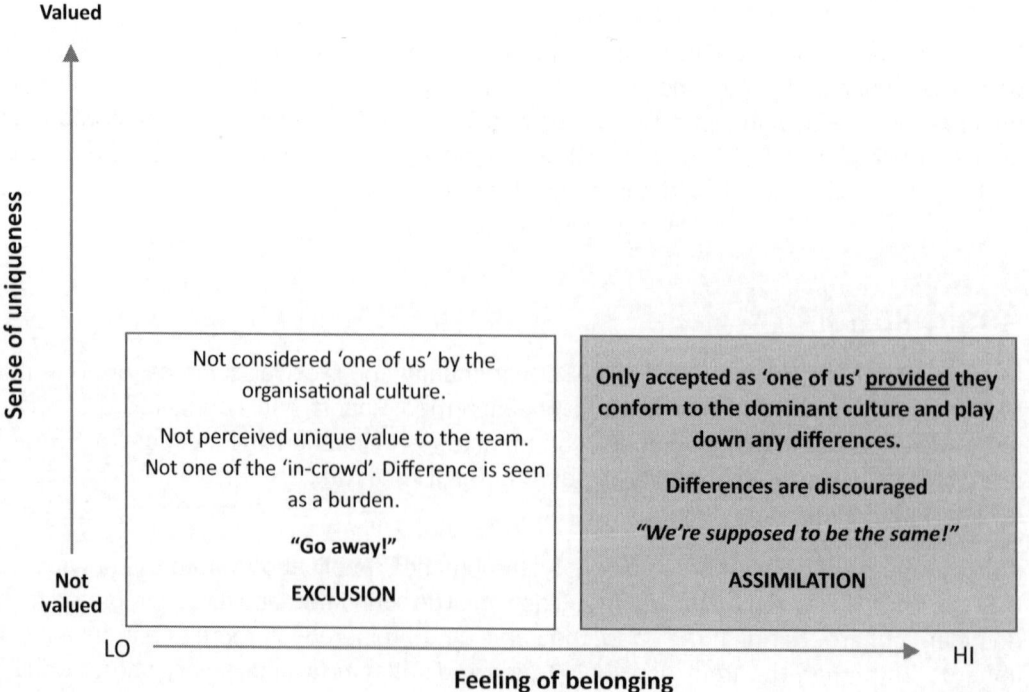

Figure 1.2 *Assimilation*

Sergeant Langston is undoubtedly a bright, intelligent and articulate officer, but there is something about him I don't like. Not recommended!

I never did find out what it was, but I could hazard a guess! My ascent up the promotion ladder continued steadily and I remained in the Assimilation box although never feeling completely in step with the organisation but having the confidence to challenge the status quo. This was tolerated only by virtue of having proved myself as operationally credible over the decades.

Differentiation

A palpable shift in culture occurred after the murder of Stephen Lawrence and the publication of the damning public inquiry report in 1999. This rocked the service to its foundations. Labelled for the first time as institutionally racist, the police service was left with little option but to undertake radical change to improve the way it dealt with both minority communities and those ethnic minorities within its own ranks who were receiving detrimental treatment.

The Home Office response was predictably to impose further targets on forces to recruit more officers from BAME backgrounds in order to reflect the diversity of local populations. This was crudely interpreted as little more than trying to recruit as many non-white people as possible. This strategy has remained unchallenged for over 20 years and progress has been tortuously slow, hampered in part by further high-profile service failures to deal with EDI-related issues.

Over the past two decades the ethnic and cultural diversity of the nation has expanded exponentially. The 2020 census shows 270 different ethnic groups currently resident in the UK with over 300 languages being spoken on our streets every day. Which of these then do we expect to be represented amongst the ranks of our police?

Exactly how the presence of melanin alone translates into increased community confidence has never been articulated. In a nation of such kaleidoscopic diversity a policy of 'representation' based on pigmentation alone is an absurd strategy to pursue.

Much of the police service languishes in the 'Differentiation' quadrant at the current time, acknowledging the necessity to embrace difference but not entirely sure of what to do with it when they have it.

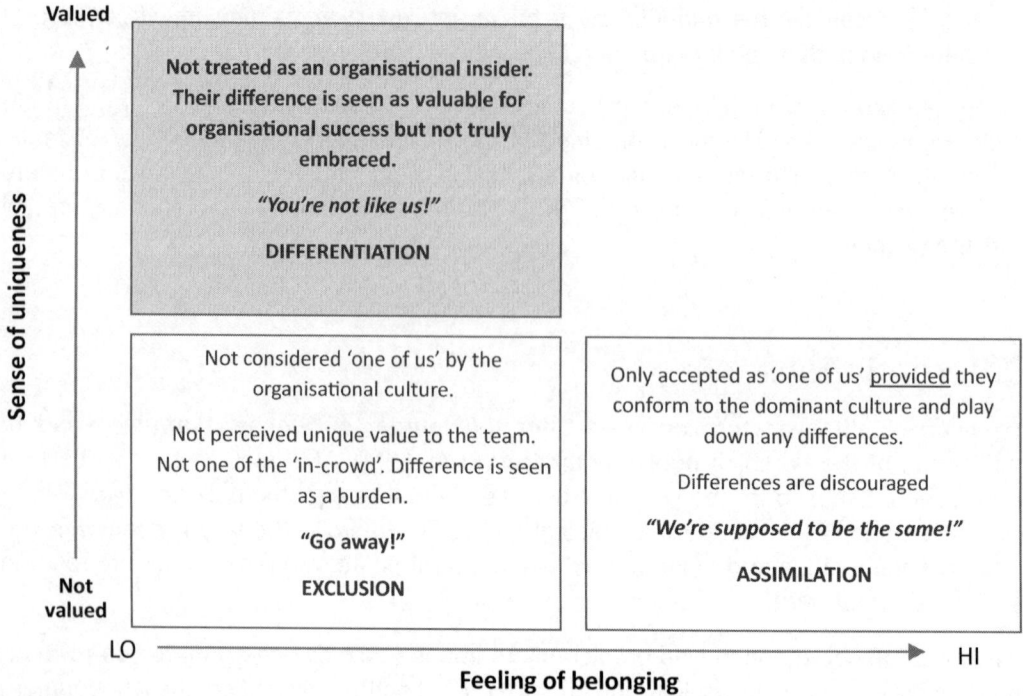

Figure 1.3 Differentiation

Inclusion

Organisationally BAME officers and staff are recognised as representing valuable political capital, essential to secure a community mandate and, in this sense, they are valued. All too often, however, they are seen as delicate flowers which have taken years to nurture to fruition and are to be protected at all costs. They are valued but more for decoration and aesthetic appearance than as organisational or operational assets. Herriot and Pemberton (1995) describe this approach as akin to nouvelle cuisine with several elements carefully displayed on a plate with the diner never quite sure which are contributing to the meal and which are solely for decoration. The service must ensure that the full diversity of its talent is properly developed and effectively utilised and not isolated from operational exposure like a skilfully carved vegetable.

The policing lack of confidence around discussing EDI issues and the misguided fear of grievances are just some of the reasons why managers shy away from giving BAME officers the essential developmental feedback they need to achieve their full potential. As a result, their progress is often hampered as they are 'damned with faint praise' at appraisal time placing them at a disadvantage to their white counterparts who benefit from 'straight-talking' from their (largely) white managers. In truth the service has not yet reached the level of organisational maturity where inclusivity has advanced beyond piecemeal pockets of good practice.

Whether ethnically or cognitively diverse, the police service has experienced difficulty in retaining people who think differently. Unfortunately, progression to the final quadrant of 'Inclusion' continues to evade much of the police service. Despite a myriad of well-intentioned EDI initiatives and worthy statements of intent, progress towards true inclusivity remains frustratingly slow. The fact remains that the service is not tolerant to difference and the dominant culture may have moved from command and control but remains predominantly one of comply and conform.

The service recruits with a certain type of citizen already in mind. Those who challenge the status quo and accepted stereotype are often sidelined or driven out or languish in silence having failed to achieve their potential. The social filters applied to potential recruits have already been discussed which weed out those citizens deemed to be unsuitable. Further changes in recent years such as police forces only accepting applicants who currently live in the force area has also impacted on diversity by limiting the recruiting pool for potential applicants. In an effort to elevate what is seen as a trade rather than a profession by many communities, the police service has now imposed a requirement for a degree for recruits (College of Police: Police Education Qualifications Framework 2020). It remains to be seen whether this will help or hinder diversity across the service.

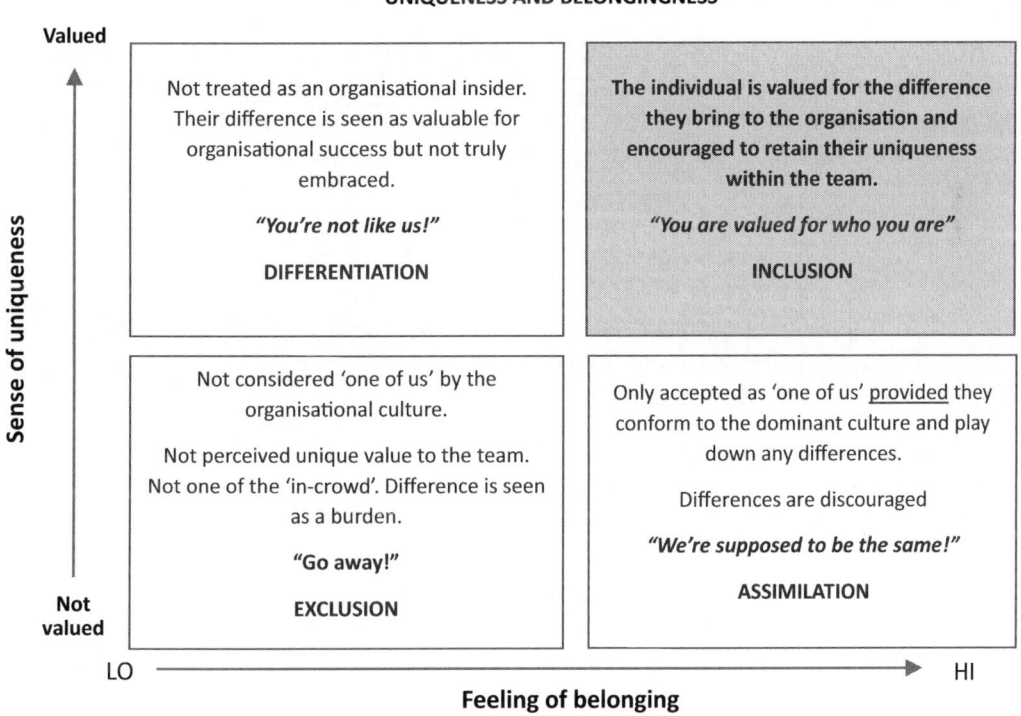

Figure 1.4 *Inclusion*

> **REFLECTIVE PRACTICE**
>
> - How can policing create a culture where equality, diversity and inclusivity can be discussed openly and freely without fear of breaching political correctness?
> - How could the police force skill up managers to be confident enough to open up dialogue on EDI issues?

A way forward
BAME advancement within policing

Currently only 4 per cent of senior officers in the service are from a BAME background. Despite fast-track initiatives and direct-entry schemes designed to bring talent through at a faster pace (College of Policing: Fast Track and Direct Entry programme for Inspector and Superintendent), it is unlikely these schemes will yield significant changes to the upper echelons of the service in the short term. Indeed, the College of Policing pilot scheme is currently suspended pending a parliamentary review into its efficacy.

Progressing through traditional routes, it typically takes 20 years to grow an officer to Superintendent level and with the high attrition rate, it would require a great number of BAME officers with potential and a strong following wind to get one of them into the Superintending ranks, let alone to the level of Chief Officer. Aside from the conscious and unconscious bias that BAME officers often face within the police service there are a number of other systemic barriers which conspire to prevent their advancement. Foremost amongst these is the inexplicable obsession to cling to the monolithic legal memory tests before allowing officers to progress to any position of leadership. While the operational knowledge of practical police law and procedure is essential at all levels, this changes with such frequency that it should be dealt with as continuous professional development (CPD) throughout an officer's career.

The current system of Sergeant's and Inspector's OSPRE exam is no more than a snapshot test of the key legislation in force at the time and tests nothing more than the ability to absorb and regurgitate information. Taking my own case as an illustration, I passed the Inspector's exam as Sergeant in 1985. Over the subsequent 25 years I advanced to Assistant Chief Constable never being required to pass another law exam. My progression was enabled through CPD and operational application of leadership principles. Advancement should be based on merit not memory. The continued requirement to learn by rote legislation which could be accessed by a phone app seems unjustifiable. As Einstein once put it: 'Never memorise something you can look up'.

The limiting impact of a legislation-based exam cannot be overstated. I have seen the service miss out on generations of BAME (and white) leaders who could not get their heads around passing the OSPRE exam. This was not for want of cognitive ability, many were graduates capable of studying at high levels but found the exam, essentially a crude memory test, one which eluded them.

The role of Sergeant remains a pivotally important rank in the service and is the gateway through which everyone needs to pass in order to access all other leadership roles. In these volatile, uncertain and changing times we need more than ever to get the best people for the job into operational supervisory roles: those who think differently and act differently and who can inspire those around them to achieve their peak performance. Supervisors who have acquired practical skills on the streets and understand how to motivate a team to deliver a high-quality service to the community.

OSPRE in my experience has done a disservice to a generation of officers by squandering a wealth of talent and failing to capitalise on the unfulfilled potential that exists on the front line. This obsolete requirement has been a stumbling block for way too many highly capable officers and represents yet another institutional blocker to cognitive diversity in the service. The requirement to pass a legal exam as a pre-requisite for a position of leadership is long overdue for retirement and the College of Policing needs to act, before the potential of the next generation is cut off at source. OSPRE is a redundant barrier to entry and should be scrapped in favour of a system of ongoing CPD with a greater emphasis on the ability to motivate and lead a team under operational pressure to provide a better service to the community.

REFLECTIVE PRACTICE

- What are the fundamental blockages which have prevented the service from advancing to the next level in equality, diversity and inclusivity?
- What steps need to be taken to overcome these barriers in order to achieve a truly inclusive workforce?

Access all areas

At the same time of initiating transformational change internally, the same effort needs to take place externally. The service needs to be more trusting of the community and allow it greater access to influence and shape the service it wants to see. All too often the police are viewed more as a symbol of oppression than a public service with a customer focus. Despite all the progress the service has made, there is a mystique about what goes on within police stations. There are sections of the community that perceive people are still being routinely beaten up in police cells or that canteens (where they still exist) are a hotbed of racism, sexism and homophobia. In order to eradicate the mythology and quell the rumour mill, the police service needs to allow the community to shine a light into every corner of its work and get hands-on.

The service has made significant inroads in recent decades to involve trusted members of the community in the debrief of critical incidents. This approach, however, is by no means universal and because of a fear of further reputational damage and litigation (both personal and organisational), the service is not as open to share its mistakes as it could be. A cultural change is needed to open up the service to more scrutiny from the community especially when things have not gone well.

This is more than simply being an observer on lay visits and ride-along schemes but a paradigm shift to *co-production*. This means inviting your harshest critic to join you at the police station and help design and deliver a service which meets their needs. The process started decades ago with Independent Advisory Groups but many of these have become toothless talking shops or overly politicised. Co-production moves further along the continuum from co-operation and collaboration and provides true accessibility and engagement, actively empowering the community to have a significant influence on local policing policy and practice.

REFLECTIVE PRACTICE

- How can the people we have let down most be used to rebuild trust and confidence in the policing service they receive?

- How can victims or their friends and families be given an 'access all areas' pass into policing processes, policies and practices and actively help to re-shape service provision?

- How can we put the community in the driving seat without compromising operational independence and accountability?

CASE STUDY

Operation Comfort: a public order operation with a difference

What follows is a case study taken from my own experience as the local commander in the operationally demanding, multi-ethnic town of Slough just West of London. In each case, and against the conventional wisdom I endeavoured to put the community in the driving seat to play a significant role in the style of policing it received:

> During a period of heightened community tension following a terrorist outrage, Slough found itself targeted by far-right groups who sought to capitalise upon the fear and uncertainty within the community and exploit tensions within the town. Racist graffiti and hate crimes showed a significant increase as shaven

headed gangs from out of town began making a regular appearance. Scuffles between these right-wing elements and local Asian youths began to develop, creating a climate of fear in the town centre and an increase in the fear of crime and the anticipation of violence. Intelligence suggested that two high-profile fundamentally racist organisations, had targeted the town with the intention of inflaming racial tension.

Radical Islamic groups also began to pitch stalls in the High Street using megaphones and explicit imagery of Western violence against Muslims. This became the focus of attention for the skin-head gangs who baited the groups and before long violent clashes were taking place. Law abiding citizens began to complain about the inflammatory behaviour of the radical Muslims, the intimidating presence of the skinheads and the Town Centre Manager reported a slump in the retail footfall as shoppers were deserting the town in favour of nearby Windsor and Maidenhead.

A downward spiral had begun with increased community tension and fear of crime and an associated downturn of the local economy. The local media also fanned the flames by characterising the town centre as a 'no-go' area at weekends.

The response was a radical and unusual one. While the traditional approach would be to flood the town with a high-visibility policing presence, this has previously shown to actually increase the fear of crime with high-profile policing being seen as a precursor of violence. *Operation Comfort* was a high-profile public order response with a difference. Its strategic objective was to both deter trouble-makers and reassure the local community. This was achieved through the *style* of the deployment which was one of active engagement.

On one particular Saturday, intelligence revealed that far-right extremists were going to up the ante and not only carry out a violent attack of ethnic minorities in the town but were also going to throw a pig's head into one of the town's several mosques. An inflammatory act of such blasphemy that it would constitute a 'critical incident' (namely an incident in which the effectiveness of the police response is likely to have a significant impact on the confidence of the victim, their family and/or the community).

The briefing for the weekend's high-profile operation stressed the importance that all officers were expected to take every opportunity to positively reassure the community and allay any fear and anxiety. This was to be done by proactively engaging with as many people as possible with a smile on their face and a approachable attitude. I remember saying: '*I want you to smile, joke, shake hands, kiss babies and pat dogs if necessary to show the community that we are there to reassure them. Don't wear your uniform on your face!*'

In order to demonstrate complete openness and transparency selected local community leaders and local politicians were invited to sit in on the full operational briefing. An unprecedented step which raised a few eyebrows from some tactical advisors. Furthermore, having heard the policing style that was being planned, the community observers were invited to go out on patrol alongside the officers to witness first-hand the operational deployment. They were given a direct dial number into the Silver Control Room to report any interactions they saw which were inconsistent with the intended policing style.

In the first operational use of diversity in the country a black Sergeant and six black and Asian colleagues from the Black Police Association were deployed with a specific briefing to engage with ethnic minorities using their enhanced cultural awareness and language skills as fully as possible. This manifested in a high-profile engagement operation using Urdu, Punjabi and Jamaican patois with shoppers and community members and reassurance visits to mosques, Hindu temples and Sikh gurdwaras. Somewhat disconcerting was the realisation that this style of talking to people while out on patrol was a novelty for many of the younger officers who privately disclosed that they would not normally talk to the public unless they had a reason (or power!) to do so. A red flag in terms of the drift away from community policing.

A police recruiting stand was set up next to the Islamic radicals pitch which attracted a great deal of attention from a wide variety of curious young people and defused the potentially inflammatory impact of the angry Muslims. Several local youngsters quizzed the officers about the extent of racism in the force and some applied to join the force as a direct result of this initiative.

Local shop-keepers welcomed the visits from the patrolling officers and one butcher disclosed that someone had unusually ordered two pig's heads to be picked up on that Saturday. This tied into the earlier intelligence about the mosque desecration and observations were mounted to intercept the offending customer, who doubtless deterred by the heightened police presence, failed to turn up, thereby averting a critical incident.

The local newspapers had several reporters and photographers on the ground ready to capture images of anticipated violence but were forced instead to report the positive policing operation that was delivered.

During the course of the operation, the Silver Control Room received an anonymous call to say that a petrol bomb had been thrown at one of the mosques. Fortunately, one of the BPA officers was already on scene at the mosque and able to quickly and calmly confirm that this was a hoax call, designed to cause panic and initiate a blue light response.

The community observers were glowing in their praise for the officers they had shadowed during the operation, reporting back that they had done exactly what was asked of them and had managed to create a positive mood in the town.

An unexpected spin-off on using the BPA serial was that their impact was exaggerated by the community. Stories began to circulate around the town about a large influx of BAME officers. In my own tour of community hubs during this weekend, I was approached by many community leaders who expressed astonishment at the number of BAME officers the force had at their disposal. Such was the impact of the targeted use of a Sergeant and six Constables from a visible ethnic background had on community perceptions.

What was equally satisfying was the feedback I received from the BAME officers themselves who reported that it was the first time in their service that they felt their diversity had been specifically utilised in an operational capacity, particularly in a public order situation. They felt empowered to use their difference as an operational asset and were encouraged to make the most of their language skills and cultural awareness, strengths that they felt all too often were best left in the locker room to avoid standing out. This was precisely why they had joined the force in the first place and yet the organisation had never deployed their specialist skills in this way before.

Ironically the day before the operation I received a phone call from a fellow Chief Superintendent, an experienced and highly regarded white colleague who urged me in the strongest terms to reconsider my plans to use the BAME serial. He warned me that it would blow up in my face and I was in danger of recreating the black regiments of the Second World War. In fact, their deployment was so successful that I received calls from many BAME officers to join the operation in the weeks that followed and the use of a targeted and well-briefed BAME serial became a standard template in managing community tension within the force.

The far-right groups were deterred by the multi-faith unity displayed in the town and turned their attention elsewhere in the country where fault lines between communities and the police could more easily be exploited.

Concluding personal reflections

In reflecting upon this unorthodox approach, I learned several things about myself. First, to trust my instincts rather than defer to the status quo and the usual way of doing things. Including community members and local politicians in the operational briefing was risky and could have back-fired. Political capital could have been made and the operation could have been compromised. However, given that the intention was to demonstrate openness and transparency, the warts and all approach was considered to be appropriate and helped to build trust with sections of the community who had low regard for the police. Empowering the observers to report back any findings of concern also sent a message to the officers that the highest standards were expected.

Using the BAME officers in a targeted deployment was also fraught with danger and it would have been easier to have taken a risk-averse approach and diluted their impact by mixing them with white officers. The Operation Comfort BAME serial were hand-picked by me from officers who I knew had the right motivation, attitude and emotional intelligence to achieve what I wanted. They were not selected on skin colour alone. They were, however, volunteers for the operation and had they objected to such a deployment (as I am sure some BAME officers would) I would have respected their decision. I was able to count on their support because of my long-standing commitment to diversity but also my own ethnicity and shared experiences made it much easier to have a dialogue about using race as a tactical option. There are many white senior officers who would not have been comfortable having this discussion for fear of being labelled tokenistic. Indeed, there is often a very narrow line to be trod between tokenism and an appropriate deployment of difference which is why the service often retreats to the safe option.

Courage and calculated risk-taking are key hallmarks of good leadership and a great deal of trust and community confidence was built during the weeks of this operation which yielded enormous benefits in later years when other critical incidents didn't end so well. While high-profile policing failures certainly occurred under my watch and were subject to intense community criticism, they did not lead to a loss of trust, and the community were always actively engaged in shaping policy and practice to deliver the service they wanted to see. This model of co-production saw the re-writing of a number of policies and procedures influenced by the experiences of victims of critical incidents and their families.

REFLECTIVE PRACTICE

- When did you last make a stand for something you truly believe in? What were the circumstances?

- Detail a time when you took an unpopular stance against the status quo or dominant culture of an organisation or environment?

- If applicable, explain how you were able to actively utilise the diversity of your workforce/colleagues?

CHAPTER SUMMARY

The service has made significant inroads in recent decades to involve trusted members of the community in the debrief of critical incidents. This approach, however, is by no means universal and because of a fear of further reputational damage, the service is not as open to share its mistakes as it could be. A cultural change is needed to open up the service to more scrutiny from the community particularly when things have not gone well.

The public order example above is an illustration of a critical incident avoided. It made no national headlines because nothing particularly newsworthy happened. Neither did the arrest, a few months later, of a terrorism suspect on the day of his wedding in front of 650 assembled guests. Elsewhere in the country this may have prompted an outcry or even public disorder, but the trust developed in the years leading up to this event allowed us to manage the situation with limited community impact. The building of trust and confidence cannot be done overnight and remains a fragile asset and can be lost at the next critical incident.

In order to build a meaningful and sustainable relationship, there is a need to get ahead of the curve by involving the community in the *formulation of strategy and delivery of services* and not simply lip-service consultation or damage limitation exercises. A philosophy of co-production with the community needs to drive neighbourhood policing. Diverse communities should influence policy development and then quality assure the practical application of those policies when they hit the ground and start to affect the lives of the community. The service should ask itself at every stage three critical questions:

1. How have you involved the community in the development of this policy?
2. How are you involving the community in feeding back on the impact of this policy on the ground?
3. How are you involving the community in the delivery of this service?

This will require a sea-change in thinking from the traditional paternalistic approach to policing, whereby the community are involved not only in the discussions but also the delivery.

The British police service remains the best in the world but must radically reform itself and refocus the attitude of its ranks if it is to retain its legitimacy with the whole of the community. It is time to abandon the mythical quest of a fully representative police service and tokenistic targets. The service needs a radical culture shift to fully embrace emotional intelligence and cognitive diversity to unleash talent and shape a more responsive service for contemporary British society.

References

Herriot, P and Pemberton, C (1995) *Competitive Advantage Through Diversity: Organizational Learning from Difference London*. Sage.

Macpherson of Cluny, Sir William (1999) *The Stephen Lawrence Inquiry: Report of an Inquiry by Sir William Macpherson of Cluny London*. The Stationery Office.

Page, S E (2007) *The Difference: How the Power of Diversity Creates Better Groups, Firms, Schools, and Societies*. Princeton and Oxford: Princeton University Press.

Randel, A E et al (2018) Inclusive Leadership: Realizing Positive Outcomes Through Belongingness and Being Valued for Uniqueness. *Human Resource Management Review*, 28(2): 190–203.

Scarman, L G (1982) *The Scarman Report: The Brixton Disorders 10–12 April 1981: Report of an Inquiry*. Harmondsworth: Penguin.

2 Building rapport

Peter Nicholas

CHAPTER OBJECTIVES

This chapter will help you:

- understand the meaning of rapport and how it can be utilised in everyday life;
- recognise the concept of 'flow' and its importance in effective communications;
- challenge your own skills base around building quality interactions with others;
- understand why recognising 'difference' and 'preference type' in self and others helps build effective relationships.

What is rapport and why do we need to talk about it?

The *Oxford English Dictionary*'s definition of rapport is as follows:

a friendly relationship in which people understand each other very well.

In this chapter I look at some of the techniques that can help you to really listen to and understand others in order to build rapport. I also explore some of the things that get in the way of you being able to do this. Whatever you do in life you need to be able to communicate and build trust. Rapport is the foundation for these relationships. Being able to build rapport is a crucial skill to develop in all walks of life, both in work and in personal life. Once you have rapport with someone you can have more constructive discussions, even if you disagree with each other. In my life as a business consultant, coaching and running communication and leadership development programmes, it has been the essential stepping stone to success.

A working definition

Over the last few months, I have discussed rapport with doctors, undertakers, CEOs of technology companies, sales directors, vicars, teachers and therapists, as well as members of the police. They all said largely the same thing:

You need to listen, be interested, find common ground, respect and value the other person, whoever they are. Building rapport is about being effective in your job.

Whatever your line of work there will be many challenges and constraints that you have to negotiate when dealing with colleagues, victims, suspects or members of the public. In many circumstances improving rapport will seem absolutely appropriate and in other cases less applicable. At times you may even need to break rapport. In one policing scenario it might be you are arresting or apprehending someone who is out of control and needs to be restrained for their safety or other people's safety. In another scenario, there will be times when increasing rapport will be essential to ensure that an increasingly escalating scenario is calmed down as best as possible.

A lot of your time, though, will be spent dealing with colleagues and the general public where building rapport is essential. In the neuro-linguistic programming (NLP) for example, rapport is about demonstrating to other people, by your behaviours and words, that you accept the validity of their experiences for them (McDermott and Jago, 2011). So, what does rapport mean in practice?

Really listening

The tools and techniques in this chapter are not a system or methodology whereby if you do ABC you will get to D. Rapport is simply honing the basic human skills you have already to tune in, be interested and care about others.

Listening
- Being present
- Using your senses
- Listening in disagreement

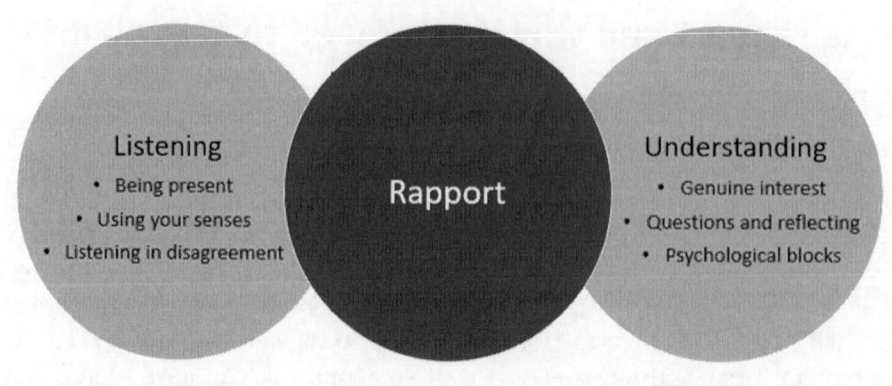

Rapport

Understanding
- Genuine interest
- Questions and reflecting
- Psychological blocks

Figure 2.1 Rapport zone

You have the power to improve your own rapport-building skills. The more you practise, the more you can improve. I encourage you to start putting the learning and theory into practice straight away. I find it useful to think about three zones of listening.

Zone 1

We can all do superficial listening, when you are not really interested in what someone is saying but are trying to make all the right noises? How many of you speak with relatives on the phone and zone out? Or how many of you check your emails on a conference call? Be honest!

Zone 2

Listening in a normal conversation, but only so we can know when to interrupt or fix their issue quickly rather than staying genuinely curious. If you are saying lots of, 'yes, ok, right, yes', you are speed listening to get to a solution, not being in an authentic enquiry.

Zone 3

Hopefully there are times when you are in zone 3 and have really done your best listening because you are genuinely interested and want to understand. What happened to the conversation, the rapport and your relationship?

This is close to what the psychologist Mihaly Csikszentmilhalyi describes as being in a state of 'flow'. Where your attention is ordered and focused; where there is a clear focus to your discussion, maybe with an opportunity to offer feedback; where there is a match between the challenges (of the individual) and the skills you have (Csikszentmihalyi, 2009).

When you find yourself in a conversation where someone is sharing their views on a subject you disagree with, you can feel attacked or affronted. When this happens your listening usually stops. Two things regularly happen in this scenario: you significantly challenge their viewpoints; you become defensive around your own position. In effect, your listening stays in Zone 2. Rapport is broken. As Covey says about this scenario, '*most people do not listen with intent to understand; they listen with the intent to reply*' (Covey, 1989).

We've evolved to the point where even though as human beings we feel we have fully developed, the brain is still the same brain that our stone age ancestors used when they were under threat from wild animals and other tribes. Goleman's work (see below) explores the impact of an amygdala hijack – which in effect means that when we feel attacked (at an emotional level) we shut down our thinking brain and revert to fight or flight mode. Steve Peters further develops this idea in *The Chimp Paradox* exploring the impact that a non-thinking brain has on our behaviours and the need for us to develop strategies for managing our reactions (Peters, 2012). As he states, *'the chimp is far stronger than you are, it is wise to understand it and then nurture and manage it'* (ibid.).

Pause for thought: the next time you hear someone launching into promoting a subject area that you fundamentally disagree with, see how long you can stay focused and in enquiry mode or what Covey describes as *empathic listening* (Covey, 1989). Be careful because the next time someone says, 'I hear what you are saying' or 'with all due respect', they really aren't listening and don't respect you.

Humans have an inbuilt B**L S**T radar and you know when someone is really listening or pretending to listen or trying to fix you. Please do not expect to be able to build rapport if you spend most of your time in Zone 1 or Zone 2. To listen in Zone 3 and build rapport you have to be willing to let go of your agenda for the conversation. You also have to get really comfortable in silence. This isn't easy for some people, it takes practice.

REFLECTIVE PRACTICE

- What type of interactions help you to listen in Zone 3?
- What are you listening for and why?
- What do you notice about what you hear?

We know therefore that listening is critical and it needs to be active listening. That means we need to be genuine because you are giving to another, what Krogerus and Tschappeler describe as, your most valuable asset – your attention (Krogerus and Tschappeler, 2017). It is this attention which creates the right environment to have high-quality interactions.

How do we achieve rapport with Zone 3 listening skills?

In the following section, we are going to outline a number of areas that relate to Zone 3 listening, where rapport can be built and effective communication is achieved. Some of these appear obvious, yet are frequently missing in effective communication. Others are more general in nature but in our experience, when they are absent from an interaction, a positive outcome is difficult to achieve.

As you go through the subsequent list, it might be an idea to score yourself out of 10 as to how you rate your communication skills and what this might mean for your abilities to build rapport on a regular basis (see Appendix A). Once you have done this, do you have the courage to hand it to someone who you trust and ask them to score you? Are there any areas of difference?

Be present

It all starts with being present. *The Power of Now* by Eckhart Tolle is a fabulous book that explores how being more present can transform your life. He talks about how the '*enlightened person*'s main focus of attention is always '*Now*' (Tolle, 1999). The importance of being present *now* in any conversation.

At business conferences around the world, I became fascinated with noticing who was present in conversation and who wasn't. At networking functions, I've seen too many people only being partially present because they were looking over a person's shoulder to see somebody who could be more useful or interesting. The irony, of course, is that I wasn't present with people and what they were saying because I was in observer mode.

And the lack of attention is getting worse; in our technologically advanced world we can spend a disproportionate amount of time staring at screens while ignoring the people around us. I have children who spend an awful lot of time on screens and I cannot always communicate with them. Then I check how much time I spend on a screen and it is often shocking. Being present in the moment of course helps with our well-being.

It is therefore no surprise that when we are in potentially rapport-building situations, by not being present, we miss the opportunities to authentically connect with others. Even if you have to be on Zoom/Skype/Teams, get your phone out of the way so you aren't distracted and switch off your email alert.

REFLECTIVE PRACTICE

- How does it make you feel when you are talking to someone and they are distracted?
- When was the last time you experienced somebody not being present with you in a conversation? How did it make you feel?

Being present is a choice. It is not down to personality or genetic disposition. You have to choose to engage. The quality of your rapport in relationships will improve if you decide to engage – properly. When you are distracted, hungry or tired this may be more of an effort.

In a virtual setting, try standing up on your calls: it encourages you to be more present and gets you more energised and animated which can assist rapport building.

Warmth and competence

When we meet people for the first time we need to know whether we can trust them or not. An appropriate amount of warmth is essential to help establish this trust. Of course, you have also to be credible and competent. In the workplace, in a serious job, we can often forget to smile and share our human warmth. There is plenty of research showing how warmth and competence play a crucial part in human engagement. There are numerous TED talks by Susan Fiske, and in her book *The Human Brand* (Fiske and Chris Malone, 2013) she talks about the evolutionary benefits of having both warmth and competence.

In their excellent article, Cuddy, Glick and Beninger also identify the real importance that warmth and competence make with respect to impression management. As they say, 'through nonverbal behaviours that subtly communicate warmth and competence information, people can manage the impressions they make on colleagues, potential employers, and possible investors' (Cuddy et al, 2011).

Genuine warmth and smiles matter. Think about when you're interviewing somebody for a job. Assessing them isn't simply about who is best qualified or cleverest. You are looking to gauge the social skills: have they got the ability to connect quickly, tune in and build rapport with you and can you easily build rapport with them? As Goleman states, *'Empathy is crucial for wielding influence: it is difficult to have a positive impact on others without sensing how they feel and understanding their position'* (Goleman, 1998).

However, it has to be an appropriate level of authentic warmth. Again, the more present you are in a situation the more you can gauge what is needed. There is no point in going in all hugs and smiles in a very serious situation. However, in day-to-day connections with people keep reminding yourself that warmth is necessary for connection and trust.

Eye contact helps to build trust

When my father first joined the army in the 1950s the sergeant major wore very peaked caps and you could never see his eyes. The lack of eye contact prevented trust being built and kept the new recruits scared. Salespeople (in those days when we met salespeople in real life) are taught to engage eye contact as early as possible because it helps them tune in to the other person and build rapport.

If you find engaging in eye contact uncomfortable take it in small incremental steps; start looking at someone in the eyes for a few seconds and then gradually increase this over time. As Chris Farmer, from the Corporate Coach Group states,

> *Eye contact is important because the primary sense for humans is sight. We take most information about other people's emotional states from what we see written on their faces.*
>
> (Farmer, n.d.)

In our virtual world remember to look at the camera on a laptop. It sounds simple but most people don't. Most of us don't look at the camera, we look down at the screen. Looking at the camera can increase the sense of connection. However, please be aware that in some cultures 'not' looking directly at someone is actually a sign of respect. The more you are present the more you will become aware of what is appropriate.

Matching the mood

I was delivering a key-note presentation to a large group of delegates. I had put together a pertinent and reasonably amusing 45-minute lecture on communications and influencing. What I didn't know, because nobody thought to tell me, was that many of them had recently found out their jobs were on the line; they could be let go within two weeks.

Fairly soon I realised that I was failing to match the mood and build rapport in the room and had to drastically change direction and re-tune, so I was more empathetic to where they were at … and just about got away with it.

As an executive coach, during the majority of conversations I simply focus on being present, listening and tuning in to the client, ascertaining their mood and how I need to pitch my reflection and questioning. I even tune into how they are breathing.

Matching isn't simply copying their mood. For those in jobs where you have to deliver bad news to people you may find that you don't want to build too much rapport. If they are upset you don't want to be breaking down with them. But you do still need to be able to tune into what is needed and show appropriate empathy.

Body language

There are whole books written about body language and its effect on human communication. My favourite is *The Dictionary* of body language by Joe Navarro a former FBI agent (Navarro, 2018). Psychologists have studied people when they had good rapport and found they often move and strike poses in very similar ways. You will do this naturally. Try folding your arms when you are talking to a person or group. Then put your hand on your jaw in an interested pose. Notice how long it is before many of them copy your pose. Yawning is also copied.

You know this and most of the time if you are present and curious it will happen unconsciously. If you want to connect and tune into others better, then become aware of tuning into their body language.

Yet, it is not just our bodies that use language – clearly the words we use and the expressions we engage with send a message to those with whom we connect. Just as we can match body expressions, so too it is important that for rapport to take place, our language must connect with another.

Listen to the language that others use.

- If someone is high-thinking, factual and logical then to connect better use efficient, structured and detailed language.
- If they are using plenty of emotional language then adjust the way you communicate to fit in with this.
- Are they focused on the action, then assist them in quickly moving towards achieving results.
- Are they big picture thinkers, then engage with them at a blue-sky level.

Trust that if you are really present and have their best interest at heart, you will probably do all the above naturally.

Be careful: over-thinking this will mean you are focusing on listening out for what language they are using and over-analysing in your own head. You will not be really present with them. Keep bringing your attention back to them and being interested.

Authenticity

You will build stronger rapport with people when you are being your most authentic self and being genuinely interested in them. People can sense when you are acting and will mistrust you. Of course, you still have to be professional and do your role but the happier you can be in your own skin the better you feel and the easier you can build rapport. People are always interested in people who are interested in them, so get interested in people. As Carole Gaskell states, learn to give unconditionally because giving without expectation of anything in return is a great way of building authenticity (Gaskell, 2003).

The ability to ask the right questions

The way you ask questions can help you to open up a conversation. Closed questions which illicit a yes or no response close the conversation down. However, open questions starting with *who, what, where, when, how* and *why* generally open up the conversation. Beware of over-using the *why* question: it can sound like a threat and you are blaming them – '*why don't you get it?*', '*why didn't you talk to me before?*', '*why did you think that was a good idea?*'

TED questions can help you follow their train of thought:

- **T**ell me more about that?
- **E**xplain how that might impact on you?
- **D**escribe the process you might need to follow?

Reflection

Reflection is an important tool to use to really understand others. Reflecting helps you to check that you have understood correctly, but it also demonstrates that you have been listening and shows that you care. People need to feel heard. Often the solution in an argument is simply shutting up and listening and then reflecting.

Reflection comes in many forms.

- Nods, facial gestures that show you are genuinely listening.
- Affirming sounds – uh hu, mmm noises.
- Single words reflected back.
- Summarising the essence of a sentence.

My favourite reflection is the *'when you say'* reflection.

- Listen out for their key words.
- Reflect 'When you say … difficult … / challenging … / problematical.
- Stop, make friends with silence.
- Let *them* finish the sentence.

Avoid saying '*I understand exactly how you feel*'. You don't! And you are making it about you not them. Remember, people need to feel understood, validated and respected. They generally do not like to be fixed.

What are the blocks that stop us building rapport?

When building rapport, you must be aware that there is stuff that gets in the way. It is fascinating that we can meet some people and seem to click with them automatically, we're on the same wavelength, we go away feeling we've always known them; other people we find more difficult to connect with.

Our first reaction is often to blame them. Our egos want us to be right and make others wrong. I often hear people saying things like:

- *Oh they're really difficult to work with;*
- *They don't communicate very well;*
- *I find it difficult to connect with them because they are a closed book.*

Some of that may be true, but what is crucial if you want to build better rapport is that you take responsibility. It starts with you. What are you doing that could be affecting the way they are behaving towards you? Stop and consider how you might be contributing to the lack of rapport.

We all need to be more aware of the unconscious bias that comes into play when we are dealing with other human beings, namely your prejudices and judgements. The more you can be aware of them the better you can handle them and ensure that they don't get in the way.

In his brilliant book *Surrounded by Idiots*, Thomas Erikson (Erikson, 2019) uses a number of different models that emphasise why some people just seem to connect with you; others almost wind-you-up on impact. He talks about different types and relates these to preferences that we all have (knowingly or unknowingly). He also colour-codes preferences. So in simplistic terms those with:

- red preferences are often driven, determined, competitive, assertive;
- yellow preferences are often expressive, creative, outgoing, unconventional;
- green preferences are often nurturing, values-based, compassionate, caring;
- blue preferences are often objective, methodical, organised, structured.

When building rapport, it is vital that we recognise our own preferences as well as those with whom we are connecting. Being flexible in our approach means that we can increase the chances that we will be able to interact at a positive and meaningful level.

And Erikson takes the concept of difference to another level when he talks about body language. We discussed aspects of body language above, but here is how he says different preference types impact on body language.

Table 2.1 Basic preference grid

Red preference	Yellow preference
• Keep their distance from others	• Are tactile
• Have powerful handshakes	• Are relaxed and jocular
• Lean forward – sometimes aggressively	• Show friendly eye contact
• Use direct eye contact	• Use expressive gestures
• Use controlling gestures	• Often move in close
Green preference	**Blue preference**
• Are relaxed and come close	• Prefer to keep others at a distance
• Act methodically	• Either stand or sit
• Tend to lean backwards	• Often have closed body language
• Use very friendly eye contact	• Use direct eye contact
• Prefer small-scale gestures	• Speak without gestures

So, we have a sense then that we can make some general comments about building rapport; yet, at the same time we need to be flexible in our approaches in order to deal effectively with another person's preference style. The understanding of difference is built on the work of Carl Jung and many organisations have sought to utilise it for the benefits of increased effective communication (see ex. Myers Briggs Type Indicators). There is clearly a skill to this which to some extent relies on an ability to stereotype which in many ways is what Cialdini identifies as a short-cutting process in the very complex and rapidly changing world of people and organisations (Cialdini, 2007).

Unconscious bias

As a police officer you have to be so aware of the unconscious bias that can lead to racism sexism and prejudice of any kind. The main thing you need to know about unconscious bias is that you generally aren't aware it is there. Even if you who think you don't have any unconscious bias, you will have plenty. You have to call it out by having conversations, raising awareness and being honest about your unconscious bias.

REFLECTIVE PRACTICE

- Imagine you are on a train and have a spare seat next to you. The train stops and a variety of people get on.
    - Who do you not want to sit next to you?
    - What is it about them that makes you feel comfortable?
    - Who would you not want to sit next to you (be honest)?
    - What is it about them that makes you feel uncomfortable?
    - Having done this: what do you think you need to do now?

We can all fear the unfamiliar or the different, which can make us less willing to build rapport.

- Phase one of combatting unconscious bias is admitting you have it.
- Phase two is creating a circuit breaker by taking a breath, pausing and asking yourself: how biased is my thinking?

Fundamental attribution bias

Remember that everyone views the world from different perspectives; my take on this fundamental attribution bias is as follows. As humans we have a tendency to wear two different pairs of glasses. One pair of glasses we generally put on when we are looking at our own behaviour, 'situational glasses'. We understand the context and situational factors that cause us to behave the way we do. In the past, I have shouted at my children while shopping because I was tired, running late or under pressure at work.

However, we tend to put on another set of 'dispositional' glasses where we view other people's behaviour. We can easily assume that their behaviour is down to their disposition or personality. They were born angry, difficult, unmotivated etc. Of course, we can't see other people's context and situational factors; therefore, we slip straight into judgements. In the shop example, on another day if someone else was shouting at their children in the same way I was, I might easily judge them as an ineffective angry parent. It is then all too easy to see their behaviour as part of their personality and fixed.

It is interesting that when we are doing exactly the same as somebody else, we can view that behaviour entirely differently depending on which glasses we're wearing. We all make judgements about how other people are: they are difficult, rude, unmotivated, cold, lazy; the list goes on. Whereas when we view our own behaviour we can explain and justify why we are behaving the way we are because we know the context. Of course, in many situations in your line of work you don't have time to consider all the factors that are at play and you have to make snap judgements. But keep looking for situations when you do have more time to reflect.

Why is this impact on building rapport? Because if you judge others instantly without considering the situational factors that might be going on it will get in the way of building rapport. Always take time to reflect and ask:

- Why might they be behaving like that?

- What is going on that I don't know about?

- What is going on for me when I behave like that?

Confirmation bias

We all have a tendency to focus on and seek out evidence that supports our existing point of view and discount anything that doesn't fit with this.

Our brains have to process incredible amount of information every single second, therefore we have built-in shortcuts that enable us to make quick judgements and decisions. Our brain has filters to make it more efficient but not necessarily more effective. Our brain deletes information that it doesn't need or that doesn't fit the story; it makes generalisations.

Our minds seek evidence to support the view that we have taken. It is reassuring to be right and so we tend to discard any evidence that is not consistent with this view. It also boosts our self-esteem/ego because we can tell ourselves, '*You see I was right*'. We like to think that our inner judge is objective and fair, balancing evidence and counter-evidence before passing judgement. Actually, we have an in-built tendency to form very rapid and often negative judgements about others. We then send out our inner lawyers to seek out evidence confirming that we are right and dismiss any evidence that does not fit with our view.

I was once due to be coaching a senior partner in a law firm. Numerous people had told me he was difficult to work with and hated being coached. I had to work really hard to defuse those stories. I went in imagining he was a distant relation I hadn't seen for years, somebody I really respected and cared for. With that attitude and intention, I had a magnificent series of coaching sessions which lasted for many months and he is now a dear friend. It is possible to transform relationships but be aware of buying in to others' stories. It starts with you and what you are taking into the conversation.

All of the above is filtered through our in-built negativity bias that can lead us to think worse of people. Becoming more aware of these thought patterns will help you to realise some of the blocks that are preventing you fully understanding others, which may be having an impact on your rapport with them.

REFLECTIVE PRACTICE

- Think about all the relationships in your life. Choose one right now that feels difficult. Here are some questions that you can ask yourself that may help you take off the dispositional glasses and put on the situational ones:

    - What have I heard others say about this person that may be colouring my views?
    - How have I evaluated other people's feedback on this person?
    - How useful are these thoughts about this person?
    - What is going on for this person outside work?
    - What assumptions am I making about their intentions?
    - What stories have I created in my mind about this person?
    - Am I looking at evidence objectively or am I looking for evidence to support my own assumptions?
    - How might the situation be seen from their point of view?
    - What is their fear?
    - Why would a decent rational person be behaving in this way?
    - What is it like to work with me?
    - How might I have been contributing to the problem?
    - What am I feeling when I behave in the way that they appear to be behaving?

Facts and stories

We all distort reality and make up stories that get in the way of building rapport. We interpret our world view of what actually happened (the facts) and make up stories. Once stories are established they obscure the facts. This is often coloured by our emotional response. We allow our feelings about a situation or person to become the truth. For instance, if somebody disagrees with you it is easy to believe that they are trying to undermine you or don't like you. What can you do to separate facts from stories? Again, use the circuit breaker: '*What am I making this mean?*'

In meetings you can easily start believing you can mind-read what others are thinking about you. Keep reminding yourself you can't. Telling stories about others is enjoyable. As social animals we like to feel aligned to others and want them to agree with our point of view so we don't feel isolated. However, this can damage relationships.

If you are hearing the words *always, never, everyone, no-one*, you are listening to a story and not a fact. Things are rarely '*they always do that / they never support me*' or '*everyone thinks it / no one cares*'.

When do you need to practise separating the facts of a situation from the story? If you practise applying these questions and shifting your judgements in one relationship, then this can be applied in others.

> **REFLECTIVE PRACTICE**
>
> - Take a moment to think about the following questions and answer them as truthfully as possible. At the end think about where your strengths are, if you have any flaws that almost feel fatal when it comes to building rapport, what you might focus on developing further that would give you a disproportionate positive advantage in building your skills base?
>
>   o   With greater rapport I will be better able to ....
>
>   o   Which will mean that ....
>
>   o   What's in it for me?
>
>   o   How will others benefit?
>
>   o   How will I know I have made some progress?
>
>   o   How might it change my job day to day?
>
>   o   How might it improve my career prospects?

CHAPTER SUMMARY

This chapter has focused on the necessary criteria that are essential for building rapport with another person. It is in a mutually trusting environment that people can form what neuro-scientists call 'empathic resonance' – a brain to brain linkage that forms an effective understanding of the others' viewpoint (Goleman, 2006).

The critical aspects of this chapter centre on how to build rapport by developing certain skills and techniques. In effective, mutually beneficial communication environments, the critical criterion are: be present – be here in the now and nowhere else; demonstrate warmth and competence to create trust; ensure that eye contact, matching mood and body language are demonstrated in an open and honest manner; ask effective questions and ensure that you refrain from introducing any type of bias into a relationship.

We know that people are different and that is what makes the world such an interesting place. To build rapport it is our duty to be flexible and sufficiently malleable in our approach to match the needs of those with whom we engage. We are conscious of the short-cut opportunity that an appropriate understanding of preference type can give us and in this sense all of the above can help us prepare for building rapport even before we connect with an individual, team or organisation.

If you remember nothing else remember this: policing puts you in the communications and relationship business. Your job is to keep exploring how and when you can put these tools into practice in every aspect of your life, inside and outside work.

It starts with being present, keeping quiet and really listening to others. Be curious about how they're feeling and what they're thinking. Become aware of the blocks you are putting in the way. Get genuinely interested in them without trying to correct or fix them and practising all of the above techniques will improve your rapport-building, which will build your confidence. People want to be around confident people so you will find it even easier to build rapport.

Start to notice what changes in conversations and relationships when you create better rapport. As with all learning it is essential that you approach this with a spirit of lightness and fun rather than homework. Become the best, most supportive coach you could possibly be for yourself; start noticing when you get it right rather than always just beating yourself up for getting it wrong.

If you have any questions, contact www.pnatraining.com.

REFLECTIVE PRACTICE

- Self-assess your own abilities using the table below.
- Then pass a blank copy to a colleague or peer.
- Are there any significant differences in the scores?

	1 Low	5 Medium	10 High
Being present			
Warmth and competence			
Eye contact			
Matching the mood			
Body language			
Spoken language			
Authenticity			
Asking questions			
Reflection			
Unconscious bias			
Confirmation bias			

References

Cialdini, R (2007) *Influence: The Psychology of Persuasion*. New York: Harper.

Covey, S (1989) *The 7 Habits of Highly Effective People*. New York: Simon & Schuster.

Csikszentmihalyi, M (2009) *Flow*. London: Rider.

Cuddy, A, Glick, P and Beninger, A (2011) *The Dynamics of Warmth and Competence Judgments, and Their Outcomes in Organizations*. Amsterdam: Elsevier.

Erikson, T (2019) *Surrounded by Idiots*. London: Vermilion.

Farmer, C (n.d.) https://corporatecoachgroup.com/blog/how-to-use-eye-contact

Fiske, S and Malone, C (2013) *The Human Brand: How We Relate to People, Products, and Companies*. San Francisco: Jossey-Bass.

Gaskell, C (2003) *Your Pocket Life Coach*. Element.

Goleman, D (1998) *Working with Emotional Intelligence*. London: Bloomsbury.

Goleman, D (2006) *Social Intelligence*. London: Bloomsbury.

Krogerus, M and Tschappeler, R (2017) *The Communication Book: 44 Ideas for Better Conversations Every Day*. London: Portfolio Penguin.

McDermott, I and Jago, W (2011) *The NLP Coach: A Comprehensive Guide to Personal Well-Being and Professional Success*. London: Piatkus.

Navarro, J (2018) *The Dictionary of Body Language*. London: Thorsons Publishing Group.

Peters, S (2012) *The Chimp Paradox: The Science of Mind Management for Success in Business and Life*. London: Penguin.

Tolle, E (1999) *The Power of Now: A Guide to Spiritual Enlightenment*. London: Hodder.

Part 2
Organisational cultures

3 Building emotional buy-in
Will Kerr

Introduction

Dwight D Eisenhower (1954) once said that *'motivation is the art of getting people to do what you want because they want to do it'*. Although written for a different time, and different context, the quote does illustrate one of the fundamental challenges of policing. In a career which usually spans 30+ years, one which prides itself on being a vocation, the emotional rationale for joining the police service can sometimes get lost – or at least diluted – by a wide range of professional and personal factors. In those circumstances, what is the emotional 'commonality' that brings a disparate organisation and (positively, an increasingly diverse) workforce together?

If emotional buy-in requires a form of emotional capital to be built into the social contract between an organisation and its officers and staff, then how can that emotional capital be built and sustained to reflect both the many roles within policing and also the myriad personalities and backgrounds of its workforce?

CHAPTER OBJECTIVES

This chapter explores those basic questions, drawing from my personal experience of holding Chief Officer roles in the Police Service of Northern Ireland (PSNI), the National Crime Agency (NCA) and Police Scotland. It particularly focuses on change programmes within these organisations where personal examples support what many academic studies (Chick, 2018 and Connors, 2020) have shown over recent years – namely that there is a direct and positive correlation between emotionally intelligent leadership and the qualities required by a truly effective transformational leader.

- In the PSNI, I consider how the Patten Commission (HMSO, 1999) change programme – framed by politics but delivered in the day-to-day lived reality of individual officers – addressed the connection between culture and emotional buy-in. In particular, how that change programme did not fully take into account the difference between cultural inhibitors and cultural enablers, nor the respective challenges or value of each, and potentially elongated the time it took for the PSNI to establish its own identity.

- In the NCA, I particularly focus on the lessons from running the NCA's CEOP Command (the Child Exploitation and Online Protection Centre) and how an intense emotional buy-in to the role/'mission' affects the relationship between the individual and the organisation – not least in terms of the latter enabling the former – but how the level of emotional buy-in also brings significant care and welfare responsibilities.

- In Police Scotland I consider the organisational 'tipping point' – when the majority of the organisation became emotionally bought-in to the new structures – from an amalgamation process that was initially very transactionally focused, to a maturing organisation that was both confident in its own identity and its connection to diverse and disparate communities across the whole country.

I outline some key areas of commonality across all of these organisations and, as well as posing some questions along the way, I explore what could be some practical and deliverable enablers of emotional buy-in within a policing environment.

The questions posed at the end of each section of this chapter are purposefully broad, appropriate for a range of readers – principally leaders but also practitioners within policing, and those with a wider interest in the value and role of policing within a modern environment, eg student officers.

Case study 1

Police Service of Northern Ireland (PSNI): transition from the RUC GC

The PSNI was created on 4 November 2001, after being renamed on the recommendation of the 'Patten Report' (the Independent Commission on Policing of Northern Ireland, chaired by Lord Patten, HMSO, 1999), the latter containing 175 Recommendations, both symbolic and structural. While many of the structural Recommendations were based on an earlier, internal review conducted by the then RUC Deputy Chief Constable Ronnie Flanagan, this section will focus on the symbolic Recommendations – argued necessary to ensure a new start, and Nationalist community buy-in to policing in Northern Ireland – and how they were implemented. This section is neither a commentary on the necessity, nor politics of these 175 Patten Recommendations, but of the approach taken to implement and embed them.

With such an expansive change programme to implement, one with a high degree of political and independent scrutiny, the PSNI approached the changes through an approach broadly aligned to the McKinsey 7S Framework (Peters and Waterman, 1995). This approach, more often used as an analytical tool for organisation health, was based on the alignment and inter-relationship of the seven component parts – namely strategy, structure, systems, staff, style, skills and shared values – all centred upon shared values at the core of the approach. The model characterises the seven elements into 'hard' elements (strategy, structures and systems) which are relatively easy to identify, and soft elements (the remaining four elements) which are less tangible and more influenced by organisation culture. While the use of this model facilitated the broad grouping of the 175 Recommendations in the Patten Report, it also helped to create a subliminal mind-set that the 'programmatic' approach to such a large and complex change programme was sufficiently flexible to adapt to the emotional mood of an organisation as it went through that change programme.

During the first few years of transition, I was serving as a public order Inspector, and then a Detective Chief Inspector responsible for CID in Belfast City Centre. I was not directly involved in the change programme, in the sense of programme delivery, but was a mid-level office responsible for managing officers and staff and saw the effect of the change programme on them through first-hand, and daily, experience. Therefore, this section is about the emotional collateral of the process, as personally experienced by myself as an individual and as a manager. It is, therefore, purposefully specific to the emotional impact and consequences on those officers and staff, rather than the professional impact, and to try and illustrate the key catalysts in their emotional journey and pose some, hopefully useful, questions throughout.

The Patten Commission changes to policing in Northern Ireland could be argued to be, in part at least, about transactional necessity. As the government had made a decision to implement the report in full, there was a political imperative for successful, and timely, implementation – hence the understandable 'programmatic' lens through which the change process was viewed and approached. The discussions in police vehicles, and generally among frontline officers, were not, in my direct experience, about the structure or process of the programme but how it made them feel. Some of the symbolic changes, not least the name change itself, were the subject of lots of discussions, but mostly in the acceptance that the decisions had been made and officers were quickly attuned to the practicalities of the decisions, reflecting their daily lived experience, and manifesting in a significant interest in, for example, the practicality of the new uniform. This reflected the simple fact that, for the majority of frontline officers, their daily duties and experiences would not change very much at all. A number of things, symbolic but important, did cause consternation and anger amongst officers and, while the decisions may have been understandable against the macro context of the politics and broader community confidence, these small things were not always communicated in an emotionally intelligent way. The one example of this, which has stayed in my memory most vividly, was that of the display of RUC Passing Out (Squad) Photographs. Many officers displayed theirs, proudly, on their office walls and, when a decision was taken that a 'natural working environment' should apply to all police properties – the understandable rationale was about creating a more natural and therefore comfortable, working environment for new officers from Nationalist community backgrounds – an initial direction was issued that these photographs should be removed. These photographs connected officers back to the start of their professional careers, and often reminded them of the reasons they had joined the police service. They had emotional resonance, and a connection, to vocational identity. Removing them, although on the face of it a relatively simple issue, was felt at a more visceral level by some officers.

So, what could have been done differently at the time to either retain the emotional connection to policing – even if relabelled and re-branded – or create a new emotional connection to the 'new' organisation? The PSNI had some statutory accelerants which assisted – not least 50/50 recruitment, which changed the religious composition of the organisation though a mass retirement/recruitment drive over ten years. However, the PSNI's change programme also missed some obvious opportunities (admittedly, more obvious with hindsight) to deliver cultural change, by using transformational leadership to emotionally ground an increasingly, and positively, diverse organisation in a core identity based on shared values and vocational identity.

REFLECTIVE PRACTICE

- How do you identify the emotional common denominator of policing – the basic emotional bond between the employee and organisation – and is it possible to do so in an institution which is increasingly representative of local communities?

- How do you sustain that emotional buy-in through a lengthy and disparate career? Is that done by a designed and regular process of emotional reconnection, or should it be more subtle and ingrained?

- What is the role of internal communications, and training (Continuous Professional Development) programmes, in contributing to sustained emotional buy-in?

CASE STUDY 2

National Crime Agency: Child Exploitation and Online Protection (CEOP) command

I was privileged to be responsible for CEOP in 2017 and 2018. As some context to the critically important work that CEOP do – referrals for online sexual abuse rose by over 700% between the creation of the NCA, in 2013, and 2018. This exponential rise in referrals reflected the massive growth of digital opportunities for the abuse and exploitation of children, and better technology to identify and locate offenders. The rise in both workload, not least the triage responsibilities that sit with the NCA for the referrals, before they are disseminated to the UK police services to action, and the emotional pressure on CEOP employees, is significant. CEOP is not a particularly large NCA command of itself, although they can – and do, to great effect – leverage the capabilities and capacity of the Agency as a whole. CEOP are, however, a group of very highly motivated, and personally committed, officers working in a very traumatic area of protecting vulnerable children and investigating those responsible for abusing them.

This particular case study, therefore, is not about a deficit of emotional buy-in, but about the challenges of addressing a substantial surplus of an emotional connection to your work. This is not an issue unique to the NCA. Investment in public protection teams has risen steadily in most UK police services over the past ten years, reflecting a growing recognition of the importance, and priority of policing vulnerable people. This rise has led to a series of organisational challenges.

REFLECTIVE PRACTICE

- What is the optimal balance of (prescribed) responsibilities which rest with the employer and the individual responsibilities of the officer/staff member (not least to seek help/support if needed)?

- Many police services have tenure policies for staff working in these traumatic areas of police work. What is the best way of using tenure policies, and with appropriately flexible timeframes, to ensure the optimal balance of professional effectiveness with a clear duty of a care to the individual?

- How does an emotional buy-in to a specific 'mission' translate to an emotional connection to the wider organisations aims?

The NCA has an extensive support architecture for officers working in this space, with a mixture of regular but prescribed support interventions/psychological assessments and a support framework for individual self-referrals. My own direct experience, of this area of policing, however, was that the staff were so personally committed to the work that there was always an ongoing risk that they could continue to work in this area even if they recognised that their emotional resilience was lowering. In these circumstances, where the emotional buy-in of the officer is so high that it could, in certain circumstances, become counterproductive – how can an organisation, and its managers responsible for this area, calibrate that emotional buy-in so that it does not start to negatively affect the individual? There are, in my experience, no particularly easy or straightforward answers to that professional quandary. The challenges of CEOP are also, of course, about the emotional buy-in of officers in a very specialised area of policing, as opposed to a more generic career. That said, with the growth in public protection responsibilities, more and more officers and staff are being exposed – some by choice, others by the need for skills development in this growing area of police work, and police services need to understand and proactively address that balance of needs and responsibilities between the organisation and the individual, otherwise the emotional buy-in to a particular role may turn into an adverse emotional disconnect from the organisation.

So, overall, that level of emotional buy-in creates an additional set of responsibilities for an organisation and its leaders and, while there may not necessarily be any easy answers in this emotionally and professionally intensive area of policing, the following questions may help navigate these issues.

REFLECTIVE PRACTICE

- How can you identify, and regularly assess, the most appropriate balance of care and welfare responsibilities between your organisation and officers/staff working in areas of potential emotional intensity? How can you approach this issue in a mutually supportive way, and one which avoids the risks of being perceived – in presentation or delivery – as a parent–child relationship?

- What internal steps can be taken to measure and assess the levels of emotional buy-in in these areas of police work? What are the ethical and privacy boundaries in doing so, and how can any such process be done in an open and transparent way with the shared ambition of supporting staff?

- Is it possible to identify particular emotional catalysts/trigger points for officers/staff working in these areas (beyond the standard post-incident procedures)? What would that process look like and how could it be implemented consistently?

- Would, or should, there be any criteria to identify mandatory support interventions?

CASE STUDY 3

Police Scotland: establishing a single national police service

Police Scotland was created in 2013, as a single national police service, and it merged eight (legacy) regional police forces and the Scottish Crime and Drug Enforcement Agency. It is the second largest police service in the United Kingdom and, by far, the largest territorial police service in terms of the scale of its geographic area of responsibility.

The creation of a single national police service in Scotland reflected political and economic imperatives, as well as professional need. It happened quickly, in terms of the structural changes, and that speed, coupled with an early transition mind-set which was characterised by the needs of an introspective and transactional change programme, meant that the process of cultural transition – in a new organisation which reflected at least nine different legacy cultures, with strong regional association and identities – was slower than it could, and should, have been. This impacted directly on the early quality of the emotional buy-in to a nascent organisation, one which was establishing an appropriate balance between national identity and local delivery. In some respects, certainly in respect of the critical issue (for confidence in policing) of local identity and relationships, the workforce was ahead of the organisation in recognising the importance of this issue, not only for public trust and confidence, but also equally importantly, for levels of staff engagement and well-being. Staff surveys highlight this issue, and it took a number of years for the organisation to mature – in terms of its own self-confidence and identity – to the point where it made the tangible connection, both in language and delivery, between local identity and an emotionally engaged workforce.

Two events significantly accelerated not only the cultural and structural maturation of Police Scotland, but also the emotional connection between the organisation and police officers/staff. The first, after a number of years of command churn, was the appointment of a Chief Constable, and experienced Deputy Chief Constables, who shared a strong value set and a clear vision for a national organisation which could operate at multiple tiers, but understood the importance of localism, and the need for respectful and consistent engagement of the whole organisation, through to every local community – rural, urban, remote or island – in Scotland. That recalibration of itself, and the language used to describe policing services and the importance of legitimacy and consent, created the environment for a different conversation with staff. It was also helped by an honest reflection by the Chief Constable (Iain Livingstone) repeatedly in public fora of the introspection- and compliance-based culture in the first few years of Police Scotland – in part, perhaps, necessary to accelerate the process and structured transition to a single service – but a transitional culture which had not encouraged innovation, and sustainable transformational change, to the extent which reflected the full potential of an organisation the size and scale of Police Scotland. Iain Livingstone was equally honest, as the new Chief Constable, about his role in the Senior Leadership Team in the early years of Police Scotland.

The second accelerant, although firmly housed on the foundations of the first, was the approach taken by Police Scotland during the Covid-19 pandemic. Between March 2020 and March 2021, against a backdrop of regularly changing Regulations and Guidance in the different countries that make up the United Kingdom as a whole, there was a substantial amount of public, political and media disquiet about how the police both interpreted and responded to this myriad of changing, often inconsistent, demands and expectations. Police Scotland decided, from the outset, to base its approach on three core elements. Firstly, a recognition that communities across Scotland would need visible and proactive reassurance, particularly during the unexpected first lockdown, so it put hundreds of extra police officers out on patrol, which surged additionality coming from specialist and back-office functions. Secondly, that because of the unprecedented nature of the pandemic, but also the critical need to maintain – and sustain after the pandemic – public trust, confidence and legitimacy, Police Scotland set up an Independent Advisory Group chaired by a highly respected senior human rights lawyer in Scotland. This Group, representing an eclectic mix of community voices and human rights groups, was explicitly commissioned to both advise Police Scotland on how it was policing the pandemic and to provide an additional level of assurance to Police Scotland's accountability body (the Scottish Police Authority). Thirdly, and although, all three of these core components each played both an individual and a collective role in setting the overall tone in which police officers bought into the still relatively new organisation, this was arguably the most impactful – Police Scotland purposefully decided not to set a rigid, or even particularly detailed, policy infrastructure for how the changing Regulations or Guidance should be policed. Instead, the corporate instructions to officers, reinforced by consistent public messaging by the Chief Constable and other senior officers, simply referred to the strong bond of trust and respect between police officers and communities in Scotland, the importance of public confidence and legitimacy to maintain policing by consent, and asked that officers use their discretion, common sense and some compassion when policing what was a wholly unprecedented pandemic.

This approach, while it may seem counter-intuitive in a command and control organisation which may have traditionally favoured consistency over discretion, has had a number of positive benefits for the organisation as a whole, not least on the emotional connection between it and officers/staff.

So, what were the positive changes that this operational stance brought about, and why were they felt so keenly? Police Scotland was helped, during its response to what was principally a public health crisis, by the fact that – built into its statutory D.N.A. in the enabling Act which formed the organisation, the Police and Fire Reform (Scotland) Act 2012 – the Scottish Parliament has purposely broadened the statutory purpose of policing beyond the confines of the traditional definition of *'prevent and detect crime, keep the peace … etc.'* to *'improving the safety and wellbeing of people, places and communities in Scotland'* (Section 32, Police and Fire Reform (Scotland) Act 2012). This had meant that the psyche of the organisation was more receptive to taking a public health-based approach to traditional policing issues – not least drugs and violence – and it has responded less defensively to the exponential growth in mental health-based demand over the past few years. It further meant that, during the public health crisis that was the Covid-19 pandemic, its organisational mind-set was less fixated on a traditional enforcement role during it, and there was a stronger resonance between the organisation and its officers, on the need to maintain public confidence and support throughout.

So, the building blocks for buying emotional buy-in had been slowly building in Police Scotland, after a rocky and transactional start, and significant leadership churn, to the point where growing organisation maturity, and a stable senior leadership tier, converged just before the pandemic started. That convergence meant that the organisation and its leadership were now confident enough to trust those core elements of discretion and common sense in the front line, and to strongly and visibly support how well they were delivering on both. The absence of an unnecessarily proscriptive policy environment on how to police the pandemic helped to address some of the transactional baggage from the first few years of Police Scotland by linking public perception of the success of the organisation not to an effective communications strategy (important as they are) but to the professional standards and behaviour of every single officer and staff member. The language used in public commentary about how Police Scotland had approached the policing of the pandemic was very much based on the mutual trust with the workforce, and that trust was increasingly manifesting itself in a, while not perfect, more adult–adult relationship.

So, what were the lessons for senior leaders in policing, or any other public service, from how to approach the management of a crisis environment in a way which maximises the emotional buy-in of staff? As with the other case studies in this chapter, these potential lessons are posed as a series of questions, reflecting the fact that every organisation has its own history, culture, context and operating environment.

Reflective practice

- What is the first thing your organisation turns to, or thinks about, in a crisis – is it policy or legal advice based, or is it about the tone and presentation of the organisational response? Is there an optimal balance of both in your organisation?

- At what stage in a crisis are your frontline staff engaged? Is it right at the onset, genuinely seeking the thoughts (and fears) of those at the point of service delivery/public contact, or is staff engagement formulaic, and usually informative only via Staff Associations?

- How well do you understand, and celebrate, the positive aspects of your organisation's culture? How can you use those positive aspects as enablers, or accelerants, during an extended crisis?

- How can you ensure that the cultural muscle-memory of your organisation doesn't default, during crisis mode, to any negative behaviours? What are the design means by which you ensure that your organisation does not default to introspection and defensiveness during a period of sustained public scrutiny?

Chapter summary

This chapter has dealt with a range of different policing agencies and, using practical illustrations, has attempted to illustrate both how important is it to have some degree of emotional buy-in from staff and also how difficult it can be to sustain that emotional buy-in and how there may be direct connection between the levels of emotional buy-in and the responsibilities of the organisation to provide additional tiers and methods of staff support.

Although all three organisations may be different in style and culture, they do share a significant degree of commonality – both in core roles and the likely motivation of those who joined them. It is likely that many of those joining all three organisations did so from a civic-minded desire to help and protect their fellow citizens, but all three organisations, to a greater or lesser extent, went through degrees of demographic and structural change over the past 10–20 years. They also, in particular the PSNI through the 'Patten' years, went through a significant churn of employees over a similar period.

A growing proportion of new employees into policing will be from the 'Generation Z' demographic. Although there is a paucity of detailed research on this issue (although plenty of headlines like 'Millennials? They aren't much cop at police work', *The Times* (2019)), a younger generation of entrants into policing may have a more transient perspective on careers generally and may not view it – certainly with changes to pension regulations which mandate a minimum retirement age of 60 – as a 'life-time' career.

The responsibilities on police leaders, therefore, now include the need to understand how this inter-generational, and increasingly diverse, workforce can both enjoy the undoubted benefits of diversity of thought and opinion, but also have a core identity based on shared values. It is those shared values – the values espoused and articulated by most policing organisations – which provide a framework for sustained emotional buy-in, irrespective of either background before joining or the length and nature of career profiles.

Those values are built into the (relatively new) Competency and Values Framework (CVF) – Transparency, Impartiality, Integrity and Public Service – and most UK police services have variants along similar lines. The CVF is used as the core tool for workforce assessments, including promotions, and research shows connections between those values and employees' wider emotional buy-in and burn-out.

As Basinka and Daderman (2019) pointed out – *'values represent people's higher emotions and cognitive representations of basic motivations'*. In other words, intrinsic values can shape the emotional connection between an organisation and its staff. Shared values, consistently and transparently displayed, can provide a strong emotional connection, and capital, in an organisation, and can transcend role and rank.

However, do police services invest enough time, and organisational capital, in the relationships between their stated values and the emotional buy-in of staff? Can you answer the following questions with tangible and practical evidence of what your organisations is doing?

- How are those values operationalised, on a daily basis, in the organisation? Are they merely articulated as standard introductions, or adjuncts, to Force Policies?
- Many services have their values built into their CVF-based promotion processes, and some into their annual appraisal systems too – but, apart from their set-piece arrangements, are the values ingrained as part and parcel of daily conversations in the organisation, at every level from corporate governance meetings to briefing rooms?
- Has the organisation actively thought about how to use their values as a consistent translation point between the emotional buy-in of staff to the wide range of increasingly myriad roles within policing?
- How can service values be consistently, and continually, connected back to the emotional motivation of the officer/staff member when they first joined policing? Can those values provide the consistent bedrock for a lengthy and variable career?

Emotional buy-in is a function of how staff feel about their organisation – their sense of worth, value and respect in their role, and their emotional participation in the success of the organisation as a whole. The anchor point for that relationship between the organisation and its employee rests within those shared values to create time, thought and effort into using organisational values to create an emotional bond between both in a consistent way to sustain emotional buy-in within an organisation. Supporting those values with a genuinely nurturing relationship with staff – where they feel supported, valued and involved – is a further way for an organisation to ensure that those values are consistently applied to all public and victim interactions.

References

Basinka, B A and Daderman, A M (2019) Workforce Values of Police Officers and Their Relationships with the Burn-Out and Work Engagement. Available at https://www.frontiersin.org/articles/10.3389/fpsyg.2019.00442/full (accessed 20 May 2021).

Chick, G (2018) *Corporate Emotional Intelligence: Being Human in a Corporate World*. St Albans: Critical Publishing.

Connors, C D (2020) *Emotional Intelligence for the Modern Leader: A Guide to Altering Effective Leadership and Organisations*. Emeryville: Rockridge Press.

Cuddy, A, Tannen, D, Jen Su, A and Beeson, J (2018) *Harvard Business Review 'Leadership Presence'*. Massachusetts: Harvard Business Review Press.

Eisenhower, D (1954) Leadership/Organisation. Available at: https://www.eisenhowerlibrary.gov/eisenhowers/quotes#Leadership (accessed 20 May 2021).

Feel, A (2019) *Emotional Intelligence for Leadership: Learn How to Manage and Influence People, Improving Communication and Leadership Skills with the Power of Emotional Intelligence (Self Esteem, Charisma)*. Independently Published.

George, B, Ibarra, H, Goffee, R and Jones, G (2017) *Harvard Business Review 'Authentic Leadership'*. Massachusetts: Harvard Business Review Press.

Goleman, D (2013) *Leadership: The Power of Emotional Intelligence*. Florence: More Than Sound.

Patten, C et al (1999) *The Report of the Independent Commission on Policing for Northern Ireland*. London: HMSO.

Peters, T and Waterman, R H (1995) *In Search of Excellence: Lessons from America's Best-Run Companies*. London: Profile Books.

Zander, R S and Zander, B (2000) *The Art of Possibility: Transforming Professional and Personal Life*. Massachusetts: Harvard Business Review Press.

4 A culture of coaching to support the next big leaps in policing

Serena Kennedy and Cameron Thomson

CHAPTER OBJECTIVES

This chapter will help you:

- understand the value of developing a coaching culture in the workplace;
- consider how best to identify and develop the potential of employees;
- explore how to engender an even stronger sense of belonging and organisational engagement;
- support personal growth, empowerment and encourage personal responsibility.

The approach

We approach this chapter drawing on our two different workplace experiences. On the one hand, we can call on 28 years of experience as a policing leader across all the various ranks and roles and the complexities therein. At the same time, we have considerable successful experience (14 years) in the field of executive coaching, specialising in cultural development. It is our contention that the requirement for significant performance improvement in policing will be best enabled by the implementation of a high-quality coaching culture. This, *apparent* soft-skill, we argue, will help police officers and staff feel more valued and help them better connect to the purpose of the organisation. As Sinek states, '*Those who truly lead are able to create a following of people who act not because they are swayed, but because they were inspired*' (Sinek, 2009). We maintain that a coaching approach will inspire people to be better equipped to address the needs of the communities that we all seek to serve.

Context

Since the global financial crisis of 2008, even greater demands have fallen on public sector organisations such as policing. As with all public services, policing is in an era defined by an expectation that we will continue to deliver an effective and efficient service to our communities, in conjunction with our partners, while delivering exceptional value for money. This has been against a backdrop of significant reductions to our budgets meaning that workforce numbers have been cut by approximately 25 per cent and the ability to invest in our workforce and organisation severely challenged. In some forces what this led to was all but the core elements of policing being stopped resulting in little investment being made in our people. Yet, people are 83 per cent of our budget.

The pledge to increase police officer numbers by 20,000 by 2023 and a more favourable comprehensive spending review, with a three-year settlement, is seeing policing start to increase the numbers across the whole workforce. Rising to this recruitment is a challenge, while at the same time we also recognise that the impact of policing through Covid-19 has changed the expectations of both our communities and staff for the foreseeable future.

We argue, that a coaching culture alone won't achieve the progress that is demanded of policing, but it will underpin the behaviours that position policing at the transformational edge of people and organisational development. We maintain that embedding a coaching culture within policing will help establish a policing context that is more enlightened, forward thinking, employee centric with an environment that can compete for talent with other industry sectors. This approach will assist employees explore the full depth of their abilities.

This approach is about focusing on behaviours and how we appropriately engage with each other, how we lead our people, how we lead our departments and how we interact with our communities and our partners. To achieve this, we need to create a culture within policing where people consider our daily interactions as teachable moments, opportunities to coach individuals towards improved performance. This is about embedding a philosophy where everybody matters and a workforce feel trusted and empowered and understanding their Why!

The difference between coaching and mentoring

> Good mentors have great answers for your questions, good coaches have great questions for your answers.

This section defines coaching and how it is used effectively to enhance individual performance.

We want to differentiate between how coaching is perceived and how it contrasts with the more traditional mentoring approach associated with development in policing. The issue for many organisations is that coaching and mentoring are regularly lumped together, conflated in such a manner that there is little distinction in people's minds between the two forms of development. Yet, the basic foundation of both is fundamentally different.

Mentoring

The traditional support mechanisms throughout policing have their foundations in mentoring. This is most typically characterised by less experienced police officers and staff tapping into the experience of more qualified colleagues in how they can:

- navigate their way around the organisation;
- conduct themselves through particular situations;
- progress their careers.

In this sense therefore mentoring is about a more experienced individual sharing their knowledge with another person. And as Clutterbuck insists, this should be '*in a relationship of mutual trust*' (Clutterbuck, 1991). Please remember, mentoring can be carried out by a colleague and peer – it does not mean the mentor needs to hold a formal rank or role.

This style of mentoring currently happens on both a formal and informal basis – its historic, traditional values are well embedded. Mentoring absolutely has an effective place in the development journey of an individual because it centres on effective approaches that include – supporting, guiding, helping, facilitating. Done well, mentoring will rightly have a significant impact on an individual's progress through an organisation. However, as with all approaches, it's important to be aware of the limitations of mentoring conversations. By the very nature of the definition, you are limited by the experiences of another person. Mentoring conversations are therefore heavily influenced by, and weighted towards, the contributions of the mentor.

Another thing to note is that these contributions will inevitably be impacted by the unconscious bias that the mentor carries – bias that has been gained through the usual mix of life experience and work experience such parental values, religious beliefs, sexual orientation and ethnicity. Nevertheless, it is a powerful way to engage in development and the mentor should also find the relationship useful as it provides an opportunity to reality test their thoughts and ideas with their mentee. Indeed, this relationship of reciprocity has been formalised within many policing organisations through the use of reverse mentoring, which provides the mentee the opportunity to connect back to the reality of policing on the front line and understand how vision and strategy are being interpreted by others.

Mentoring conversations are of high value, yet can be inhibited by the hierarchical nature of the relationship. It is therefore important to set the boundaries to the relationship at the beginning: a clear understanding of need and requirement in order to ensure that no form of parent–child dependency relationship develops (see Harris, 2013).

Coaching

Coaching conversations have their foundation in exploration and curiosity. They are about using the power of "open" questions to unlock latent talent, create moments of pause for the coachee. This is about helping another person to understand their own decision-making processes, and exploring the foundation of limiting beliefs. Like mentoring, one of the foundation pillars of an effective coaching relationship is for the coach to create an environment of psychological safety for the person they are coaching.

Parsloe and Wray suggest that coaching is a relationship that enables learning and development to take place in a safe environment thus helping making a significant difference to performance improvement (Parsloe and Wray, 2016). This is a really important point to make at the outset. People engage in coaching not just because it is a *good to have*, but rather because there is a performance improvement expectation during and at the end of the professional relationship.

Each coaching session will have a process and, in this sense, it is the coach who manages the process and the person who is being coached provides the content. There are many models available on the market for coaching but perhaps the one that has the most lasting utility is provided by Sir John Whitmore in *Coaching for Performance* (Whitmore, 2017). In the GROW model there are four stages that can help the individual explore their own needs and requirements. Rather than it being a simple cosy chat, it is about taking them through a structure in order to achieve performance improvement. Whitmore suggests the following.

- **G**oal – what is it the individual wants to achieve?
- **R**eality – how real is this issue for the individual?
- **O**ptions – what options might the individual want to choose?
- **W**ay forward – how can you agree a commitment that will ensure the goal is delivered.

As we demonstrate, coaching is about concentrating on thought processes and decision-making rather than just outcomes; centring on future potential rather than historic performance. Consider also the helpful work of Amy Edmondson around establishing a positive psychological contract in order to make coaching an effective relationship (Edmondson, 2018). Coaching has got real utility across many types of organisations. The importance of the coaching relationship, for example, is also emphasised in the sports world of James Kerr looking at the approach to performance adopted by the All Blacks. He explores the constant need to build connections, reinforcing belonging and using coaching conversations as a platform to enhancing performance (Kerr, 2015).

Perhaps a push-pull analogy might help in making a clear differentiation between coaching and mentoring? In mentoring the mentor is trying to *push* new knowledge and previous learned experiences into the individual in order to help them problem solve. In coaching the coach is helping to *pull* out from the coachee their knowledge and experiences in order for them to self-solve some future issue in question. In other words, they want the relationship to flow towards positive outcomes (Csikszentmihalyi, 2002).

Two types of questions might best emphasise the difference between the approaches. When a person comes with an issue:

1. a mentor would assist by saying: *'Have you tried doing "X" to solve the problem?'*
2. a coach would assist by saying: *'What else might you do to solve this problem?'*

Reflective practice

- Think of a situation in the workplace where it would be appropriate to utilise your mentoring skills to assist an individual with their learning?

- Think of a scenario in the workplace where it would be more appropriate to use a coaching approach to help someone with an issue in question

- What do you notice about the speed of the interaction? Is it quicker to coach or mentor? Why?

The case for a coaching culture

In this section we want to consider in more detail as to why organisations are embedding coaching within their culture. We look at the deep cultural benefits that accrue and how coaching creates a culture where staff feel more engaged, trusted and empowered.

As a nationally regulated public service that operates in a complicated, nuanced, cross functional environment with a variety of competing stakeholder considerations, where do you even start to embed a coaching culture that is going to land with frontline officers, staff and senior leaders?

We are conscious that historically, policing has been associated with a 'command and control' style of leadership and this is a difficult style to unlearn. Policing has very much led through the hierarchal structures that can lead to a 'parent–child' relationship (see above) and in this sense it makes culture change problematic. That said, we accept that there are many situations in policing when an authoritative 'command and control style' is needed and as leaders, we draw on experience and training from public order command, firearms command through to being the senior investigating officer on a kidnap case.

We also acknowledge that coaching is just one form of leadership. Goleman (1998) helpfully outlines the range of leadership approaches that an individual needs to develop and their utility. Nevertheless, from a people-focused perspective we believe coaching gives disproportionate positive impact on both well-being and performance improvement.

64 • *Behavioural Skills for Effective Policing*

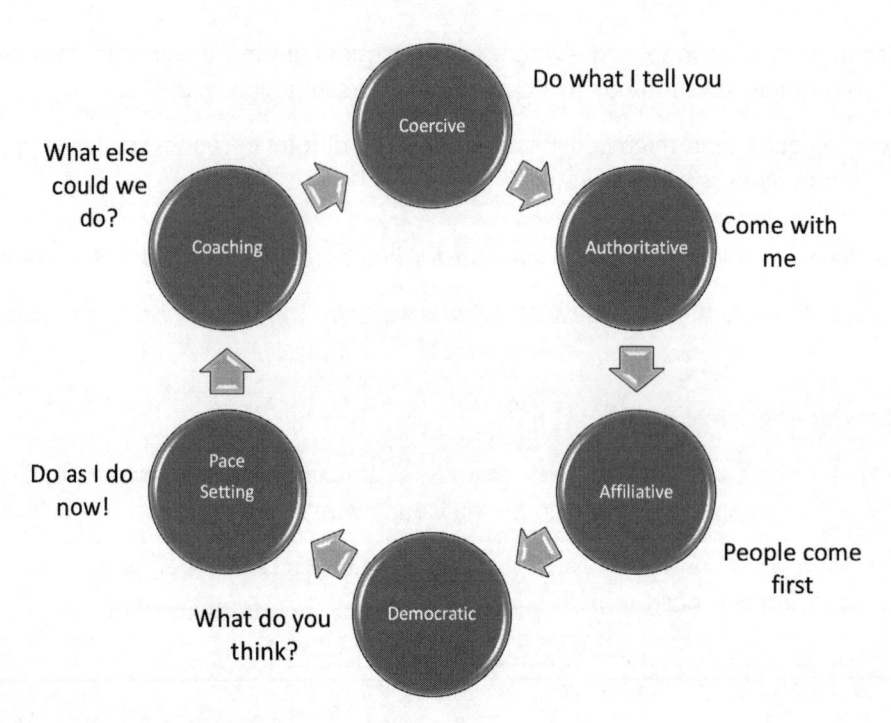

Figure 4.1 Leadership styles

We would argue that in the past, there has sometimes been a reluctance to use coaching proactively – as an opportunity to develop the leadership style of an individual, the culture of a team or indeed a whole force. It is our contention that this is because the true value of coaching was not yet been fully recognised by leaders and in fact was only seen by the dominant leadership culture as a remedial tool should there be a perceived deficit in someone's performance.

Alternatively, from our perspective, a coaching culture starts by being clear about the results that are required and carefully defining what success will look and feel like. Drawing on successful change programmes across the public and private sectors, these should include:

- attracting and retaining top talent;
- developing the behaviours which give the confidence and skill to challenge our 'status quo' and affect positive performance improvement;
- recognising the limiting effect of our current approach;
- achieving top-level buy-in that emotionally embraces and models the cultural shift being sought;
- embracing partnerships with external providers and communities that will support the career success, standards and ethics sought.

The development of the behaviours that we want to see in people as individuals, in leading teams and in leading organisations through creating the environment for a coaching culture to flourish is absolutely essential if policing is going adapt to the challenges ahead as articulated in College of Policing 2040 report. As they clearly state:

By exploring how policing's operating environment might change over the longer term, police leaders can identify what action should be taken now to prepare current and future officers, staff and volunteers for the challenges that lie ahead. (College of Policing, 2020)

This report sets out challenges in relation to well-being, inclusion, community cohesion and partnership. Leaders at all levels within the organisation including leading-self are going to need to be able to lead in a much more collaborative, caring and compassionate style to deliver against these challenges. A coaching approach to leadership facilitates these issues.

This is about creating a far more powerful emotional connection running throughout the organisation in order for leaders to facilitate a more people centred coaching approach to performance improvement. This then gives individuals the self-confidence to shape their own destiny. As Goleman suggests, by increasing self-confidence it facilitates growth in self-worth and capabilities. Achieving this means that individuals are more confident in:

- presenting themselves with self-assuredness, ie have presence;
- voicing views that may be unpopular and going out on a limb for what is right;
- being decisive, able to make sound decisions despite uncertainties and pressures (Goleman, 1998).

It is also, as Kouzes and Posner argue, about *proximity 'you have to get close to people if you're going to find out what motivates them, what they like and don't like, and what kinds of recognition they most appreciate'* (Kouzes and Posner, 2017). After all, real commitment is putting our emotional weight behind that which we initially were sceptical about.

An essential ingredient for success is creating focused development programmes that underpin the direction of change. Currently, the benefits of focused development programmes in supporting and encouraging the progression of staff that are underrepresented in both leadership positions and specialist teams in policing is recognised by the College of Policing, the Superintendents association and the National Black Police Association. All have bespoke programmes specifically aimed at addressing issues that may impact on individual's confidence and aspirations. Coaching is utilised in order to support staff with broader cultural challenges when transitioning into different roles and police forces.

Leaders need to be encouraged to understand the benefits of creating the environment where a coaching style of leadership can flourish in order to increase the productivity of the workforce. Coaching creates a movement within our mindset from one that is fixed:

- that avoids challenge;
- expects rewards without too much effort;
- avoids regular feedback;
- blames others for mistakes;

towards a growth mindset that:

- encourages challenge;
- sees hard work as essential;
- views feedback as constructive;
- uses set-backs as a wake-up call (Dweck, 2017).

By developing coaching through a growth mindset approach, it has the potential to create a successful organisation that is empowered and resilient. It is also about being flexible about how coaching can be utilised as this short, non-police case study demonstrates.

CASE STUDY

Company One, who deal with vulnerable children, have a policy that staff members will not be disciplined for *poor performance*. Instead, in a mindset that centres on positive learning, they are committed to a culture of coaching that will improve performance. In this sense poor performance is discussed with individuals, explored for cause and effect and an action plan is agreed an implemented.

At the same time, they do reserve the right to apply discipline for *poor behaviour* because they want to ensure that those whom they select to work within the organisation constantly exhibit the positive behaviours the organisation embraces.

This is not about adopting a soft-option to performance and behaviours; but it is about creating a growth mindset that seeks to maximise the impact of every employee within the organisation.

Coaching for Performance underpins the philosophy of Company One as it transitions towards being acknowledged as a world-leading centre of excellence in its specialism.

Critical success factors

Momentum is shifting in the world of employee development. There is now a recognition that mere training alone does not create embedded sustainable cultural change and performance improvement. Traditional training is typically centred on developing the technical skills of individuals with long-held, uniform, beliefs being imposed on trainees. Success depends on several factors, not the least of which are the skill of the trainer, the motivation of the trainee and the opportunity to implement newly learned skills with effective evaluation, revision and reimplementation. This would be supervised by co-colleagues who subscribe to the original training methods.

Effective coaching, by its very definition, adapts to the learning style of the individual employee. Coaching is fluid, non-linear and explorative. Coaching deliberately creates an environment where the coachees' talents are nurtured in the style that suits them. Coaching goes far beyond the old adage – *being treating how we would want to be treated ourselves*; towards a far more progressive mindset of – *treating people how they want to be treated*. To that extent, coaching creates the greenhouse that nurtures fragile growth in a safe environment.

CASE STUDY

One such example can be seen in the culture at Company Two, a specialist finance provider to the UK transport sector. Company Two have embedded a specific in-house coaching programme aimed at developing their senior and middle management personnel, equipping them with the coaching skills to develop themselves and their colleagues around them. This is already paying dividends with increased performance levels, reduced attrition rates, stronger engagement and increased satisfaction levels among staff and wider stakeholders.

We have now entered the age of coaching and policing needs to fully engage with this approach. Coaching is fundamental to creating sustainable behavioural upgrades and is the primary enabler for people realising their full potential and delivering in high-performing organisations. The most successful cultures on the planet are, at their heart, coaching cultures.

- FC Barcelona (sport).
- New Zealand All Blacks (sport).
- South West Airlines (air travel).
- Barry Wehmiller (manufacturing).
- GSK (pharmaceuticals).

The above organisations have all recognised that if they invest in their people and through coaching create a culture where people feel connected to the mission and values of the organisation, then performance will significantly improve. In the above cases the organisations and the teams have seen significant increases in performance whether that be on the pitch, delivering performance results, excellent customer service or productivity and profitability.

An excellent example of this is to be found in *The South West Airlines Way* by Jody Hoffer Gittell (2005). Here she discusses how a '*warrior spirit*' and '*servant's heart*' have been coached into the culture in order to achieve outstanding connectivity and performance. The airline, founded in the early 1970s is synonymous with service, performance and have delivered profitability across every trading quarter since their inception.

> **REFLECTIVE PRACTICE**
>
> - How would you describe the culture within your organisation?
> - Does your organisation value its people?
> - How does it demonstrate worth?
> - Where might a more coaching approach add value to performance improvement?
> - Where would a coaching approach give your organisation a performance edge?

The emotional shift

From a policing perspective, embedding a coaching culture takes much more than the occasional engagement. It requires an emotional shift in perspective that weaves coaching into the fabric of policing. Creating a culture where a coaching style of learning and leadership is seen as a positive and a behaviour that is rewarded through progression opportunities and promotion processes needs to embedded right across the organisation.

Time needs to be taken to explain the 'why' to the staff so that they understand the mission and values of the organisation, the behaviours that are expected and what will be rewarded and recognised.

So, what would be the critical success factors needed in order to embed coaching into the culture? We believe that there are elements that need to be present from the outset or the risk of failure increases significantly. Vital among these is the emotional buy-in and participation of the senior leadership across the organisation. If they don't get involved then coaching becomes something that is done to others and not experienced by everyone. Conversely, it is vital that the availability of coaching is not perceived as being more readily available the higher up the organisation an individual is placed. This is about a way of doing business centred on equality of opportunity.

Coaching therefore needs to permeate every level of policing and be part of the DNA of organisational behaviours. We will know when we have come close to achieving the goal when the following are in place.

1. There is clear and repeated evidence of a growth mindset across the organisation.
2. The leadership mandate is bought in, and actively engaged, in coaching.
3. Coaching is readily available to, expected of, and practiced by officers and staff.

4. There is an expectation that developing coaching skills is a critical part of personal and organisational growth.

5. Coaching and feedback are a routine part of how policing does its business.

6. Engaging in difficult conversations becomes a core competency (see Scott, 2017).

The structure

Added to the above success factors is the need to have a structured approach that maximises the opportunity for learning. A discipline in planning, executing, reflection and having clear next steps to ensure success. The following case study demonstrates where initial success was achieved and then allowed to escape due to time pressures and the demands of the everyday role. This change process has ultimately resulted in a positive change in culture, yet if we knew what we know now – we would have created an even more structured approach to the process. This is a case study that demonstrates how precarious cultural change can be.

CASE STUDY

A coaching culture in policing

In 2016 Merseyside Police developed a new force strategy which focused on putting the communities first and at the heart of its decision-making. The new Chief Constable Andy Cooke QPM also wanted to further develop the values-based leadership that had been started by Sir Jon Murphy QPM through a 'just triology' of:

- just listen;
- just think;
- just talk.

C C Cooke recognised that this values-based leadership needed to be the golden thread throughout the organisation to link in new force strategy, with the new targeting operating model and a value-based leadership approach. As such, he took the bold approach to invest in personal development for every single member of staff within Merseyside Police.

Following the completion of a personality questionnaire each member of staff irrespective of rank, grade or role received an individually created personality profile and attended a half-day session which explained the different types of personality, how people may respond as individuals and also interact with other members of their team and with their line manager.

The session also made the connection between these profiles and the force strategy. The majority of the sessions were personally opened by CC Cooke but if he was not available, one of the other Chief Officers opened the session. This demonstrated to the organisation just how important these sessions were to the Chief Constable but also provided an opportunity to explain to the workforce why it was so important to the success of the force in delivering the force strategy and the new target operating model.

The energy and desire for change within the organisation was high and the sessions were extremely well received by the organisations. There was very little negativity from anybody that attended.

The sessions created momentum and individuals, teams and leaders took the learning back to their workplaces and found ways to use what they had been taught about themselves. The sessions created a legacy within Merseyside Police; people still talk about their profiles and they are still used to some degree at a team level to understand team dynamics.

The environment was set for a successful transition and change in culture, and yet progress stalled and momentum faltered.

As a result, the opportunity to maximise this incredible investment in the short term was lost, some staff moved on and interest transitioned to other competing actions and (inadvertently) organisational disappointment and frustration ensued.

The senior leadership team knew that this investment could not be a one off and that they needed to go back to the profiles, the sessions and look at what next in relation to embedding a coaching culture.

On reflection, the issues that should have been addressed were as follows.

- There were no agreed or defined next steps to follow up the investment.
- A change in senior leaders with less of an emotional connection to the profiles.
- Organisation busyness.
- Financial investment required to mainstream the learning and change the culture.

The relationships

We want to further emphasise something we identified at the start of the chapter. A coaching culture demands that professional objectivity between coach and coachee is maintained. Therefore, the balance between coach and coachee is a negotiate space based on mutual respect. This is not about rank or role! On the one hand the coach must feel uninhibited and able to ask the coachee anything. On the other, the person being coached must respect the willingness of their coach to make themselves (potentially) personally uncomfortable by exploring patterns of behaviour and performance matters that may be getting unintended results. It is clear therefore that the psychological contract within the relationship is agreed and formally set.

This is what we class as a *familiar/remote professional relationship*: familiar, in the sense that areas of behaviour, skills, attitude, values can be fully explored; remote, enough to maintain an atmosphere of objectivity, unhindered by personal bias. Both parties must be willing to observe these dynamics in order that the sessions can be *in the zone*. We spoke earlier of the need to have flow within the coaching relationship and this is essential because it creates an environment where both parties are fully invested, there are clear goals and there is a healthy balance between levels of challenge and sense of reward. Coaching will instinctively gravitate towards a feedback conversation that explores personal blind spots and behavioural improvements. These are often the hardest peer-to-peer conversations of all.

To ensure that the coaching relationship remains healthy, the work of Martin Seligman can assist (Seligman, 2011). In his book *Flourish*, he contributes to our understanding of the coaching relationship by identifying criterion that can create a sense of well-being. These are:

- positive emotions;
- full engagement;
- positive relationships;
- meaning;
- a sense of accomplishment.

In achieving all these, his argument is that we create a positive symbiotic relationship of well-being where an individual can fully achieve their potential. Effective coaching therefore requires navigating the narrow path of psychological safety and objectivity.

REFLECTIVE PRACTICE

- What circumstances could you imagine that would derail the embedding of a coaching culture in policing?

The business of coaching: making the connections

'Coaching' is about unlocking a person's potential to enable fulfilment.

'Culture', from the Latin 'Cul-tis' which means (literally) to care.

(Coyle, 2018).

Policing is moving much more to a place where it is working with partners and communities to enable individuals and families to reach their full potential. This applies to all our stakeholder groups, be it our communities, our staff, our partners – put simply, it's why every member of the police service gets out of bed in the morning.

By embedding a positive coaching culture across our organisations, we potentially replace the inhibitions created by an interventions-/corrective-based approach with the confidence to be creative, to experiment, learn from errors and be vulnerable in the spotlight of our peers. In turn, we will create the platform that will serve our ability to innovate and build trust across all ranks.

In doing the research for this book and in implementing cultural change programmes we have engaged with a number of people listening to where they perceived that a coaching approach added to our abilities to connect more authentically within, and external to, the organisation. In summary, they look like this.

- Experiencing a more mature approach to personal development, staff will be more engaged across all ranks and grades. Given that there is a significant war on talent this has the potential to make policing a more attractive sector for high-performing individuals.

- It also provides a greenhouse platform – a career-long commitment to the development of officer and staff talent. Individuals, experiencing a constructive learning environment have the opportunity to nurture their own talent and develop an appreciation of their growing potential.

- Coaching places the growth of the individual at the heart of organisational intent. For these reasons it has a strong commitment to supporting officer and staff well-being. We achieve a more rounded approach to the "balance" sought around work/personal life. It is therefore not too much of stretch to suggest that it will have a positive impact on retention rates.

- Developing personal and organisational communication, and comprehension, styles. Appreciating (and experimenting) with other perspectives and diversity of thought develops better appreciation of others' viewpoints.

- When people feel a certain degree of control of their own destiny it helps grow officer confidence and self-belief.

However, the approach is not just people centred though that is a significant element. There is a real business case for embedding a coaching culture across organisations. Financial considerations form a fundamental part of modern policing. It's no longer enough to merely deliver savings – modern policing demands a tangible return on capital employed. Such returns require to be measurable and capable of being articulated through our balance sheet. We argue therefore that the financial benefits of a fully functioning coaching culture are clear and immediate through:

- increased wellness and resilience;
- organic talent development;

- reduced recruitment and absence costs;
- tangibly enhanced inclusivity.

> **REFLECTIVE PRACTICE**
>
> - What personal benefits can you anticipate accruing from a fully functioning coaching culture?

Does this stuff work?

We have been keen to identify the critical success factors that are associated with the creation of a more coaching approach to leadership and communication within organisations. We have considerable experience in working cross-sector, and so to utilise learning from elsewhere we want to demonstrate the practical impact that coaching has on cultural change. Embedded within these change processes is a desire to make the organisations more efficient while at the same time create high-quality services to customers and communities. In other words, values, behaviours and actions are aligned. We have practical, day-to-day experience of both.

Company One: this is a facility that is transitioning from being public sector financed to being privately financially self-sufficient within seven years. In this period it seeks to be recognised as a world-wide centre of excellence in the support of vulnerable children and their families.

Company Two: are an investment backed organisation that provide finance to the transport/haulage sector. They have grown rapidly with five acquisitions in the last five years and are located on six sites throughout the United Kingdom with over 110 employees. They have utilised a coaching culture approach to overcome the challenges of bringing together cultures that had, until recently:

- been in competition with one another;
- not known one another beyond a superficial level;
- no particular care or bonds with one another.

The collaboration that emerges from an embedded coaching culture recently made them an investment target for a larger financial institution (deal now complete).

While these organisations are different from policing in many ways, the challenges, complexities and perhaps outdated practices had to be overcome. The benefits that have accrued are numerous. Here are the top ten key practical changes.

1. Buy-in at the highest level has permeated the whole organisation. Senior staff modelling desired behaviours have facilitated lower-level buy-in and created an increased sense of oneness.

2. Improved staff engagement (confirmed by data led surveys) as staff sense the sincerity around their individual development.

3. Willingness to embrace peer to peer accountability rather than vertical accountability. This is a direct result of peers being increasingly clear about what they can expect of one another.

4. Improved levels of trust attributed to increased sense of willingness to be personally vulnerable.

    a. Peer to peer vulnerability has become expected – this is now the bedrock of organisational performance.

5. Increasingly productive difficult conversations, resulting in constructive professional conflict.

    a. Increased willingness to talk about what's NOT going well – these reflections have improved performance and engagement.

6. Organisational non-negotiable behaviours are improving. This is a result of improved understanding, regular dialogue and willingness to have fierce conversations.

7. Improved sense of comprehension of individual behaviour leading to stretched thinking to accommodate individual styles and preferences.

8. Staff turnover has reduced as the belief in the sincerity of the principles of the coaching culture grows. This has offered the benefit of reduced recruitment costs.

9. Improved decision-making with decisions being made with clear intent.

10. Improved relationships with suppliers and community. General stakeholder buy-in is strong (and appreciated) – this has included stakeholder feedback around organisation blind spots!

Key takeaways

- The key elements of the coach–coachee relationship are where they believe the best IN one another, want the best FOR one another and expect the best OF one another.

- Coaching builds cultures that overcome the cynics, the naysayers and outdated practices – the objections are the same across all sectors.

Reflective practice

In order to make this cultural change happen in policing it might be important to reflect on three questions.

1. What is policing outstanding at and how could we better coach this into the culture?
2. Has policing got any fatal flaws in how it does its business and how can we coach that out of the culture?
3. If you were in charge, what are the three to five things that you would break over the next 12–18 months in order to make change happen?

What about team coaching?

The principles that underpin the creation of a coaching culture across an organisation are exactly the same when discussing the team environment. Indeed, we would argue that within teams the principles are experienced in a more intense manner because of the close proximity of peers and work colleagues.

At the heart of every successful team is the need for trust; embedded in how they do business is self-confidence; in moments of deep crisis is the ability to have fierce conversations; in order to perform at the maximum efficiency, is the need to respect diversity and difference; to stop people being disruptive, is the need for effective feedback; at the heart of everything is clarity around intent and a deep-rooted connection to values.

One of the critical points in team coaching is the need for each and every member to focus on their connectivity with the other parts of the team. A critical success factor is therefore now how each individual is performing. Rather it is about the interface between people and how these help performance improvements when dealing with other aspects of the organisation, partner agencies and communities.

In coaching teams, it is also about helping them achieve their mission as a whole, assisting them prepare for potential hazards that lie ahead. In his excellent book *Leadership Team Coaching* (2017), Peter Hawkins asks two great questions in this zone.

1. What are the top five ways our plans can be derailed?
2. What might we discover in a year's time that we already know?

Once again this is about taking time to reflect on an area of business, slow down the thinking and make change happen in a sustainable way. He also emphasises the need for teams to understand:

- their primary purpose;
- their strategy;
- their core values;
- their vision for the future.

These are all areas that rest heavily within a coaching approach to change.

Perhaps the one issue that is even more emphasised when working within a team is having the self-awareness and the self-assuredness to be vulnerable in order to improve personal and team performance. Being vulnerable is about being willing to be open. It's about being willing to be emotionally exposed and showing a little more of our authentic selves. When we are willing to move to this psychological place we are liberated to speak up about what we really think, rather than being inhibited by how we want others to react – we are willing to reveal our true selves and bring our whole selves to work. We believe that, ironically, it's only through being willing to be truly vulnerable that enables us to move towards being invulnerable.

The willingness to forego our need for self-preservation is counter intuitive for most, but for police officers and staff it's instinctive – we are better placed than most as we put ourselves in harm's way, daily, for a living!

Reflective practice

- What are you most vulnerable around (in a professional context)?
- How would you encourage a growth mindset?

Professionalising the service

The College of Policing is quite rightly leading the approach to professionalise policing. Never has the need for the officers to have the skills, knowledge and values to meet the demands and expectation placed on the police service in the current climate.

For several years comparisons have been made to the training required for the professions of nursing and teaching and questions raised to how the training given to police officers compares, which is quite right considering the position they hold and the decisions that they are required to make and the impact that these can make on the trust and confidence in policing of our communities.

The College of Policing has developed the Police Constable Degree Apprenticeship and Police Forces around the country are developing apprenticeship programmes for Police Community Support Officers, Custody Detentions Officer and Call Handlers. All of these programmes being developed to ensure that the policing family deliver a truly professional service.

Andy Marsh QPM the Chief Executive Officer from the College of Policing outlined in his article in the *Daily Telegragh* (8 November 2021) that *'policing is not a vocation, it is a profession'*. The development of every officer needs to reflect this, with a permanent focus on modern skills that the jobs requires and an adherence to the high standards that the public expect.

The College of Policing also recognises the importance of leadership in professionalising the service. They have developed leadership and management resources for people working within policing. These resources include developing coaching and mentoring skills especially to support the development and progression of officers and staff who are currently underrepresented in policing.

CHAPTER SUMMARY

Drawing on our experiences, and hopefully having convinced you that a coaching approach would produce more positive outcomes for your performance, we want to be explicit about what we think are the core elements that will help move an organisation forward. This is not about so-called soft skills; rather it's about embedding change in cultures that are both traditional in outlook and robust in confronting change.

Critical issues

1. A coaching approach underpins required organisational behaviours and moves the culture in a transformational manner.
2. Coaching needs to be forward-thinking.
3. This is about empowering employees to explore their own value and take personal responsibility.
4. Coaching requires emotional engagement and connection throughout the organisation. It is a requirement from leaders at *all* levels.
5. Coaching creates moments of pause – in order to slow thinking down.
6. The whole concept of coaching centres on performance improvement.
7. The attitude to coaching needs to move from a remedial tool towards forward facing improvement.
8. At its core coaching has deep-rooted respect for diversity and difference.
9. Coaching requires the organisation to think about its ability to adopt a growth mindset.

10. Coaching is a structured process and requires considerable planning and commitment.

11. Coaching is slower than mentoring. It is quicker to tell someone (mentoring) than to ask them what they think (coaching). In a world that values speed the danger is coaching gets replaced by telling-managers who are under pressure.

12. Senior leaders must create the environment within which they encourage other leaders and managers to slow down, engage appropriately with the needs of the people they are leading, and ultimately let them flourish.

Conclusion

Modern policing faces huge challenges on how we will adapt to the demands of the expectations form communities, government, partner agencies and, perhaps most importantly, our own staff. We maintain that embedding a coaching culture will provide the platform through which we will develop and retain talent, improve performance and increase our return on investment in our people.

We know we cannot mentor our way out change because that only harnesses what we already know. Rather, for policing to be transformational it needs to allow our people to flourish in order to create new thinking and new ways of doing business. We need to utilise our coaching approach in order to slow down so that we can continually generate sustained success.

Further reading

Edmondson, A (2018) *The Fearless Organization*. New Jersey: Wiley

Collins, J (2011) *How The Mighty Fall*. New York: HarperCollins

Bungay Stainer, M (2016) *The Coaching Habit*. Toronto: Box of Crayons Press.

Syed, M (2015) *Black Box Thinking*. London: John Murray Press.

Williams, D and Howell, E (2021) *Leadership Moments From NASA*. Toronto: ECW Press.

References

Clutterbuck, D (1991) *Everyone Needs a Mentor*, 2nd ed. London: Institute of Personnel Development.

Coyle, D (2018) *The Culture Code*. Kent: Cornerstone Digital.

College of Policing (2020) *Preparing Policing for Future Challenges and Demands*. https://www.college.police.uk/article/preparing-policing-future-challenges-and-demands

Csikszentmihalyi, M (2002) *Flow*. London: Rider.

Dweck, C (2017) *Mindset*, 6th ed. London: Robinson.

Edmondson, A (2018) *The Fearless Organization*. New Jersey: Wiley.

Gittell, J (2005) *The South West Airlines Way*. New York: McGraw-Hill.

Goleman, D (1998) *Working with Emotional Intelligence*. St Helens: Bloomsbury.

Harris, T (2013) *Im OK – You're OK*. London: Cornerstone Digital.

Hawkins, P (2017) *Leadership Team Coaching: Developing Collective Transformational Leadership*, 3rd ed. London: Kogan Page.

Kerr, J (2015) *Legacy*. London: Constable.

Kouzes, J and Posner, B (2017) *The Leadership Challenge*, 6th ed. New Jersey: Wiley.

Parsloe, E and Wray, M (2016) *Coaching and Mentoring*. London: Kogan Page.

Scott, S (2017) *Fierce Conversations*. London: Piatkus.

Seligman, M (2011) *Flourish*. London: Nicholas Brealey Publications.

Sinek, S (2009) *Start with Why*, p 8. London: Portfolio Penguin.

Whitmore, J (2017) *Coaching for Performance*. London: Nicholas Brealey Publications.

5 Leading effective teams
Dee Collins

CHAPTER OBJECTIVES

This chapter will help you:

- consider what an effective team looks and feels like to work within and lead;
- explore real and hypothetical situations;
- consider team theories and how they can be applied in practice;
- develop your reflective learning to facilitate a more effective leadership approach.

What makes an effective team?

My formative years were dominated by my love of sport and in particular team sport. I graduated from 'pirates' and 'British bulldogs' at primary school to netball, hockey, tennis and volleyball in my secondary education. I thoroughly enjoyed being part of a team who worked hard and energetically, who understood one another's abilities and played to our strengths. I recognised my own areas to improve upon and that we all had something positive to contribute. I quickly understood that if everyone pulled together with a common shared purpose then the results were more likely to take a positive direction. Having a strong team captain, who recognised and valued the different skills within the team and who motivated us all to want to do our best, inspired me to not just attend the regular training sessions, but to also undertake additional activities to help me improve as a team player. During my time in further education, I committed a lot of my time to team sports, captaining teams, building rapport, relishing the challenges and learning practically what worked to make us successful (and importantly what didn't). Joining the Police was an obvious choice for me as I viewed them as a whole as a professional and dedicated team (fired up by wonderful stories from a friend's dog handler father).

A starting point for this chapter is perhaps *'what is an effective team?'* There is a great deal of research and material about this, with differing views from writers and academics. There is a shared view though that teams that perform well don't 'just happen'. A team is a group of people who have the same aim, ambition and outlook that drive their ability to work together to achieve common shared goals. There are two important aspects to consider – Team Building, ie, likeminded individuals who contribute towards the shared vision, and Team Work, ie, the ability of every individual to understand one another in a group and efficiently undertake tasks. Underpinning each team is culture, where to work together effectively individuals need to trust and respect one another; see Lencioni (2002) who states, *'Remember teamwork begins by building trust …'*.

There are a number of characteristics that have been identified by many authors as being a key part of effective teams.

1. Clear direction

    - A clear sense of purpose and measurable outcomes.
    - This unifies the group, and every team member knows what that purpose is and how they contribute to it.
    - Need to communicate the team goals and desired outcomes.
    - Leave some flexibility for the team to achieve the goal.

2. Clear communication and open doors

    - Communication is crucial for building a sense of being collegiate.
    - Aim for open conversational relations between all team members and don't talk unsupportively behind each other's back.
    - Adopt a genuine 'open door' to share thoughts and ideas.
    - Don't forget to listen and hear.

3. Generate a spirit of collaboration

    - This will generate more creativity and different approaches to problems.
    - Successful teams tend to have strong leaders who keep everyone on the same page and keep any squabbling to a minimum.

4. Set out the team rules about how you are going to work together
    - This helps to keep the team on track and eliminate any ambiguity.
    - Develop these rules together to form a 'team contract' or something similar that can act as a touchstone/anchor.

5. Set out defined roles for each team member
    - Skill sets.
    - Specific roles.
    - Different styles of thinking.
    - Someone who does detail.
    - Creative thinkers.
    - someone who will monitor progress etc.

6. Encouraging difference
    - Set out common goals but encourage alternative views and ideas.
    - Collectively by doing this you will generate a wider range of ideas to choose from.

7. Mutual accountability
    - High-performing teams accept responsibility as individuals and as a team.

8. Team trust
    - Trust is essential for teams to be effective.
    - Trust enables team members to share their views freely.
    - Team building exercises, development and problem solving activities help to build trust.

9. Decision-making
    - The leader brings together different views and formulates group response.
    - Develop the decision-making process and any hierarchy.
    - Consider how to record decisions and how to best share them with the wider organisation.

10. Efficient use of ideas
    - Develop ways of being able to work together through challenges such as workshops, board-blasts, concept thinking, sharing thinking etc.
    - Use facilitators where appropriate to enable all team members to participate.
11. Enjoy working together
    - People get satisfaction from working well together; this improves overall well-being.

By utilising these 11 characteristics team leaders can map out and plan what they need to consider if they want to build a successful high-performing team. Most of the components within this list will have been applied to many of the recent Great British Olympic teams during the 2021 events at Tokyo.

REFLECTIVE PRACTICE

Think about the elements that contribute towards being part of an effective team in your current work environment.

- How many of these elements do you recognise and how many are missing?
- What would you do as a leader or team member to make a team more effective?
- Is there anything else you would add to this list?

Effective teams theory

It is reputed that Helen Keller once said, '*Alone we can do so little, together we can do so much*'.

There are many theoretical models to consider when building a team or becoming a new member of an existing team. The characteristics of an effective team summarise the numerous different approaches that have been cited during the last 50 years. In my experience, while some leadership traits can appear instinctive or intuitive many of the skills needed to build well-performing teams can be learned or adapted using some of the theories that work for you.

The first consideration when working with teams is building the team in the first place, or having been appointed as the leader of a team new to you – determine/assess the effectiveness of that team and build upon it.

John Adair's Action-Centred Leadership model

John Adair's Action-Centred Leadership model (1973) is helpful when addressing the early stages of developing a team. He suggests that there are three key elements to consider in order to develop an effective team – Individual needs, the needs of the team as a whole, and the actual task/purpose of that team. By carefully balancing these three areas and giving each interdependent aims, plans and support, a team is more likely to be successful. In current thinking, the culture underpinning the team and providing for individual and team well-being and resilience is critical to team success too.

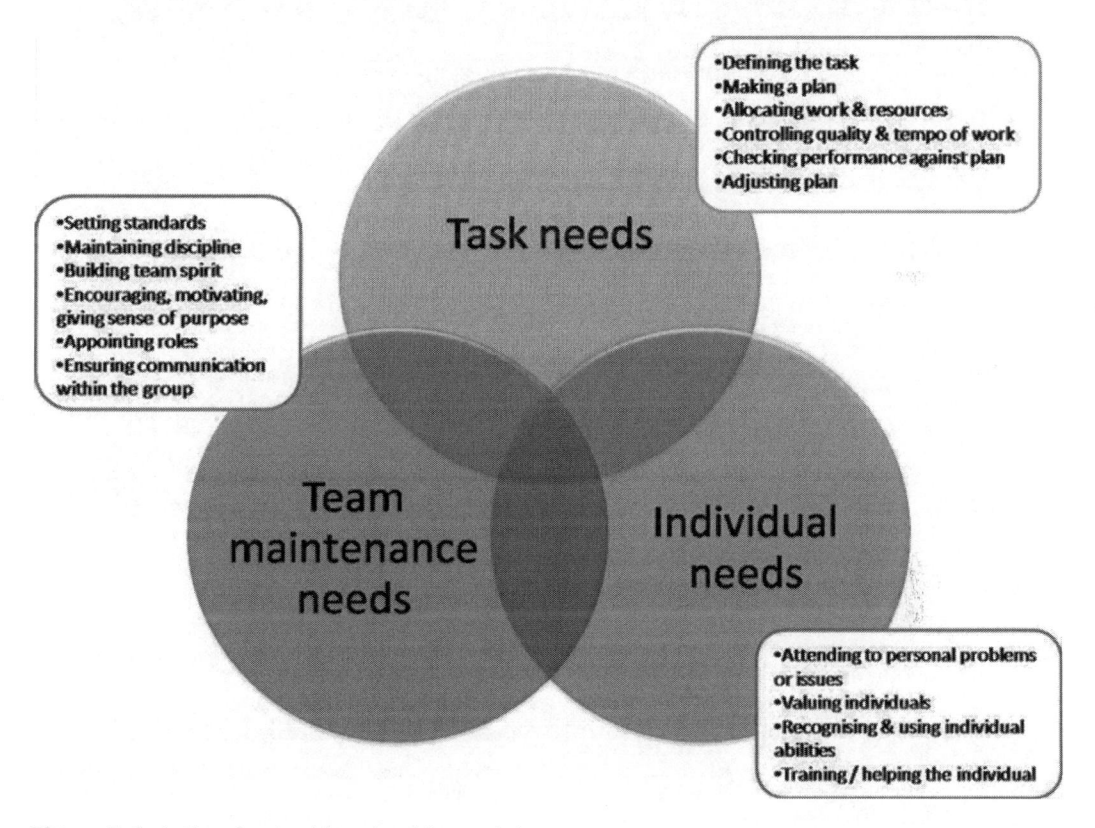

Task needs
- Defining the task
- Making a plan
- Allocating work & resources
- Controlling quality & tempo of work
- Checking performance against plan
- Adjusting plan

Team maintenance needs
- Setting standards
- Maintaining discipline
- Building team spirit
- Encouraging, motivating, giving sense of purpose
- Appointing roles
- Ensuring communication within the group

Individual needs
- Attending to personal problems or issues
- Valuing individuals
- Recognising & using individual abilities
- Training / helping the individual

Figure 5.1 Action-Centred Leadership model

As a huge admirer of the leadership skills (rather than management skills) of Ernest Shackleton and his infamous Imperial Trans-Antarctic Expedition in 1914–1917, think about how each of these three key elements will have been considered by him in the race to survive the disaster that ensued.

Myers-Briggs theory (MBTI)

Myers-Briggs theory is an adaptation of the theory of psychological types produced by Carl Gustav Jung (1921). It is based upon 16 personality types and acts as a useful reference point to understand individuals' personalities and therefore how they are more likely to behave, operate, work with others and deal with stress. Katharine Briggs and Isabel Briggs Myers's theory proposes four preferences in how an individual deals with issues (see Figure 5.2). I have become convinced that understanding how each individual team member thinks and reacts can significantly assist in building a diverse and thereby broader thinking team. The greater the diversity of thinking within the team, the more likely that effective, creative and successful ideas and solutions will be put forward.

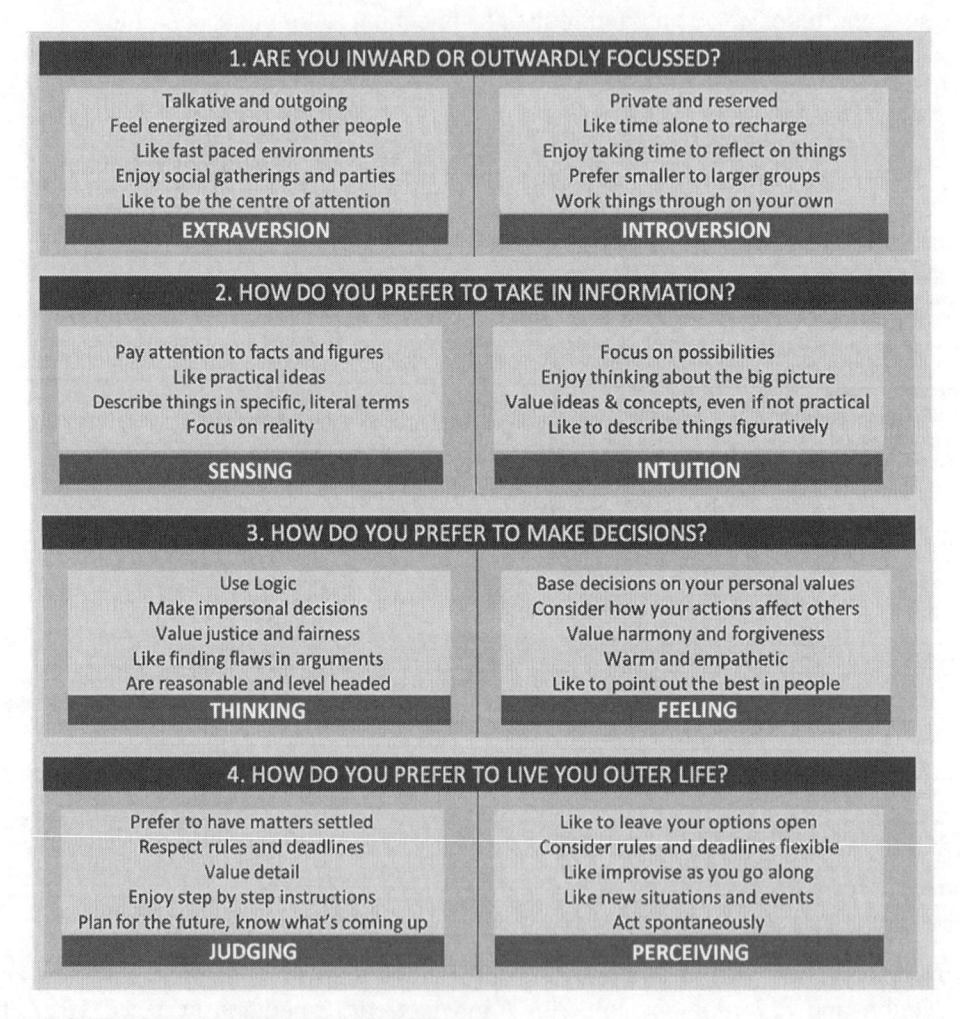

1. ARE YOU INWARD OR OUTWARDLY FOCUSSED?

EXTRAVERSION	INTROVERSION
Talkative and outgoing	Private and reserved
Feel energized around other people	Like time alone to recharge
Like fast paced environments	Enjoy taking time to reflect on things
Enjoy social gatherings and parties	Prefer smaller to larger groups
Like to be the centre of attention	Work things through on your own

2. HOW DO YOU PREFER TO TAKE IN INFORMATION?

SENSING	INTUITION
Pay attention to facts and figures	Focus on possibilities
Like practical ideas	Enjoy thinking about the big picture
Describe things in specific, literal terms	Value ideas & concepts, even if not practical
Focus on reality	Like to describe things figuratively

3. HOW DO YOU PREFER TO MAKE DECISIONS?

THINKING	FEELING
Use Logic	Base decisions on your personal values
Make impersonal decisions	Consider how your actions affect others
Value justice and fairness	Value harmony and forgiveness
Like finding flaws in arguments	Warm and empathetic
Are reasonable and level headed	Like to point out the best in people

4. HOW DO YOU PREFER TO LIVE YOU OUTER LIFE?

JUDGING	PERCEIVING
Prefer to have matters settled	Like to leave your options open
Respect rules and deadlines	Consider rules and deadlines flexible
Value detail	Like improvise as you go along
Enjoy step by step instructions	Like new situations and events
Plan for the future, know what's coming up	Act spontaneously

Figure 5.2 *The four dichotomies of Myers-Briggs*

The first pair of styles is 'Extraversion and Introversion' and concerns how an individual directs their energy. Extraversion focuses energy on dealing with people, situations and things in an overt and active way. Introversion focuses energy inwardly and deals with ideas, information and theories.

The second pair of styles is 'Sensing and Intuition' and concerns the type of information that an individual prefers to process. Sensing involves a person's preferring to deal with facts, descriptions and what is known. Intuition focuses on ideas, possibilities and what isn't known.

The third pair of styles is 'Thinking and Feeling' which reflects how an individual makes decisions. If a person decides based on logic or analysis then their preference is for thinking. If values are at the heart of decision-making then the preference is feeling.

The last pair of styles is 'Judgement and Perception' and concerns how an individual prefers to live their life. If an individual prefers plans and structure, they have a judgement preference. If someone prefers spontaneity, flexibility or dealing with issues as they come along, then their preference is perception.

Putting each of these pairs together through a specifically designed personality questionnaire develops an individual overarching personality type and a description of how a person is likely to think and work including when under stress. By determining what each individual team member's personality preference is, a team leader can assess where the collective strengths and areas for development may be. It relies on all team members participating in the process, and also does need refreshing from time to time as people can and do change. That said it is a very useful tool that can help to predict what may happen when teams come together.

By way of example, when I was a new Inspector and getting to know my team, it struck me that while I thought I was being extremely clear in my requests of individuals and the team, it became apparent that my messages were not always landing, or that a piece of requested work didn't arrive in the format I was expecting. To summarise, simply, I am an ENFP and was talking to a team of predominantly ESTJs! Understanding this theory and how to adapt my communication style to facilitate a better shared conception of what was needed.

Belbin team roles

Dr Meredith Belbin (1981) and his team conducted extensive behavioural research to determine eight specific roles that need to be undertaken in order for a team to become a highly effective and performing team. The list of roles has developed over time and now includes a 'Specialist' role. Most individuals will have two or three roles that they are most comfortable with undertaking; however, within each role there are strengths and weaknesses. Therefore, depending on the task or objective that the team is tackling, the balance of the roles needs to be considered and discussed.

- Resource investigator: this person has an investigative inquisitive mindset and uses this to scope out ideas and concepts. They are frequently very outgoing and enthusiastic individuals who enjoy seeking out opportunities and developing a network of contacts. They can be over optimistic and risk losing their enthusiastic momentum after the early stages of the project/plan.

- Team worker: this individual works hard to bring the team together and uses their adaptable approach to help identify and complete the work that is needed to achieve the task. They are good listeners and diplomatic and enjoy working in a co-operative collegiate way. They can tend to avoid confrontation or be less willing to make difficult or unpopular decisions.

- Co-ordinator: this person is skilled at keeping the team focused and on track. They are good at identifying which piece of work is best suited to whom, and also at delegating fairly. They help in clarifying objectives and identifying or developing talent. Co-ordinators risk being viewed as allocating too much work to others and perhaps not having their fair share of the workload.

- Plant: this is a highly creative person who can solve problems in imaginative ways. They are free-thinking and innovative with a tendency towards being forgetful or easily distracted. They are particularly good at board blasting and making suggestions as they see issues from many differing perspectives.

- Monitor evaluator: this person provides the logical and rational view to problem solving weighing up each piece of information in an impartial way. They can provide balance in decision-making and are often strategic in their outlook. Their complete focus on the problem may not inspire some team members and they like to have a lot of information before arriving at a decision which could be problematic if there are tight deadlines to be met.

- Specialist: this individual brings specialist subject matter expertise to a team. Their skills and knowledge can significantly assist a team to better understand the issues they are dealing with. They tend to focus on technical information in a relatively narrow field, and risk overloading the team with detail.

- Shaper: this person is full of drive and helps the team to keep moving forwards, particularly if the team is starting to lose momentum. They are bold and can thrive on pressure and enjoy challenge and fast moving problems. If things are going in the way that they would prefer they can be prone to being seen as aggressive or having a fixed view.

- Implementer: an implementer is someone who is good at turning strategy into action. They are practical, efficient, reliable people who enjoy getting the work done. They can be a bit inflexible, particularly if a new approach is needed and their plans have to change or a good new idea is suggested.

- Completer finisher: this individual helps to finalise a project or piece of work and enjoys undertaking the final accuracy checks or finessing the final product. They are strong at searching out errors or areas of weakness and risk spending too much time repeatedly going back over and over a piece of work.

Belbin's profiles assist both individuals to better understand where their own natural fit within a team best sits and helps the team leader determine if they have all of the necessarily skills, experience and behaviours to develop into a high-performing team. In my case as a Chief Constable, I recognise I was a Shaper/Plant – full of ideas and energy to get things done. I absolutely needed a Team Worker/Co-ordinator to both keep me (and the team) on track and also to provide a degree of pragmatism to what ideas I might have.

Tuckman model of group development

Bruce Tuckman (1965) first proposed his model for group development in 1965. He stated that in order for a team to grow collectively, deal with issues, face up to challenges and deliver results they needed to move through four phases of development (see Figure 5.3).

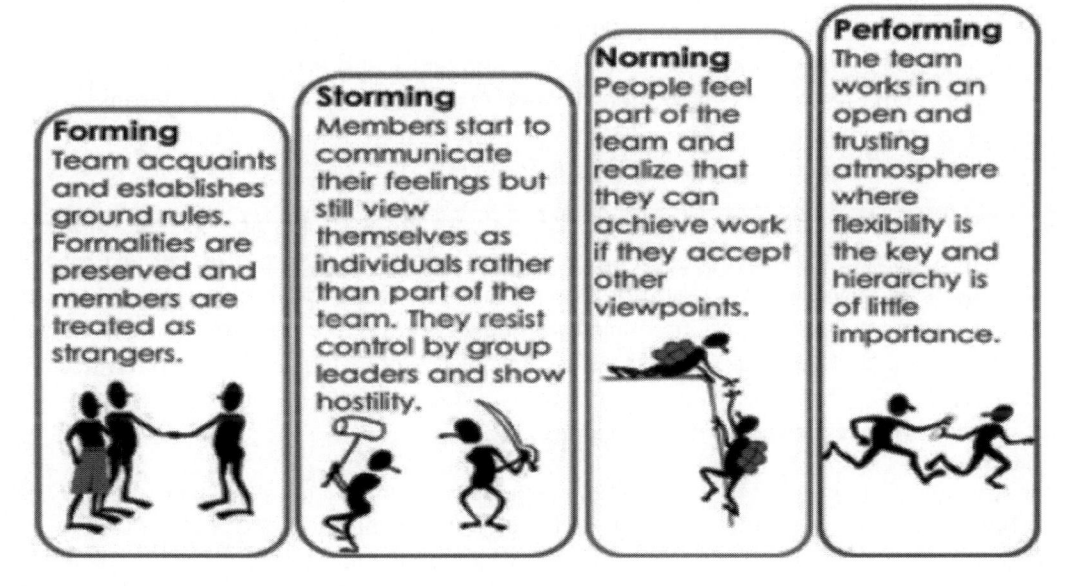

Forming
Team acquaints and establishes ground rules. Formalities are preserved and members are treated as strangers.

Storming
Members start to communicate their feelings but still view themselves as individuals rather than part of the team. They resist control by group leaders and show hostility.

Norming
People feel part of the team and realize that they can achieve work if they accept other viewpoints.

Performing
The team works in an open and trusting atmosphere where flexibility is the key and hierarchy is of little importance.

Figure 5.3 Tuckman model of group development

- Forming: this stage is at the start of the process when individuals come together and learn about their purpose. They identify the goals, aims and objectives and begin to address how to achieve their desired results. Initially team members will operate independently and need time to understand the collective strategic intent. Meetings and discussion tend to focus on the task in hand, how to approach it and who is going to do what. The focus of individual's activity is self-centred until each team member begins to share thoughts, concerns and ideas and risk the potential for conflict. Getting to know one another and being able to express thoughts and feelings takes time and energy and the team leader needs to find ways of facilitating this.

- Storming: the second stage of team development is where the group start to work together and gain one another's trust. They learn about how each other works, what their preferences are and how they learn. The atmosphere and working environment are positive and reserved as confidence grows in sharing or raising more controversial and debatable ideas. Some team members may find this phase generating feelings of anxiety or disorientation and so the leader needs to be clear about what the ambition is for the team and how they want the team to work together. Spelling out what they expect and need from each team member is key. If disagreements or conflict arise then they need to be addressed as soon as they emerge; see below regards managing conflict. Tolerance, respect, patience and participation will be essential if the team is to move onto the next phase. There are occasions when a group may jump straight from stage 1 to stage 3.

- Norming: once any conflict or tensions have been resolved and mutual trust is established the team are more likely to move towards working to the common shared goals. Team members will feel responsible and accountable for their part in the team's success. Ideas can be exchanged in a safe environment and colleagues ideas bounce from one contributor to another enabling greater co-operation and collegiate decisions to be made.

- Performing: when all team members are aware of their roles and contribution to the team, they are focused on achieving the ambition; they are more likely to start to deliver with a greater degree of success. Everyone feels supported and competent and become increasingly empowered to make decisions without having to discuss them collectively knowing that such a decision will fit within the overall plan. Disagreements are managed well and recognised as being healthy provided the way they are managed is accepted by all.

Every team will go through different phases continually dependant on changes of strategy, ambition, plans or team membership itself. Recognition of each phase is helpful to the team leader, particularly when new to a team which may also be new or well established. Healthy adult debate is to be encouraged but tempered with agreement on what is or isn't acceptable behaviour. Setting out a team agreement or contract of how everyone wants to work together can be a helpful touchstone for all to anchor their approach to working together. In my experience at any level within policing or any other organisation most teams go through most of these phases especially when newly brought together or a change in key roles. As a leader it is vital that you facilitate the movement through these phases and ensure any outstanding matters are resolved to avoid them being resurrected (unhelpfully) later.

Harrison Assessment

A newer tool for policing and the broader public sector is the Harrison Assessment which was established in 1990 founded by Dan Harrison PhD Organisational Psychology (htttps://www.harrisonassessments.eu). The tool uses predictive analytics to help organisations select, develop, lead and engage their talent. It has been used within the private sector for some time. Through a series of questions within a structured questionnaire the tool can predict job performance where behavioural competencies are measured including emotional intelligence, work preferences and personality style. The tool assesses the type of work that individuals enjoy and therefore where they are more likely to focus their energy when working within the team.

The approach has also developed a team building tool that generates the strengths and challenges of a team, identifies the best role for team members and assesses the potential for working effectively together or where points of conflict might arise. Strategic teams in particular could utilise this methodology for improving their effectiveness, creating cultural change or identifying where the difficulties may lie. A strength of this approach is that it identifies paradoxes within an individual profile where areas of strength or weakness could come into conflict rendering the individual behaviour to go against their preferred norm. This usually happens when the individual is under stress and can therefore greatly assist the team leader to be able to predict what might happen should stressful challenging situations occur.

While this leadership tool is relatively new to policing, I believe it could be invaluable for teams who are struggling to perform to the best of their potential as it addresses a number of elements of the previous theories together and in particular where leaders will tend to operate under pressure or as a paradox to their normal behaviour.

REFLECTIVE PRACTICE

- Visit the online opportunities within the Harrison Assessment (see website above) to take part in free tests to determine more about yourself.

- Consider how you could best use this information for your own self-development and also how to build your team?

Case study 1

Turning under-performance into effective performance

I was a newly promoted Inspector and was assigned to a shift that, in the view of the management, was significantly underperforming. There were several members of the team who had worked together for some time, alongside a number of new recruits who were each trying to gather evidence of their operational competence via a complex portfolio and assessment process. Up to my appointment the team had had a series of temporary or acting-up Inspectors and it was evident the team felt somewhat unloved or uncared about.

I considered all of the theory I had learned thus far in my career and decided to speak with every member of the shift to determine the root causes for the concerns and also to gain a clear understanding of their aspirations and potential. One long serving member of the team who had 'seen it all' helpfully said '*what this team needs is consistent leadership and someone who makes decisions*' and then added *and they don't even have to be the right decisions – just make one*'.

The Adair model was particularly helpful as I set about understanding individual needs, what the team themselves thought of their own capabilities, what they wanted to achieve as a collective and that their operational performance needed to improve. We worked together to ensure that individual plans were drawn up to help them achieve their personal and professional goals, and also put support mechanisms in place to encourage development. I held regular team meetings, where as a group we discussed how things were going and generated a culture where views could be expressed without sanction provided, they were respectfully delivered and had some evidence to withstand scrutiny. I didn't accept criticism of other teams and the view that this team were constantly having to 'mop up after others'. My view was that by being clear in how we wanted to work together, with the view of doing our best, and demonstrating the values of fairness, respect and trust, our performance as a team would improve and also the team would enjoy working with one another.

Within a few weeks the sense of collective responsibility and camaraderie was palpable. The results began to speak for themselves. The experienced Officers and Staff began to take a positive interest in developing the newer team members; people began to develop greater expertise in differing operational strands which supported their own ambitions but also the performance of the team as a whole. Other teams began to notice and team leaders asked about what we were doing and how we had shifted momentum in such a positive way. Going to work was an absolute pleasure – a sign for me that everything was working. By spending time getting to know and understand each individual team member and setting out a clear and compelling vision/purpose, what had been a fairly dysfunctional team became a strong performing and successful team.

Reflective practice

Imagine you are assigned to a new underperforming team.

- What things would you consider prior to arrival, on first landing, and then over the first few days and weeks to encourage and develop that team?
- How will you know that the team is starting to perform more effectively?

Case study 2

Leading a team under difficult circumstances

In 2014, under difficult circumstances, I was asked to take up the challenge of leading a Police Force. The circumstances of this event were sudden and unexpected, the reasons for which are not for discussion here. That said the impact and consequences for the senior team were enormous. I had only been part of this team for a relatively short period of time and in truth I was still finding my own feet, building up rapport with those I worked alongside and had line management responsibility for. My predecessor had been appointed 12 months earlier when the force was facing huge challenges around finance and overall performance and there were no comprehensive plans for leading through austerity in the way that many other Forces had undertaken. Swift and autocratic decisions had had to be made to get the Force back 'on track' but this had left the senior team and the force in general confused and uncertain about why the changes had been brought in, and where the direction of travel lay. An overarching vision had been articulated but without consultation or participation. The senior team did not feel valued and there was sadly an increasing lack of trust not only between colleagues, but also between the senior team and the rest of the force.

I recognised that there were some deep seated cultural and systemic issues to consider. The Force had faced some significant upheaval for the previous three years, had had two very different leaders in terms of personal style and vision. The workforce worked hard and were proud of what they delivered. However, in the view of Her Majesty's Inspectorate of Constabulary, the Force was in a fairly precarious position as the strategic plans to improve were not robust enough. It was evident that the senior team were working independently, rather than as a cohesive team, and some members were anxious about an uncertain future. Figure 5.4 helps to illustrate what I thought I saw was going on within the team with the dysfunctions to the left of the pyramid and the ways to develop improvements to the right. I'd be interested to know how you might have approached this dilemma and on reflection what other ideas you might have.

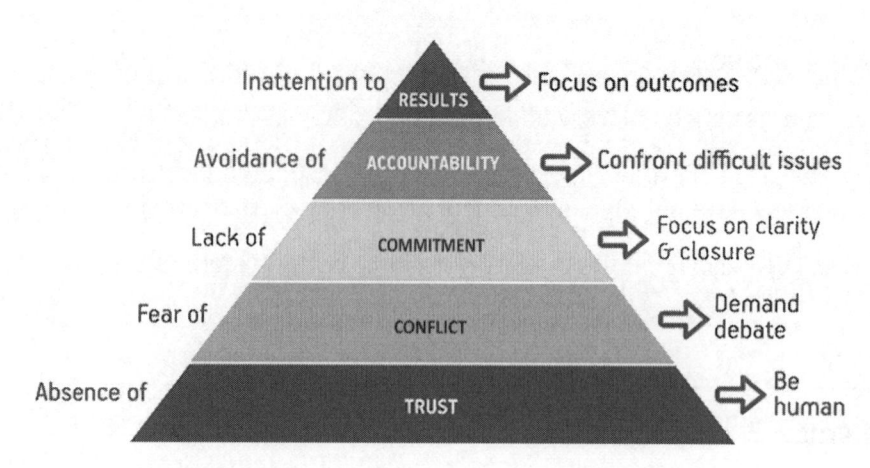

Figure 5.4 The five dysfunctions of a team

I considered everything I had learned about working in teams, some of the theories outlined within this chapter, what approach had been taken in similar circumstances in other places and how I might best address this challenge. I drew up the list of 11 areas (as I've presented earlier in this chapter) of the key areas that I felt I needed to work on to help the team and more widely the Force to become more effective and improve performance.

1. **Provide clear direction**. I consider myself to be a relatively practical person who recognises that most of us prefer straightforward and concise messages. As human beings we like to feel connected to the raison d'etre of an organisation especially if our own personal values have synergy with those of the service, agency or company we work for. The force had an 'overarching vision of keeping people safe and feeling safe'; however, what was missing was how are people expected and are able to deliver against that vision. I spent some time with the senior team drawing up a simple effective response incorporating the vision, the values we aspired to and what our policing purpose is so that every single member of the force could identify how they contributed overall to delivering the vision of keeping people safe. We worked on developing this plan together which secured collective buy-in and also a sense of empowerment. Starting with this strategic vision and plan enabled the team to revisit the 'forming' phase of Tuckman's theory and helped to build confidence within the team.

2. **Encourage clear communication and open doors**. A clear vision and plan can only be effective if everyone knows about it, understands it and acts upon it. I discussed at length with the team and our media experts how could we share the plan with the whole force and beyond so that we were all

pulling in the same direction. I encouraged everyone to share their thoughts and ideas, particularly what worked within their own areas of responsibility and how the plan needed to be embedded within the systems and processes operating throughout the organisation. I stressed that unless we as a team could discuss, share ideas and then set out a broader communication approach, then the plan was less likely to be successful. I encouraged all of us to feel able to approach one another with thoughts about how things could improve, and also where any tensions might lie. As the team leader it was my responsibility to facilitate these discussions, and to ensure that they were fair and open. My building up confidence to talk about our collective common goal of keeping people safe, the team started to realign their own individual approaches with their own teams towards that same shared vision.

3. **Generate a spirit of collaboration**. The team were starting to feel more in tune with what the Force needed, and we started to seek more feedback from the workforce about what could help to deliver against the plan. As a team leader it is far better to generate an environment where everyone feels part of the team and work well together. Professional and personal details were shared which helped us to better understand one another as well as what our individual and collective aspirations were. When one team member found something difficult or perhaps had some personal dilemma within their own private lives, team members stepped forwards to provide support and, on occasions, covered roles and areas of work to allow the individual some time and space to resolve those matters. Where ideas or contributions differed, we would explore 'why' together to minimise the risk of conflict, but also because together we could make more effective decisions.

4. **Set clear rules**. I have worked within several teams during my career. Where I felt I performed best was when I was very clear as a team member what the rules were of how we would work together. As a team leader I had the responsibility of setting those rules which include reporting processes, regular update meetings, how we would give each other time and space to set out our thoughts and concerns, and also the tone of what was then shared with the Force when decisions had been reached. In some places this 'team agreement or contract' can be written down and act as a touchstone for individual team members. If anyone acts outside of these rules then it is for the team leader to address and establish why. In this case the people in the team were keen for me to articulate a road map so that they could better understand the rules of engagement and sign up to them.

5. **Establish defined roles for each team member**. In this case this was fairly apparent given the portfolio of responsibilities each team member had. I quickly reviewed those portfolios to ensure I had the most appropriate person

leading in each area and, if necessary, to move one or two work streams around. Looking at Belbin's Theory for the cross-cutting projects I tried to ensure we had balanced teams working across our critical areas. Most importantly of all where there were areas of overlapping interest, that the information and decision-making was shared between interested parties, rather than risking decisions being made in isolation which could then impact on other areas of business without the portfolio holder knowing. This necessitated openness and a willingness to share ideas at an early stage.

6. **Encourage difference**. I have always been an advocate of valuing difference particularly within a team setting. Having varying views and diversity of thought enables a broader span of potential solutions to problems to be aired, discussed and debated. Sharing team members' MBTI profiles or using Harrison reports could have enhanced understanding our differences even further. I chose to explore our contrasting styles and ideas through regular dedicated discussion/planning days giving both time and space for us to be creative and also to consider next steps to improve performance or evolve as a Force.

7. **Mutual accountability**. It is important as a team leader to encourage everyone who is part of the team to not only be accountable for their own actions and decision, but also collectively as a team. Being viewed as cohesive and collective by the rest of the organisation is critical for consistency of messaging and that we are working well together. If something didn't work or needed to be changed, we would discuss it together, accepting that without some elements of failure we would continue to grow and develop as a team.

8. **Team trust**. In this case the trust within the team in the early stages had been affected by swift decisions being made, huge changes in strategic direction without explanation and a reluctance to then go to the team leader when things were not going so well. I made it clear that as their leader people had to feel confident and able to not only give me bad news, but also that there would be no adverse reprisals. We needed to collectively agree that there needed to be a fresh start and took the opportunity to discuss together what were the concerns, what would help in moving forwards and air any grievances to get them out into the open. I then steadily worked through what issues had been raised always linking my thoughts and words to the overarching purpose of our team and that we needed to work together to improve together and learn together. 'Clearing the air' can be a risky strategy, especially if there are any deep rooted disquiets. On this occasion the team were both willing and ready to move forwards and seized the opportunity.

9. **Decision-making**. I alluded to the importance of decision-making within the first case study in this chapter. Making decisions collectively within a team enables all views to be shared to then come to an agreed position. By achieving consensus and then communicating the rationale behind a

decision, it is more likely to land within the organisation or other interested parties in a positive or successful way, even if the decision may be unpopular. To help make the team effective at decision-making is a key role for the leader and ultimately it is for the leader to have the final say, albeit it is the team as a whole that is accountable for the decision outcome.

10. **Efficient use of ideas**. When a team leader has generated an atmosphere and environment of trust and inclusivity, then there is the opportunity for all team members to feel able to put ideas forward and bounce those suggestions around the group. Sometimes within policing creativity can be stifled, particularly if the risk appetite is low or the ambition of the team isn't sufficiently challenging. In this case I would bring in guest speakers, or work with the broader senior leadership team to generate discussions and ideas to stimulate fresh thinking. Over time the team became adept at being creative and keen to seek out what others were doing in various other agencies.

11. **Enjoy working together**. When I first started leading the team, morale was low and the energy levels were concerning. In fairness what they had just experienced was a shock, and the uncertainty that it generated was palpable. By working together, using models such as Tuckman and Belbin, developing trust and confidence in one another and the team as a whole, the feel-good factor noticeably improved. Team members enjoyed coming to work despite the many challenges we faced and the fact that we enjoyed working together rippled throughout the organisation in a positive way. The performance of the team, and the performance of the Force, turned around, and, best of all, the demanding work could still be fun too.

Reflective practice

- If you had an opportunity to give me feedback on how I approached the scenario, what would you say?

The importance of diverse inclusive teams

It would be remiss of me not to mention in this chapter (and while I have your attention) the absolute importance of having a diverse and inclusive team to achieve truly effective performance. I have spent a considerable part of my career championing diversity because I truly believe in the need for the broadest spectrum of representation, thinking and understanding of the people we work with and alongside. Inclusion is an incredibly timely and sensitive topic currently, both within policing and beyond. Working in the public sector delivering key services at a time of great anxiety with Covid, Brexit and economic concerns means that now more than ever teams have to not only understand the significance of inclusion, but truly embrace it to become even more effective so that messages, operational activity and culture are understood and well communicated. There is a plethora of information and advice available via the internet. In my view the consequences of not addressing the issue of understanding the challenges around inclusion are well articulated by Neil Basu, the lead for National Counter Terrorism within Policing, in his article in *The Guardian* dated 6 August 2019.

CHAPTER SUMMARY

We have looked at what defines an effective team. If a team leader applies theory to practice, and understands what motivates and develops teams, then they can and will succeed in making those teams and the individuals within those teams more effective. Some models of team building have been considered and some ideas for reflective practice have been suggested. Two case studies have been outlined to demonstrate practically what can be undertaken to make teams more effective. Work takes up a huge part of our lives and therefore if we wish to remain resilient and well in work, then the investment and time to develop ourselves and our teams is business and personally critical. As Jim Stovall the American author once wrote,

> You need to be aware of what others are doing, applaud their efforts, acknowledge their successes and encourage them in their pursuits. When we all help one another, everyone wins.

The benefits of spending time as a leader building your team are illustrated below – invest in your people and encourage them to deliver their best and performance will improve. It is also important to consider how as a member of a team you can also utilise some of this theory to determine how you could contribute to being part of an effective team.

References

Adair, J (1973) *Action Centred Leadership*. London: McGraw-Hill.

Belbin, M (1981) *Management Teams: Why They Succeed or Fail*. London: Heinemann.

Jung, C G (1921) *Psychological Types*. London: Routledge.

Lencioni, P (2002) *The Five Dysfunctions of a Team: A Leadership Fable*. New Jersey: Wiley & Sons.

Tuckman, B W (1965) Developmental Sequence in Small Groups. *Psychological Bulletin*, 63(6): 384–399.

6 Challenging conversations
Suzette Davenport

CHAPTER OBJECTIVES

This chapter will help you:

- explore what a challenging conversation is and what makes it so;
- explore academic models on the subject;
- better understand police culture, leadership and application;
- identify how positional power or authority affects conversations;
- apply the theory to an experience;
- transfer learning to a future scenario.

Introduction

Challenging conversations occur in all aspects of our lives – both personal and professional – and are of varying levels of importance or significance. While undertaken by individuals they stretch beyond into teams and across organisations. Given the complexity and diversity of modern-day society, pressures for success and to succeed (whatever that may be) the need for them is arguably even greater. Despite this requirement, they are often feared rather than embraced (Scott, 2011) for a number of reasons, leading to them being avoided completely or engaged in half-heartedly. There is much academic study into the subject: a panoply of ingredients are explored, models or approaches offered on how to approach them and improve how they are dealt with and their outcomes.

This chapter will focus on 'challenging conversations': what they are, why they are challenging – what makes them so. In this chapter we will look at some theoretical models that can be used to better understand both the elements of a challenging conversation and, therefore, what preparatory work can be undertaken to achieve better outcomes for all concerned. The consequences of both not having that conversation and the potential to get it 'wrong' will also be explored. Being effective requires knowledge, skills and application. Application in particular is dependent upon motivation, and difficult conversations are an everyday requirement in policing, be they with the public, partners or colleagues.

Self-awareness and values

People approach challenging conversations in different ways with a range of factors affecting their thinking and behaviours. Academics have sought to understand and document what some of the influencing factors are, for example personality type or general approach to interpersonal conflict (Thomas and Kilmann, 1974). Others have sought to understand and document effective approaches, dependent upon context: for example, Fisher and Ury's (1983) principles of negotiation, which focus on negotiations in a business context, and Scott's (2011) *Fierce Conversations*, which looks at individuals, teams and organisational success. At the heart of all these studies is the potential for unhealthy conflict, whatever the context, to be avoided.

Policing context and culture have developed enormously in the last 30 years shifting from a largely transactional leadership approach to much more of a transformative approach: '*developing an organisational culture of learning and challenge which prioritises the relational aspects of leadership*' (Davis and Silvestri, 2020). Underpinning this is a clearer examination and understanding of leadership styles and how they are underpinned by values. However, I believe that the two positions are under constant challenge which can be seen at operational and strategic levels. In my own experience the pressure to achieve positive HMIC grades often results in short-term tactical responses from leaders regardless of my overall messages of '*if we do the right things in the right way, properly, we will achieve longer term sustained improvements*'. However, years of 'new performance management' and a generation of supervisors and leaders being successful with such approaches often results in reverting to transformational responses. The current focus on the importance of well-being is positive, but Covid strains have in some places, at times, resulted in supervisors operating in a manner that undermines that intent (Fleming, J. and Brown, J, 2020). Such tensions are rarely discussed or explored.

Effective leaders '*know thyself*' (Socrates). They work hard to understand their personality type, what motivates them (their drivers), their values or moral compass. They are self-aware both in terms of their mood and thoughts on that mood. Importantly they are aware of how their behaviours affect others. Such self-awareness enables them to recognise what affects their own behaviours and adjust accordingly to achieve the most effective outcomes. Goleman's Five Elements of Emotional Intelligence (1996) and Covey's (1989) *The 7 Habits of Highly Effective People* provide useful insights into how to be more effective, professionally and personally. I was fortunate to be introduced to both these works early on in my career, and while I cannot claim that they have always been fundamental to my approach and thinking, certain aspects have guided my thinking and approach, particularly when approaching challenging conversations.

For much of my police career, I was a supervisor, manager and leader. I became convinced that setting out expectations and standards clearly and early, ensuring I was true to them and tackling problematic issues or difficult people was fundamental to being effective. Policing now has the Code of Ethics that should be central to such an approach but in its absence, years ago, I formulated and tested my own version of the same which I would set out to colleagues when taking up new roles. Policing invested in me: developing me, my understanding of leadership and management and enabling me to develop a range of necessary skills. Underpinning these were my values which often prompted me to ask, query, challenge and at times refuse to comply when I was uncomfortable with what I saw, heard and felt. Knowledge, experience and reflection bring both wisdom and the opportunity to try again. At times, when in reflective mode, I wonder *'what on earth made me do or say that'* (as in the subsequent case study).

REFLECTIVE PRACTICE

Think of the things that are important in the way you live and work.

- What are your top three values?
- Why these?
- Are they consistent in all aspects of your life?

What is a challenging conversation?

There are various definitions: The Advisory, Conciliation and Arbitration Service (ACAS) states that a challenging conversation is one where emotions and information need handling sensitively in a variety of circumstances; the Chartered Institute of Managers (CMI) adds to this that the subject matter is potentially contentious and is therefore likely to *'elicit strong, complex emotions that can be hard to predict or control'*. In the work context, that may be to:

- address poor performance or conduct;
- investigate a complaint or deal with a grievance;
- deal with a personal problem;
- tackle personality clashes;
- resolve differences of opinion on an operational or managerial issue.

In 2010 a survey by the Centre for Effective Dispute Resolution stated that 72 per cent of line managers were uncomfortable having difficult conversations (Lewis, C. 2011). Further research by the Chartered Institute of Management (CMI) in 2015 showed that 55 per cent of 18,000 surveyed did not think that they had the skills to undertake such conversations. The CMI's 2020 research suggests that cuts in training budgets have made the position even more problematic. This latest survey indicated that inappropriate behaviour/feedback on poor performance and promotions were commonly cited as the most difficult conversations to have in the workplace and 61 per cent of respondents wanted to learn how to manage workplace conversations with more confidence.

In the UK, the top three hardest conversations we have are all work related.

Pay	Colleagues Inappropriate Behaviour	Feedback on poor performance
33%	31%	30%

Figure 6.1 The hardest conversations at work

This reflects my experience in policing and is arguably exacerbated due to the 'team' and thus relationship-based nature of policing and the culture that emanates, often making such conversations even more difficult. As a police officer, the support of colleagues in attending and managing incidents is of fundamental importance; your life can depend upon it. This contributes to a culture of needing to be accepted and included as part of the team. It can result in tolerating, accepting and even sometimes engaging in behaviour that falls below the Police (Conduct) Regulations and/or the Code of Ethics as set by the College of Policing and similarly enshrined in legislation. That desire to be part of the team, even the one you are responsible for supervising can affect whether potentially difficult or challenging conversations take place at all. Given that until relatively recently all warranted officers started as constables and worked their way through the ranks, for some those previous working relationships, allegiances and loyalties (sometimes misplaced) affect a willingness to challenge. As Daniel Coyle states *in The Culture Code* (p 25), '*when you receive a belonging cue, the amygdala switches roles and starts to use its immense unconscious neural horsepower to build and sustain your social bonds*'. This often results in some leaders recoiling from their leadership duty as they are not prepared, often subconsciously, to break the bond of 'belonging'.

The policing rank hierarchy adds another layer of complexity to relationship management. However hard I tried to genuinely engage in 'adult' conversations with the varying elements of the police family (officers/police staff and volunteers), conversations generally felt the least open and engaging due to the power dynamic that my position of authority afforded me.

Why conversations can be challenging

Conversations can be challenging for a number of reasons, not least as there is the potential for conflict. In the workplace it may be that:

- you are delivering bad news;
- the emotional stakes are high;
- you do not want to upset someone;
- you may be concerned at the reaction;
- you are concerned it will affect the relationship;
- it relates to a more senior officer;
- you might not agree with a given task requiring such a conversation (eg organisational changes).

Patterson et al (2011) in *Crucial Conversations* set out the following reasons for conversations being challenging.

Table 6.1 What makes conversations challenging?

They are:		They are:
positively intended		negatively intended
planned		belittling
factual	Stakes are high	for retribution
respectful, honest	Opinions vary	one-way
action focused	Emotions are high	heated
collaborative		with hidden agendas
raise EQ		prejudiced
adult-adult relationships		parent-child relationships

Adapted from Patterson et al (2011)

Benefits of those conversations

While at the time those conversations may appear difficult or daunting, the benefits can be tangible, for example sending clear messages about those standards and expectations. I have never liked or endorsed the use of foul language at work as I believe that if it is acceptable within, it is likely to be used more generally with members of the public. Even in difficult circumstances professional behaviour is of paramount importance – arguably in such circumstances it is even more important. As a leader there is a duty to help others improve and without feedback, how can they? Taking such action appropriately instils respect and confidence and has the potential to spread, resulting in overall improved personal and therefore organisational performance.

Consequences of not having those conversations

There are a range of consequences of not having the conversation that makes a positive difference:

- tolerating poor performance and the individual thinking their behaviour is acceptable;
- that behaviour affecting others' views on what is acceptable;
- tension as others may feel they are working harder to compensate;
- reduced effectiveness or productivity;
- depriving someone of the opportunity to improve;
- well-being issues;
- different standards or treatment in teams resulting in some members feeling they are treated less favourably.

Approaches to challenging conversations

The approach taken to a challenging conversation will depend on the particular circumstances and intended outcome. Too often insufficient planning and thought is given to both, resulting in sub-optimal outcomes for all concerned. As with much in policing, planning is key and as the adage goes, failing to plan is planning to fail.

Academic theories and guidance to enable effective approaches and conversations are abundant. However, my experience is that few people, for a variety of reasons really consider and apply them. Courses aligned to supervisory promotions are often focused on the law/policies and procedures and technical skills rather than how to lead and manage people effectively. A greater focus on 'people' issues and *how* to effectively lead and manage people would result in better outcomes all around. While the College of Policing is in the process of developing a range of tools, the 'Fierce Conversations' toolkit is not yet populated. Some forces' learning and development departments provide fact sheets to assist, but what is a really core skill does not receive the focus it warrants.

Negotiating conflict

So, conflict, or its potential, is central to thinking about challenging conversations. Understanding your default approach to dealing with conflict is a good starting point. Kenneth Thomas and Ralph Kilmann (1974) developed a theory in the 1970s that those people more comfortable with interpersonal conflict were much more likely to engage in difficult conversations. The theory became known as the Thomas-Kilmann Instrument. Interpersonal conflict is at its heart: where two peoples' concerns are not compatible, so they are in opposition, especially if it is a matter they care about. Kilmann identified two key dimensions when approaching a potential conflict or difficult situation: assertiveness (how your own needs are satisfied) and cooperativeness (the extent to which you are prepared to satisfy the others' needs). From that, five broad approaches or behavioural patterns are described reflecting the 'intention' in the interaction.

1. Accommodating their needs or concerns at the expense of your own/the objective.
2. Compromising to find a solution that is at least partially acceptable to both.
3. Competing to ensure that your own needs are satisfied.
4. Collaborating to achieve a win-win, properly satisfying both.
5. Avoiding the situation or maintaining neutrality.

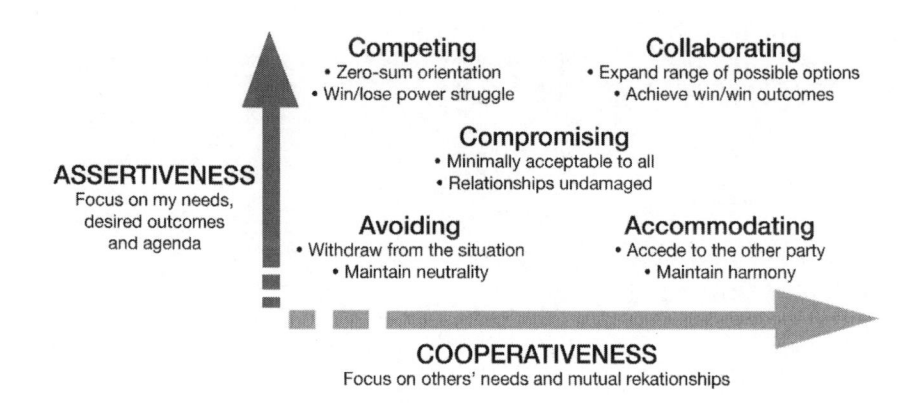

Figure 6.2 Thomas Kilmann's conflict modes

Intention is a useful thing to consider in a police context. On whose behalf are you operating and to what purpose? Your own? Your supervisor? The department you work for? The broader police service? The public? At times, there will be a mix of these and sometimes they will not all align which creates an additional layer of complexity. For example: as a first line supervisor being expected to motivate team outputs or productivity (fixed penalty tickets/stop searches) to deal with disorder outside nightclubs when you do not believe the tactic will be effective, and you are concerned at the negative impact it may have on community tensions.

Likewise, effective negotiating skills are important in policing, and there are elements of those skills that can assist with challenging conversations. Fisher and Ury (1983) in their work on negotiations described a good negotiation as one that is '*wise, efficient and improves relationships*'. Not unlike Thomas Kilmann's 'collaborating' mode which seeks to ensure that both parties' needs are satisfied, it is fair and (given that it is business-focused) the agreement endures. They claim that where parties adopt positional bargaining, where the negotiation is adversarial with winners and losers, it does not provide an effective platform (as it produces unwise agreements). However, their 'four prescriptions', which are based on a principled approach, do provide an effective platform.

1. Separating out the people from the problem: being objective and not drawn into personality issues.
2. Focusing on interests not positions: being clear on what the respective underlying interests are.
3. Inventing options for mutual gain: being creative and not constrained by positions.
4. Use of objective criteria: agreed beforehand.

REFLECTIVE PRACTICE

Think of a situation that you found challenging or difficult.

- What was the situation?
- What was the issue?
- Who was involved?
- How did you go about tackling it?
- How confident did you feel about it?
- What was the result?
- How would you tackle a similar issue next time?
- What would you change and why?
- How might the above models help with your thinking?

The impact of effective self-awareness

There has been much discussed, debated and written about leadership and its importance across all employment sectors (private, public and voluntary/charity sector). Leadership in policing is well studied, with particular reference to its distinct cultural paradigm (Davis and Silvestri, 2020). Over the last 35 years, roles together with expectations and requirements have been increasingly documented with growing levels of accountability. So how does an individual's leadership approach impact on challenging conversations?

What drives us to have challenging conversations? It could be: the consequences of not having the conversation now evidently outweigh the potential consequences of having it; the sense of public duty; the last resort (but hopefully not); or, maybe, it just feels like it is the right thing to do. From a personal perspective, my strong sense of personal responsibility, to speak up or speak out when I thought I should, was driven by values of fairness and justice together with compassion and humanity. From my experience as a leader within policing, it is my honest held belief that understanding your value set and what motivates you is vitally important.

Evidence from Zydziunaite's (2018) research on those engaged in the medical profession is that your value-set underpins your leadership approach. My leadership journey was supported by police and academic study, from which I came to believe that the very best leaders know themselves really well and they are, therefore, able to operate in other than 'default' personality mode. For example, my Myers-Briggs Type Inventory (MBTI) shows me as a strong introvert, so I am energised in quiet, reflective mode. Policing attracts extroverts with that for many years being considered a dominant personality trait. As a leader ensuring that I engaged with everyone effectively, and not close down those with the opposite trait required me to work really hard to be positive and welcoming when they came into my office or I was with them for long periods of time – they simply wore me out! So, knowing the people or circumstances that that were likely to create discomfort and thereby consciously choosing appropriate responses in-keeping with their position and role is crucially important. I found theories and approaches outlined in Goleman's (2004) *Emotional Intelligence* and Covey's *The Seven Habits of Highly Effective Leaders* insightful and helpful – material that has shaped my leadership journey.

One of my defining leadership journey moments resulted from of an exercise I undertook during my sergeants' development course. It was a self-assessment relating to conflict style based on the Thomas-Kilmann Inventory, ascribing characteristics or associated personality traits (Figure 6.3 and Table 6.2).

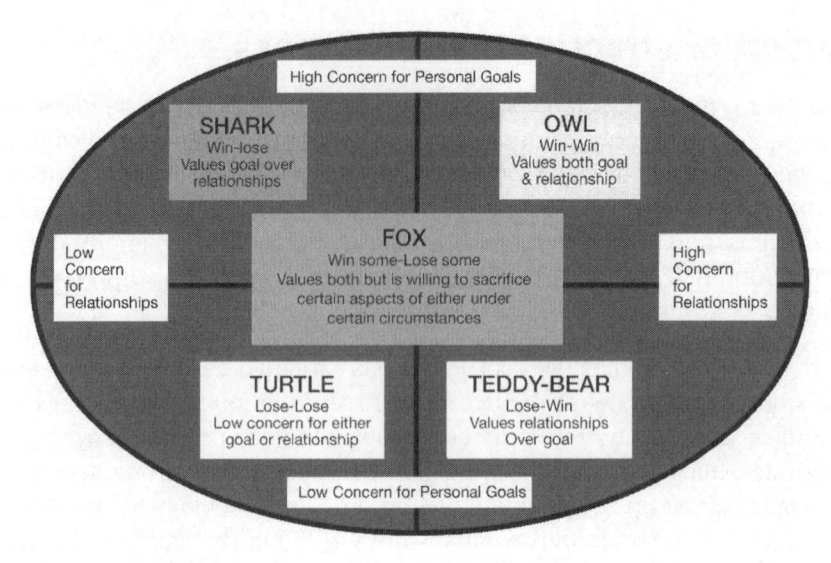

108 • Behavioural Skills for Effective Policing

Figure 6.3 Conflict typologies

Table 6.2 The pros and cons of conflict typologies

Animal type	Strengths	Struggles
Turtle (Avoiding)	Easily looks past conflict Thinks most conflicts will resolve themselves Calm De-escalates emotions in conflict	Minimises conflict Denies conflict Avoids conflict at any cost
Teddy bear (Accommodating)	Likeable in most situations Wants and needs harmony Will accept blame to bring peace	Gets taken advantage of Enables others by shying away from conflictLow self-esteem Confidence is derived from others liking them
Shark (Forcing)	Strong Courageous Brings conflict into the open Will confront bullies	Pushy Tactless Hurts people's feelings Escalates emotions Creates barriers Ruthless
Fox (Compromising)	Communication Willingness to compromise Crafts intelligent solutions	Deceptiveness Manipulation
Owl (Collaborating)	Integrity Builds trust and deeper relationships Open-minded Pragmatic in finding solutions	Requires mutual approach where quick response is needed Too deliberative at times

Given my background and life experiences even in my mid-late twenties I considered myself to be reasonably thoughtful and skilled. My self-assessment was as an Owl followed by a Fox. The vast majority of my peers identified me as a Shark. A classis Johari's window (Luft, 1969) moment where what I thought I was and presented was not what others saw or interpreted. When looking at the Shark characteristics I only internalised the 'struggles' and not the strengths, resulting in years and years of working tirelessly to address those 'struggles' in the way that I presented myself in general, and specifically my approach to dealing with conflict. For example, trying to be warm and engaging with people in person. In written communication I know I am task-focused, and even now in emails I nearly always address the task in the email and then remember to add the pleasantries before pressing 'send'. When dealing with conflict in particular I worked really hard to choose my language carefully and maintain an approach that was as low key as possible.

The work of Daniel Goleman and Frank Covey helped me to better understand myself. Goleman's 1996 seminal work *Emotional Intelligence* helped me think about the type of person and leader that I aspired to be and hopefully that people would want to work with and for. Goleman centres on how we understand and express ourselves; how we understand and relate to others and cope with the daily demands of life. It describes a range of skills and conscious abilities that can be worked on to improve performance in everyday life: '*much evidence testifies that people who are emotionally adept – who know and manage their own feelings well – are at an advantage in every domain of life*' (p 36).

Goleman's Five Elements of Emotional Intelligence (1996) are as follows.

- Self-awareness: being aware of your own emotions and your impact on others; being able to self-monitor and behave accordingly.

- Self-regulation: managing your emotions and therefore your response, expressing yourself appropriately.

- Internal motivation: having a passion to fulfil inner needs, being highly conscientious and setting goals.

- Empathy: recognising and responding to others' emotions.

- Effective social skills: building relationships and connections with others.

Covey's (1989) *The 7 Habits of Highly Effective People* are about the desire to learn (why and how things happen) and how to become a more effective and better leader. He presents a set of principles (habits) to build upon and from. Understanding your own values and leadership approach enables more effective performance, especially when the stakes are high. As Covey says (p 6), understanding '*the inner truth about the inner motivations, character and ambitions of those who hold power*' is crucial. As police officers we hold power; we exercise it every day over the public. As a supervisor and leader that is what we do with colleagues and the organisation.

So why is this important for leaders? Well, policing is a people business and therefore knowing how you operate with the range of people you encounter is of critical importance.

When there is the potential for conflict it is even more important. Habit reflects what we repeatedly do and our habitual tendencies are rooted in our personalities. To be effective those habits need to be positive ones. Insightfully Covey (p 17) states that *'the way we see the problem is the problem'* ie it is our perceptions borne out of our background and experiences that frame it in a particular way. This is represented in the way we engage in challenging conversations. Our habits therefore affect our specific behaviours.

Table 6.3 Covey's seven habits

Habit	Behaviour
One: Be proactive	Take responsibility for your life.
Two: Begin with the end in mind	Define your mission and goals in life.
Three: Put first things first	Prioritise and do the most important things first.
Four: Think win-win	Have an 'everyone can win' attitude.
Five: Seek first to understand and then to be understood	Listen to people sincerely.
Six: Synergise	Work together to achieve more.
Seven: Sharpen the saw	Renew yourself regularly.

Every day both professionally and personally there is the potential for conflict. So, think about your interactions, how you approach them and, then, specifically how you deal with conflict.

REFLECTIVE PRACTICE

Think about a recent situation that you found challenging or difficult.

- How self-aware are you of your negotiating approach?
- How did you take responsibility?
- What were the most important things to do first?
- What was your intent or mission?
- How could you ensure win-win?
- Did you listen sincerely?
- Did you seek to work with and not against?
- Did you reflect and identify how to improve?

Approaching the conversation

Having thought about Covey's and Goleman's insights, your values, leadership, the way you communicate with and relate to others, it is now time to think about how to approach those conversations.

It depends on the type of conversation (performance or coaching) and level (individual or team) as to whether it is spontaneous or pre-planned. Patterson et al (2010) identify two types of conversations. The first type is 'open ended' where through dialogue, sharing views and exploring assumptions, new understanding emerges. In this type of conversation there is no one or right answer. The second seeks a 'fixed outcome' with some decision/ agreement or priorities identified. Regardless of the type, in order to achieve the intended outcome, the advice is to plan, carefully. Researchers, academics and experts may emphasise slightly different things or there may be a different emphasis dependent upon the nature of the conversation, but they agree that there are three distinct parts. The elements set out in Table 6.4 are worthy of consideration with the last column providing an example of my use of it.

As a senior leader I have used elements of Table 6.4 often. One such example related to one of my team who were engaged in some critically important and sensitive national work. It required in-depth knowledge of the law and operational practice. They enjoyed the work immensely. But they were increasingly being drawn away from the force and their responsibilities. Their regular and continued absences were starting to affect delivery of force priorities and harmony in the team. The matter had been discussed on a number of occasions during monthly performance review meetings, but little changed. I researched carefully time spent away from the force and projected absences, portfolio performance matters and spoke to relevant people.

So far I have talked about the fundamentals of challenging conversations: individuals whose interests are not the same, be that at an individual level, a team level or organisational level. That there is the potential for conflict during those conversations which can be negative, but not always negative. Two approaches to conflict have been outlined looking at levels of co-operation and assertiveness. Your default mode is likely rooted in your personality, but awareness, experience and honing of skills enable supervisors, managers and leaders to choose their approach when dealing with challenging conversations. I know that my early leadership approach was mostly driven by my personality and value set.

One of the toughest challenges to tackle in the policing hierarchy is having a difficult conversation with a more senior officer or member of police staff. The greater the difference in the rank/role, arguably the more difficult the challenge.

The example below represents a set of circumstances that resulted in me operating way outside my authority. I will describe my approach and the result. I will then consider, using the conflict model how I could have approached the matter differently. I will also reflect on how my experience affected my response when being challenged by officers or staff much more junior in rank/position.

Table 6.4 Preparation

Before	During	Afterwards	Scenario
Recognise the need.	Be professional: language, tone, body language.	Manage their reaction.	Continued absences from force: key force and regional meetings missed.
Be clear on what the issue is:	Be aware of your emotions as well as theirs.	Stay engaged.	Portfolio priorities slipping.
• What are the facts?	State the intention of the conversation.	Offer appropriate support.	Cover continually provided by other team members.
• How does it manifest?	Identify what the issue is in clear but non-inflammatory language: facts, evidence, behaviour.	Arrange further check-in/meeting.	Team disharmony and 'sniping'.
• Specific examples?			Presence/focus/delivery/team
	Identify the impact for: you, them, the team, the organisation, the public, relationships.		Compiled a report setting out the issues and effects of absences to support the conversation.
• Impact (on who/what)?			Meeting arranged to discuss current and future work pressures.
• Why it is important?	Listen carefully as it may change your perspective.		I reflected that I may not have been direct enough about the impact on the force of the national work.
Has your behaviour or approach contributed in some way?	Throughout: be open, be respectful, have integrity, be truthful.		I stated that I needed to have a difficult conversation. That I knew how committed to the force and the national work they were. That in the absence of solutions that they could offer to mitigate the identified issues that they would have to choose between the two.
	Watch for their reaction and stay on track: denying, defending, deflecting.		
Seek advice or support.	Engage and agree: options, resolution, further conversation, next steps.		They agreed that it was a difficult situation but until I had set it out in writing the totality had not been appreciated.
What is the best outcome?			It was agreed that they would discuss how the national work could be undertaken without them and/or a secondment sought to enable a replacement.
How to start the conversation?			
What is your opening line?			We worked together to provide support to business areas and acknowledge to the team absences were having. They moved to work full time on that work enabling succession recruitment.

Case study 1

Personal example: managing upwards

I had worked in a mid-sized force for nearly 20 years. I had been supported in my development and been promoted to superintendent. The senior leadership of the force had been stable for a number of years. There were clear boundaries to operate within. New senior leadership arrived which disrupted the equilibrium. Trusted leaders had to prove themselves again, others competed with them. The new approach in general sought to instil a less formal culture with a greater sense of team approach and focus on transformational leadership, or at least that was the apparent intent. However, further leadership changes brought a particularly contrasting style and approach particularly in respect to discipline and conduct matters in the force. This was both an uncomfortable and confusing time for many.

There was a palpable shift from what I perceived to be a democratic, engaging learn from mistakes culture, to a more authoritarian one, specifically in relation to potential conduct/misconduct matters where the initial assessment of conduct assumed the worse without due diligence being undertaken in respect of context or 'agendas'. Allegations of bullying and racism, without foundation, resulted in colleagues who I considered hard working committed officers being unnecessarily suspended. This act despite the stance of regulations and rhetoric is rarely seen as a neutral act. The approach resulted in unwarranted suspensions and officers' careers being ended prematurely. Having disrupted what was known, and without surety of new boundaries being established and reinforced, the leader was appointed to a different senior policing role, not staying to work through the current created challenges and settling the organisation back down. I felt (rightly or wrongly) that the organisation and people within it, including me, were being let down. Given the oral nature of policing, there was much conversation about what was happening in force and the impact of the tenure. The unfairness of the approach and the impact on morale. It affected me and how I felt about my leaders. Having a strong sense of responsibility and loyalty I was not just going to let it happen around me without saying something. I also knew that I was affected emotionally by the events and that I would need to prepare carefully.

So with carefully crafted prompt cards in hand, my challenging conversation with the leader went something like this:

Boss: *Thank you for coming to see me: why do you want to see me?*

Me: *I have asked to see you to talk about how I and others feel about what has happened in force over the last few months and the impact that it is having.*

Reply: *What in particular?*

Me: *The approach that you have chosen to take in respect of conduct and discipline.*

Reply: Yes?

Me: I think that it is damaging the force and the people within it. People who have been long serving loyal officers who have worked tirelessly.

Reply: I have to do what I think is right.

Me: You and others have come from elsewhere, forces with different approaches and cultures and you do not really understand the culture of this force. I think that you have superimposed approaches that are appropriate elsewhere, but not here.

Reply: There have been a number of things that needed tackling.

Me: But the approach in my view is not taking proper account of the nature of this force. It is a not a metropolitan-type force, it is a county force where the geography means that there are groups of more senior officers that know each other well and are close to each other.

Reply: There have been serious allegations relating to corruption being investigated and this must be done thoroughly.

Me: I accept that that should be done but believe it should be done through proper investigation and with a mindset of seeking to establish the facts, not pre-determining guilt.

Reply: Guilt has not been pre-determined. We do need to establish the facts and will ensure that those affected are supported.

Me: I am disappointed that having started to change how we do things in the force, you have taken a course of action that has resulted in people being treated badly and in a way that they do not deserve, and now you are leaving for a new job. It feels like things have been destabilised and you are not going to be here to see the force through the impact of that.

Reply: The timing of the opportunity is unfortunate, but I will leave the force in good hands.

Me: Unfortunately, I do not have your confidence. I have grown up with this force and feel incredibly loyal to it and the people. Leaving does not help us put right the things that need to be put right.

Reply: Thank you for sharing your thoughts with me.

On reflection I:

- was true to myself in speaking out;
- had the courage to raise both the matter and how I felt about it;

- did not just gossip behind leaders' backs.

However, I had not:

- really worked through my intentions;
- sought the permission of colleagues when I said others felt the same way;
- considered solutions or what would make the situation better, or the part I could play.

Reflective practice

Consider carefully what we have explored around difficult conversations.

- If you were to give me feedback on how I approached and then managed the interaction, what would you say?

Case study 2

Steve

Steve is a popular team leader. He has been on the team for a number of years. He has a very direct style often putting team members in the spotlight, in front of other team members, regarding their individual contributions. He is very competitive and wants the team to be the 'best' performers in the station. He is good to work with and learn from. He likes to socialise, but not everyone is able to join in due to other commitments or choice.

Paul is a popular member of the team. He has been on the team for some months and has promotion aspirations but recently failed his promotion assessment. Recently, you notice that Paul has been consistently the focus of Steve's attention for a number of reasons. He has also had a number of short sickness instances. These have resulted in even closer scrutiny from Steve. Paul now infrequently socialises with the team.

You recognise that there is growing friction between Steve and Paul, and it is starting to affect the remainder of the team. You are Paul's colleague and Steve is your supervisor. You have recently been on your promotion development course and learned about dealing with conflict.

Reflective practice

While case study 1 reflects a specific set of circumstances, potential disagreements or conflicts with those that supervise are not uncommon.

- So, reflecting on your experiences and the information in this chapter, how would you deal with the set of circumstances outlined in case study 2?
- Using Table 6.4, prepare for conversations with both Steve and Paul.
    - What are facts?
    - Examples?
    - What is the impact?
    - Why is it important?
    - How do you feel about the conversation?
    - Has your own behaviour contributed in some way?
    - What advice or support do you need?
    - What will your opening line be?
    - During the conversation what behaviours should you focus on?
    - What is the best outcome?
    - What actions could be agreed to resolve the situation?
    - What support will be available?

CHAPTER SUMMARY

This chapter has explored what challenging conversations are, why they are challenging and what preparation may be undertaken to make them more effective and less damaging. It has identified that one of the central features of them is conflict or the potential for conflict. The Thomas-Kilmann model of approaches to conflict has been considered together with how that model has been adapted by others (Johnson) to enable people to think about their own approach to conflict, specifically how I viewed myself as an 'Owl' but how colleagues perceived very different behaviours and how such behaviours might impact on others.

The chapter has sought to consider the importance of personal values, how they underpin leadership approaches and affect our perceptions, our reality. The importance of 'knowing thyself' and thereby being able to 'choose' behaviours to achieve best outcomes through practising Goleman's Five Elements of Leadership and Covey's *7 Habits of Highly Effective People* has been made clear, striving for continual self-improvement.

A personal case study was shared, identifying in the context of models explored, how effective that challenging conversation was from my perspective. I then reflected on conflict models and elements of Goleman and Covey. From that a future challenging conversation was proposed together with a template based on the provided advice.

Further reading

Thomas Kilmann Instrument; Animals Exercise Sheet: https://rrcnegotiationsandconflictresolution.files.wordpress.com/2018/02/test5.pdf

What Are Your Values? - Decision-Making Skills from MindTools.com

Videos

Susan Scott. *What to be Mindful of and How "Fierce Conversation" Helps your Business*. YouTube

Johari's Window. https://www.youtube.com/watch?v=XKkK6x5rchg

References

ACAS (2010) *Challenging Conversations and How to Manage Them*. Available at: https://www.acas.org.uk/acas-guide-to-challenging-conversations-and-how-to-manage-them (accessed 2 April 2021).

Chartered Management Institute (2015) *The Ten Most Difficult Conversations*. Available at: https://www.managers.org.uk/knowledge-and-insights/news/top-10-difficult-conversations/ (accessed 2 April 2021).

College of Policing (2021) *Communication, Negotiation and Influencing Toolkit*. Available at: https://leadership.college.police.uk/course/view.php?id=35 (accessed 2 April 2021).

Covey, S (1989) *The 7 Habits of Highly Effective People*. New York: Simon and Schuster.

Coyle, D (2018) *The Culture Code: The Secrets of Highly Successful Groups*. New York: Random House Business.

Davis, C and Silvestri, M (2020) *Critical Perspectives on Police Leadership*. Bristol: Policy Press.

Fisher, R, Ury, W and Patton, B (2012) *Getting to Yes: Negotiating Agreement without Giving In*. New York: Random House Business.

Fleming, J and Brown, J (2020) Policewomen's Experience of Working During Lockdown; Results of a Survey with Officers from England and Wales. *Policing: A Journal of Policy and Practice*.

Goleman, D (2020) *Emotional Intelligence: Why It Can Matter More Than IQ*. London: Bloomsbury.

Lewis, C (2011) *Difficult Conversations: Tacklers Not Dodgers*. Cheltenham: Globis Mediation Group.

Luft, J (1969) *Of Human Interaction: The Johari Model*. California: Mayfield Publishing.

Mullins, L (2007) *Management and Organisational Behaviour*, 8th ed. New Jersey: Prentice Hall.

Northern Care Alliance (2019) *Challenging Conversations*. Available at: https://www.pat.nhs.uk/community-services/CF2/CF2%20Challenging%20Conversations%20Toolkit.pdf (accessed 2 April 2021).

Patterson, K, Grenny, J, McMillan, R and Switzler, A (2011) *Crucial Conversations: Tools for Talking When Stakes Are High*, 3rd ed. New York: McGraw Hill.

Scott, S (2011) *Fierce Conversations*. California: Berkley Publishing.

Thomas, K W and Kilmann, R H (1974) *Thomas-Kilmann Conflict Mode Instrument*. Tuxedo, NY: Xicom.

Zydziunaite, V (2018) Leadership Values and Values Based Leadership: What Is the Main Focus. *Applied Research in Health and Social Sciences*, 15(1).

Part 3
Operational learning

7 Firearms: emotional management
David Hartley

CHAPTER OBJECTIVES

This chapter will help you:

- explore the difference between training and reality – are you ready?
- recognise the presence of emotions in complex incidents;
- understand potential leadership pitfalls – who are you taking with you?
- explore potential solutions;
- consider CPD – the New Dimension and Cultural Challenge.

Introduction

Policing brings unique challenge in the nature, scale and variety of leadership and command scenarios, but the one which often evokes most interest is when you encounter the 'firearms job'.

This is not to say that the specialists involved, from the cop with the gun to the Strategic Firearms Commander (SFC), are not well trained and tested. They all are. But when routine becomes the exception, emotions and behavioural skills can become critical factors.

This chapter explores how those emotions can manifest and how current training and continuous professional development (CPD) will prepare those involved, to a point. It looks at the key role of emotional intelligence, which through its presence or absence can have quite a profound impact upon performance. The chapter largely explores the issues from a command perspective, but the factors, skills and behaviours extend right across policing roles.

Training versus reality: are you ready?

It's another day at work. You may be a duty Armed Response Vehicle Officer (ARVO), a duty Tactical Firearms Commander (TFC) or a duty SFC. The daily routine is under way, even before landing at work.

Didn't sleep so well last night, far too hot – I must sort that smart thermostat I've been meaning to get, kids were demanding this morning – I'll spend some time with them tonight, need to focus on their homework, car test is coming up – I must book that in, I'll make a note, right today – Ah, Force Performance Day, better check I have no actions, why do I always seem last minute, anyway, doesn't start until 9.30am, so I've time to check. Oh, I'm duty cover too, I'll give control a call, pop on the radio and let them know my movements and availability, should be fine, nothing much ever happens on a Wednesday.

As a general rule, nothing usually does happen on a Wednesday. But what happens when it is not a normal Wednesday?

Like Wednesday 2 June 2010, when Derrick Bird began his trail of murder in Cumbria or Wednesday 13 March 1996 when Thomas Hamilton began the Dunblane Primary School massacre or Wednesday 19 August 1987 when Michael Ryan began his series of random shootings known as the Hungerford Massacre, or Westminster Bridge, or Manchester Arena, or London Bridge, or Moat in Northumbria, Cregan in Manchester, Reading Park, or Streatham. They all started as a normal day at work.

Now in private coaching, perspective is a powerful tool. The executive under pressure to deliver to timescale can bring great balance with perspective and context: '*It's not life and death, it's a deadline, I can deal with the worst outcome, it's just a sale/contract*'. But what when it is life and death? What then for the man or woman in the Arena (Roosevelt, 1910)?

This is where the skills learnt and practiced in the training environment are now put to the test in reality, yet the emotional foundation influencing our behaviour from which critical decisions are made will be pivotal in driving effective performance.

The service has evolved and advanced its practice, processes and application of command and decision-making to high levels of sophistication – and through pass/fail courses builds rigour to the selection and preparedness of those in key roles and functions.

The evolution of the National Decision Model (NDM)(College of Policing, 2014) and its application throughout service delivery should be proudly celebrated; we see its use right from a front line member of staff justifying what force was used on a violent drunk through to a covert armed unit making an armed interdiction. British policing arguably leads the world in the sophistication of NDM.

So surely, all is well. Do we not have trained and accredited staff and commanders, assessed and fit for role? We do.

Emotions in high-risk incidents

The missing investment is psychological preparation. After the courses' occupational and operational 'pass' how psychologically match fit (mind fit if you will) do you remain? What is your attitude? Your mindset? Is it a proactive, developed, realistic one operating on calm, logical reality with supportive beliefs all in perspective, or is it a reactionary mindset, emotionally driven and spontaneously reacting to a void of psychological preparation? This is the untapped next evolution of command effectiveness.

If we see the vehicle for success being a finely tuned car – this is the NDM, the training, the knowledge and CPD. This is your capability. If driven correctly it can provide a smooth, supportive and entirely functional journey. The most appropriate decisions made at the right time with the right audit trail. The confidence that whatever the outcome, we demonstrably did our best.

But what if a dysfunctional driver gets into the vehicle, a driver whose behaviours are reactionary, emotionally driven, based upon unrealistic thoughts, beliefs and emotions? It will be a rough ride, possibly a chaotic one, and it may well end in a crash, regardless of how well tuned the engine and the car is. Therefore, I intend to examine the driver, not the tuning of the engine.

So how do we make sense of this? How do we recognise emotions? How do we recognise if they are adversely affecting our performance? Surely, we are who we are? Some people's character may be described as calm, some energetic, some blunt and short tempered, some logical – is that not what we take into high-risk scenarios?

Well, if you make no investment in understanding yourself, have no effective 'emotional radar' and have invested little or no time in your beliefs, values and mindset, then you will default, and it is pot luck whether that default serves you well. Probability says it will not, particularly at a time of crisis or high risk, where, without this investment you are likely to 'react' rather choosing a more effective 'response'. Let us explore these emotions a little more.

Have you ever thought what your beliefs and expectations are of policing? Have you ever done so for more complex and higher risk scenarios? I have seen, many times, competent and professional colleagues have adverse reactions in more extreme scenarios. The organisational gravity of the incident faced directly relates to the scale of that behavioural change and the impact upon the role they perform.

> **REFLECTIVE PRACTICE**
>
> - Cast your mind back. Can you bring to mind your own examples when you have seen, or experienced yourself, circumstances of 'losing it', 'red mist', 'raging', 'withdrawing', 'hiding', 'coming apart' or 'wobbling'?

All my examples involve trained and accredited staff, so what was happening? Well, the psychological mind was providing a series of thoughts, these have been accepted, leading to emotional behavioural change. Let us delve a little further and try and unpick.

> **CASE STUDY 1**
>
> Join me as Gold (Strategic Public Order Commander) overseeing the latest Far Right Nationalist march and protest. It has been a summer of protest and intelligence says 400 from this group are to arrive and our local Muslim youth groups have had enough, they are to give a direct reception to make it clear that the protest is not welcome a Northern city. The operation is planned meticulously, it is resourced appropriately and has excellent and experienced command and support at all levels. I have a very experienced Silver (Public Order Silver Commander – equivalent to TFC in an armed operation). All is good. All is good until a series of attacks take place on the protest group from convoys of local Muslim young men. Intelligence didn't suggest this. A member of the march is seriously beaten, is unconscious and the ambulance updates are worrying. I listen to developments. Silver becomes increasingly autocratic, takes the airwave directly and begins barking instant directions, the tone becomes intolerant, Bronze (Public Order Operational Commanders) don't like it, frustration grows, blame begins emerging, a further assault, command tension rises another notch, voices are raised. I go to the Silver Suite and upon arrival Silver is now red of face and the default communication is at shouting level.
>
> The car – the capability, the plan, the contingencies, the resources and the structures – underpinned by NDM, all remain fully functional and available to be driven well. However, the car is now erratically swerving around, we haven't crashed yet, but it's getting near.
>
> So, what has happened to our driver of this operation? Our Commander? Instant reactive decisions are being made, black and white thinking is underway, each new challenge is greeted with increasing anger and frustration, blame is present and NDM is absent – the whole command suite has become nervous, edgy and tense.

CASE STUDY 2

A complex inner-city estate in a Northern city is suffering at the hands of OCGs (Organised Crime Group) and intelligence suggests we have a house central to drug dealing and arms supply. It is fortified and by its location protected and hard to tackle with conventional tactics. After a significant planning phase, a Dynamic Entry is the preferred armed tactic to best dominate the premise and secure evidence. With many hours of audio recorded command considerations, I approve the authority for this operation. My TFC (Tactical Firearms Commander – the Silver for armed operations) is a trained specialist; our staff are trained specialists. Detailed briefings are made, rehearsals practiced again and again, contingency explored and briefed. We are ready, it's a 7am strike, we have visual control of the premise, the convoy rolls. As the convoy is at a point of no return, 30 yards from the premise, an unanticipated and unannounced incident unfolds on the front drive of the target premise. I believe we call this 'sods law'. As the police convoy approaches, at that very time a hostile OCG attack takes place on the same premise, at the same moment. Two vehicles, with five in each, have crashed onto the forecourt of the house and a large armed fight is taking place between 15 men as our first van arrives. Mayhem. Our first armed officer out of the back of the van is hit by a fleeing vehicle and has his foot run over, he collapses to the floor screaming in pain. The airwave exchange between the Bronze Operational Firearms Commander (OFC) at scene and remote Silver (TFC) was one of confusion and disorientation. In an impressively short amount of time, control was in place, the initial tactic modified but executed with success and a number from the garden conflict also arrested.

As the remote SFC this seemed to me like a highly professional reaction to complex circumstances. Order and clarity were restored very quickly.

The debrief brought a different picture with honest and professional disclosure from the STFC (Specialist TFC) and his Tac Ad (Tactical Advisor). As the chaotic scene emerged over the air, with a large, unanticipated armed fight underway and radio traffic then dominated by screams and updates of officer down and Tactical Medical Support (TacMed) required, the STFC encountered an emotional response. This was one of silence initially, then anger, then blame and focus on 'how can this be happening'. It took a great relationship between the Tac Ad and STFC to literally be shaken back into focus and core role. A great demonstration of teamwork. The driver of our command car lost focus for a short space but was prodded back into effective action by our trusted passenger, the Tac Ad.

Case study 3

My next example goes back to my days as a Specialist TFC and is the closing phase of a containment on an armed subject. The subject was wanted for murder, was armed with a shotgun and was speaking with negotiators. A firm containment was in place and a negotiated resolution was both anticipated and hoped for. A full Silver Suite was in operation with a formal Command Loggist, and this officer was of Chief Inspector rank. After a period of negotiation, the subject, without warning, committed suicide. While this was not the preferred outcome, no one else was injured and all involved had done their duty and their best to avoid this. As this news was delivered over the air, the Loggist had an emotional collapse. He slumped in his chair, threw all papers, laptop and phone to the floor and entered an extended period of emotional breakdown.

What thoughts were flowing in that colleague's mind to fuel such an emotional reaction? To those around in the Silver Suite it was both worrying and unnerving: *'If the Loggist is so upset and worried, something must have gone wrong, we must all be at risk and in trouble'*.

Unlocking the emotional context

We now have three core examples from my experience and can begin to unpick the drivers around the emotions to then later look at pre-incident work and preparation that can minimise the occurrence in future complex and high-pressure scenarios.

You may think that having such emotions when faced with these scenarios is a very natural reaction and only experience can develop the resilience to avoid it becoming destructive. There is much merit to that view, and I agree to a point. We cannot turn off our emotions, but what we can do is be alive to what thoughts we are being offered, what 'beliefs and truths' they are based upon, how we have influenced those beliefs, and how we have rehearsed and programmed for the unexpected, the unknown and high impact. I also believe that 'experience' can have hidden risk. Of course, the learning through exposure to new, different and complex challenges is the primary way to develop skills through reflection.

The hidden risk is the confirmation bias that repeated operations with the desired outcome makes us wise, prepared and ready for exceptional challenge. A commander with an experience of 40 different armed incidents may be viewed as being experienced. The nature of armed policing may lull us into a false sense of security in that most subjects we encounter are compliant in the face of an organised and prepared police operation. The vast majority of armed operations I have led as both TFC and SFC have been resolved without resistance and conflict – I would estimate the percentage compliance to be over

98 per cent. So, by the nature of the probability of compliance, we could see operations with an adequate primary plan, but pretty flaky contingencies and poor psychological preparation be deemed a great success and part of a growing impressive portfolio of command. *The vulnerabilities will not be exposed or tested until the 2 per cent arises.* Therein lies the hidden risk. A car on cruise control takes very little driving. The challenge is when the driver needs to take control.

I have seen this materialise for several candidates arriving for the Specialist Firearms Command Course. They may be the lead candidate for the force, and sometimes the region, with an impressive portfolio of successful operations, all in the 98 per cent. The moment the course presents the test of complexity, pressure, unexpected and impactive developments (death and injury), ie, the 2 per cent, then the emotional reaction begins making our driver dysfunctional at the wheel.

A highly emotional and stress reaction to the 2 per cent complexity is common, the more severe reactions have seen candidates up and leave the course, instantly. If this were a live incident, there is no acceptable option of leaving.

If you remain sceptical that enhanced psychological preparation is of any use, indulge me while I present a number of questions for you.

How much dedicated psychological preparation have you invested in your role? Be honest.

Now let us compare ourselves to professional sports people. Their investment in the technical skills and coaching (core capability) will be similar in hours and focus to policing, but for many they will have similar hours of psychological support from a mind coach or sports psychologist. It is an industry. An industry to help people play games well. To help them play games well when it is the cup final, championship fixture, Olympic final or title match. That is their 2 per cent. But it is a game. Policing's 2per cent isn't, and unfortunately there are often no qualifying heats and no advance warning when that day at 'Wembley' may arise for us.

We know emotions cannot be turned off and we know emotions can, in the extreme, be detrimental to the task. So how do we understand emotions? How do we manage them? How do we prepare for the 2 per cent?

The pitfalls: who are you taking with you?

What do I mean who am I taking with me? There is only me, isn't there? (Price, 2019)

So you have never had that voice telling you to beware, that you're at risk, not good enough, others are better, out of your depth, this always happens to you, you're an imposter, what will people say, this can't go wrong, this could be career ending, this will influence promotion/selection ... sound familiar? Of course, they are. From where do those thoughts, that inner conversation, flow?

I have always found simple reference and clarity in Professor Steve Peters – The Chimp Paradox – Mind Management Model (Peters, 2012). The complexity of the human brain and our psychological interplay are made entertainingly clear, by breaking the brain into three working systems.

1. There is you. The Human. This predominantly being the frontal cortex – where we have our logical thinking, our compassion, our rational thinking, self-control, where our law abiding and societal responsibilities live – this is our cognitive functioning. This is where evidence, rationale, perspective and shades of grey can flourish. Well, they can flourish if this next character doesn't spoil the plan.

2. Second is your limbic system – the thalamus and amygdala – the Chimp. This is the primitive system that hasn't evolved since we were primates. This is where emotions flow from. This is the second voice in your head. This is a very powerful part of the brain and is hardwired. I will explain in more detail its core drivers. Policing amplifies all these core drivers. Higher risk incidents elevate further still. This is what was fully in control in the command examples given, the Human didn't get a look in.

3. Third is the Computer – the programmable part of the brain that stores learnt beliefs, behaviours and skills. Both the Chimp and the Human can store programs in the Computer, these can be very helpful and supportive, or they can be destructive. You can decide what goes in there. This is the start of developing an emotional radar and emotional quotient.

A very simplistic breakdown of the flow of neurons when any 'event' takes place is this; the senses pick up the new information and it goes first to the Chimp for instant analysis – predominantly is this a risk to our life or security? If it's not a life risk the Chimp then checks the Computer – *Do we know what to do here?* If there is a learnt programme, there it will run it and not take over. If threat and risk is anticipated for you, or there is no learnt programme, then the Chimp steps up 'I'm in Control'. The Human is frozen out chemically for around 20 minutes and the body is offered a range of emotions and chemicals for the challenge ahead. If you are facing a true violent threat to your safety all of this can be very helpful – this is the Fight, Flight or Freeze response. If you are a police officer operating as part of an armed operation, particularly if in command, we don't want to be unleashing the Chimp.

Let us explore further the core hardwired drivers I spoke about for this emotional and primitive part of all our brains and look how that dynamic is influenced in our world of policing.

The Chimp part of the brain makes assessment against:

- survival;
- security;

- sex;
- territory;
- troop;
- status/power/ego.

So this part of the brain is looking for any threat to our person, our security; it is looking to secure the next generation – sex (I will leave that for another study within policing); it is looking for security in its territory and it needs a troop, a team, a group to be part of. It thrives on status, power and ego.

REFLECTIVE PRACTICE

Please pause again for a second and reflect on these hardwired drivers and reference them to your world and your experiences.

- Can you bring to mind experiences where you have felt someone is over-reacting, is out of perspective, having a dis-proportionately emotional reaction?
- Once you have the example reference, the bullet points above, and see which were at play – it could well be more than one.

Exploring the context

Let us explore these together for broad policing, then I will sharpen up into the management of armed or higher risk incidents.

Policing is a uniform business. From day one we become part of a troop, we wear the same clothes, we begin talking the same language and we come together to re-affirm that troop on a daily basis. We operate as part of hierarchy, we have ranks. The Chimp loves that.

Policing does, on occasion, see life and safety at risk. We rely on the troop for survival, security and safety. Survival, security and troop are daily headlines in policing.

Policing has defined territories both geographic and functional – A District, B District, Uniform, CID, Neighbourhoods and Specialists. We take our troop into other territories on a daily basis, often where they are not welcome – we enter homes, we arrest, we search – the Chimp is on high alert in these circumstances, *'Your safety is at risk, we're in foreign territory, there is another troop, you need to affirm your status'*. The limbic system is naturally agitating.

Policing by its nature brings order, control, compliance and regulation – status, ego and power are all activated.

So, policing in general is like a Chimp activation exercise, so what then when we move to the 'firearms job', what we see then is many of these areas aggravated, elevated and amplified. We set the foundation for Chimp to take control at the very time we would prefer it to be asleep in the corner while the Human runs the show.

A firearms job, by its very nature brings to the fore the considerations of life and death, security and safety are raised, we are part of command and control so the troop is tight and is on high alert, rank and status is built in, we are invariably operating in unfamiliar territory with risk – so the Chimp is naturally rattling the emotional bars of the cage.

So, when I ask who are you bringing with you? You perhaps now understand who or what I am referring to.

Back to our analogy of the car of command. The car is tuned, fuelled, primed and ready to be driven. You get in the driver's seat. Who is getting in the passenger seat to offer you thoughts, emotions and behaviours? If you have worked hard and established shared values, beliefs and thresholds your passenger will look after you and offer you helpful feelings and emotions for you to consider. If you haven't, beware, you could be about to be hijacked by your Chimp.

The role of values

So, how can values, beliefs and your truths have a profound impact on what happens? Well, this is your programming of the Computer – the first reference point for the limbic system. Let me explain by contrasting some unhelpful, but perhaps far more common truths, values and beliefs against some more helpful.

Unhelpful

- We must always save life.
- No one should get hurt.
- Things should go to plan; no one should make mistakes.
- The subject will do as we expect.
- It's right or wrong, no grey areas.
- The goal posts shouldn't move.
- My career depends upon this.

- *I have to show I'm the best.*
- *I can't show weakness, I must make the right decisions.*
- *The Chief Constable (CC) and Police and Crime Commissioner (PCC) will judge me on this, what will politicians say?*
- *The IOPC (Independent Office of Police Conduct) are not balanced and are a threat.*
- *The media will be watching and will slaughter me if this doesn't go well.*
- *The media should be fair.*

More helpful

- Principle of best effort – *by using the team around me, thorough planning, with an unassailable audit trail, I can demonstrate I did my best regardless of outcome.*
- *We will work to the strategy, but sometimes people may be hurt or die despite our best efforts. Sometimes it may be necessary for people to be hurt or die to achieve strategy.*
- Things do not always go to plan. *I have a comprehensive primary plan, contingencies and 'what if' contingencies, but things may still arise. With my training and the team alongside, there is nothing we can't deal with. We will do our best.*
- Senior Officers will be naturally interested – it may take time to explain the full detail, it is their job to enquire and be interested, particularly if harm or injury is caused. *I have an audit trail of decisions made at the time. I am happy to be judged on how I responded to what I knew at the time.*
- *The press and media will always be interested and will be rarely balanced and fair. Their job is to attract clicks and sell papers, not present fair and balanced commentary on the police. Don't expect fairness.*
- *I can't control the press they make a living from the safety of their office armchair, that safety is provided by us.*
- It is natural for others to be acutely interested in the decisions made, it may need patience to fully explain the complexity. *I expect the IOPC to be interested, it is part of our transparency and integrity. It will take time but is needed.*
- *This is not a competition and results are not guaranteed. By focusing upon best effort, we can increase the probability of achieving our preferred outcome.*
- *My career won't be defined by one incident, it will be defined by core and consistent commitment, professionalism and transparent best effort.*

Let us return to my examples, to explore what was at play. In the Far Right protest example when sporadic attacks with a serious, potentially fatal assault took place, where do you think the Commanders' beliefs were centred? I suspect quite a few were at play – no one should get hurt, things should go to plan, no one should make mistakes, the subjects will do as we expect, the goal posts shouldn't move, my career could depend upon this, I have to show I'm the best, I can't show weakness, I must make the right decisions.

Similarly, with the lively Dynamic Entry – when a total surprise unfolded, which was unexpected and unlikely, where do you think the STFCs' thoughts were? I don't think initially it was referencing *'With my training and the team alongside, there is nothing we can't deal with. We will do our best'*. I suspect the thoughts to mind engaged *'No one should get hurt, things should go to plan, no one should make mistakes'*. It took the Tac Ad to provide the timely *'shake'* to bring perspective and belief in the team ability.

Similarly, the Loggist who reacted emotionally to the death of a subject. I suspect the beliefs taking prominence were

We must always save life, my career depends upon this, the CC and PCC will judge me on this, what will politicians say? The IOPC are not balanced and are a threat, the media will be watching and will criticise.

I'm sure all of us have experienced similar scenarios and incidents where we have suffered an unwanted and detrimental emotional reaction, so what is happening to us?

As the new information is encountered, exacerbated in the 2 per cent – the attack, the death, the unexpected, the unfair – remember the first reference point in the psychological mind, in an instant, is to the limbic system to establish if we know anything about this, do we hold any knowledge in the Computer, and on account of that do we see any risk to us? That could be perceived risk to our survival (sacked), security (job and position), status (rank and role/CC/IOPC), troop (our team) and territory (moved position or role).

If our truths and beliefs see more of the unhelpful list of beliefs, then the probability of the risk being believed to be a clear and present current danger is high. What then occurs is a very primitive hardwired reaction – blood flows to the muscles to prepare for a fight or flight, it flows away from the other organs, colour drains from the face, the neck flushes, our mouths become dry and tunnel vision develops. The cognitive part of the brain is chemically frozen by neurons as now is the time to act, not to deliberate and consider – the limbic system is in control, your Chimp, and it has decided it is life and death (for you), even when the development may be nothing of the sort.

You are either ramping up for a battle or to run from the threat. The third reaction is of course *Freeze,* where the behavioural change is to freeze all functions until the threat has passed.

I have seen this very tragic state in a number of firearms command assessments where the candidate is not moving or processing, even when encouragement is made to take a breath, relax, spin the model, there is an inert, blank response. The beliefs behind the assessment process are likely to be deeply unhelpful and out of perspective, '*If I fail this, my reputation is at risk, I may lose my current job, everyone will laugh at me, I will be a failure*', so when the first difficult paper feed is encountered, high risk is registered from those beliefs and a freeze option selected.

Paradoxically, the very thing the candidate feared is activated to 'protect' them. The 'person' they brought with them to the assessment has actually sabotaged their own performance.

These are the pitfalls we may encounter. These flow from that psychological interplay between you and your limbic system where your truths and beliefs, if unhelpful, out of perspective and out of context will lead to unhelpful emotions and behaviour, reducing the effectiveness of decision-making and command.

All deeply unhelpful, uncomfortable and, thankfully, absolutely avoidable.

Solutions

So, if avoidable, what are the practical things we can do?

We need to ensure the vehicle remains tuned, fuelled and ready to go. We must refresh our technical knowledge, exercise skills and continue to learn and reflect through CPD. There is no easy option to ensuring the skills needed are optimal. We are then match fit. We have the capability. How then do we ensure we are mind fit?

This takes a degree of darkened room personal reflection, and it must be personal to you. Your values, your truths and your beliefs can only be yours. This is preparing for command – this is not a one-off task of listing a handful of reference points, rather an ongoing journey of refining, modifying and developing. By identifying your truths, values and beliefs, which are balanced, with perspective, in context and with fair expectations you have a firm platform to make a profound impact on your mindset and purpose.

Just like any other skill, emotional skills need exercising. Writing your truths down can really help to embed them and this becomes almost a written summary of your culture.

Audio recording them can be highly effective, and although listening to yourself speaking your own thoughts may seem a little odd, by once or twice a week, replaying them on your commute is an easy way to confirm, embed and develop your truths. This method places them as a headline reference in your Computer. You are deciding what platform your emotions will flow from, rather than it being a matter of luck. You are choosing to respond rather than react.

When a particular incident, challenge or operation is being pre-planned, it is good practice to develop your truths bespoke to the challenge. Further, as the operation goes live, just as we would warm up for physical exercise, it is wise to psychologically warm up – working through what your values are, what you truths are, your beliefs, what success looks like and hopefully an over-riding desire for best effort, rather than a focus on binary outcomes.

You are then ready. Match fit. Mind fit.

So, what happens when the operation is live, and things are changing dynamically? You have now programmed both the skills and the reference point of beliefs that will keep you calm and in focus. The efforts made in advance will significantly reduce the probability of a Chimp hijack, but it doesn't remove it. This is where your emotional radar will come to the fore.

Just as we have IQ for academic intelligence, we have EQ (Emotional Quotient) for our emotional intelligence. Developing your own EQ to recognise when you are being offered thoughts and emotions which are unhelpful and then being able to quickly reference your own truths and beliefs to bring balance.

Let me give a personal example of how this can translate into practical effect. The benefit can sometimes be tricky to identify as it is often the absence of a destructive emotional reaction, rather than the presence of an unhelpful one.

My example is drawn from a siege where I acted as Hostage Negotiator and was part of a team of four that negotiated with a man in siege with his two children as hostages. He had filled the stairwell to his flat with furniture, had petrol ready to pour over it for any entry attempt and had repeatedly brought his children to a balcony with a knife to their throats. We negotiated for three days and had inconsistent rapport as his mental health through drug abuse fluctuated wildly. Outside of any intelligence the subject produced a firearm on day three and became extremely aggressive, and over the space of the next three hours fired 11 shots at the armed containment. We continued to negotiate by telephone and then by spoken word at the house door, with ballistic protection, as the threat to his children intensified. At a critical point while he was engaging armed containment officers, we managed to extract both children. When there was only him left in the house, he shot himself.

Not the outcome you would ever want. The death of another human being is as significant an event as can be imagined. The emotional reaction to this will be directly related to your core truths and beliefs. If you were to quickly reference the 'unhelpful' list earlier, it would be fair to say a highly emotional breakdown, with anxiety and fear would dominate and the psychological damage in the short and longer terms could be significant. It will come as little surprise that the list of more helpful beliefs is indeed my own truths drawn up over many years and with those as a foundation, I had no unwanted emotions. I had sadness and regret that the man had taken his own life, but had and still have no fear, anxiety, catastrophic worries of implications for the future, no fear of judgement or reprisals. The impact then and now is one of best effort, perspective and realistic expectations.

In summary, by adding a new element of psychological preparation and warm up to command or incident management, we can significantly alter the probability of unhelpful and destructive emotions, and we can face the 98 per cent or the 2 per cent with equal confidence and assurance.

This approach is not restricted in its application to complex and high-risk incidents. It is equally effective to roles in unarmed policing, response policing, community policing and indeed business or family life. You are developing a platform for a considered emotional response rather than a pot luck 'reaction'.

Culture and CPD

So where next as we strive to continually professionalise and improve the service we offer?

Clearly, the purpose of this chapter has been to identify the personal opportunity of exploring your current beliefs, your current truths and values and assessing whether they serve you well. Are they formed accurately, with perspective, and with broader context?

Herein lies the wider challenge – how far does your team, force and national police culture influence and set the baseline for your personal beliefs? Broader organisational culture has a huge influence on personal beliefs; indeed, it can form many of them, the culture around us can pervade and influence to a point that they may replace or dull our own values and truths.

If the command and control environment invites more autocratic leadership, that is underpinned by more unhelpful and intolerant beliefs, the real danger is then that the 98 per cent reinforces those beliefs *'That this is the way things should be done'*. This may only come apart when the 2 per cent is engaged, and that is the very time we would very much prefer that not to happen.

How far does Firearms CPD and seminars support such development?

Let me see if my experience of CPD seems familiar? We come together two or three times a year, it's a large conference format, we have healthy mixes of roles and ranks, Firearms Command Training facilitate the day and the key areas covered are:

- change to national threat;
- change to attack methodology;
- change to APP or CoP guidance;
- key lessons learnt – case studies;
- paper feed exercises.

These are extremely professional days, and all the above are vital. They are retaining, refreshing and renewing the learnt skills and knowledge. The programming of the Computer. The engine tuning of the car. Refreshing our capability.

How many times have you talked about or received update on your psychological CPD?

We had that the first time in our last round of CPD. Our lead Firearms Command Trainer, began the session with himself and an empty chair centre stage, and asked the question *'who are you bringing with you?'* (Price, 2019). The session ended with breathing skills, mindfulness and emotional awareness.

That session was an eye opener to the first conversations on emotions and behavioural skills. This is not sports psychology; it is policing psychology.

Let me return for a final time to the car analogy.

If we have an unhelpful culture and from that flows unhelpful beliefs, we will be more prone to looking backwards *'When this happened before I felt vulnerable, I was criticised, there were reprisals, I was warned, I was compared to'*. If these occur, you have an unhealthy fear-based culture (Grange, 2020). When it comes to the car, it may be finely tuned but it will be dominated by a huge rear-view mirror, your thoughts will be in the past, forming catastrophic projections for the future. You cannot drive well if half your view is blocked looking backwards.

CPD can then bring this element of psychological balance to the fore; it can become a point of discussion and development and can reference organisational and personal culture.

British policing leads the way in terms of our professionalism and sophisticated approach to command and decision-making at all levels. These skills are elevated further still when we consider complex, higher risk or armed incidents.

We have so much to be very proud of. Our collective strength is the desire to continually improve, striving to be better.

Psychological development is part of that effort: expanding, promoting and evolving emotional skills and the critical interplay to our emotional response and then our behaviour.

A highly functional driver in a finely tuned car leads to a very smooth ride.

CHAPTER SUMMARY

This chapter has provided some thought provoking references and models for understanding our performance under pressure. You have seen that thoughts define emotion, emotions influence and drive behaviours which in turn will either bring out the very best or the very worst of your capability.

A fully serviced and tuned car along with a functional driver makes for a successful journey, or if you like, a fully prepared technical and practical capability combined with a supportive and prepared mindset leads to best performance.

The take away point is that this is under your own influence. You can decide. You can build and invest in the right preparation, the right environment, stimulate the best response (not a reaction) to lead to supportive and helpful behaviour which maximises your capability.

Our performance under pressure at the time of high risk is our canary in the coal mine for broader police culture. It can be a reveal to a fear-based or fearless culture.

I will close with a reference to the culture of the All Blacks Rugby Union team (Kerr, 2013). At times of acute pressure, they have an approach which describes the 'Blue Head' or the 'Red Head'.

- The Red Head – one of tunnel vision, panic, outcome focused with catastrophic anticipation, or
- The Blue Head – one of calm, engaged focus, balanced, problem solving, consumed in process not outcome.

If you have sense of fear as the Red Head seems very familiar, fear not. Take my assurance that 'reactions' and Red Head traits can be developed and changed. They are not sealed in your DNA. Anyone who covers destructive emotions and behaviours with a *'That's just the way I am'* response is just lazy to an investment in their development. This is absolutely an area you can develop, train, improve and exercise.

As we are the police service, I think quite naturally we should all aspire to be a Blue Head.

References

College of Policing (2014) National Decision Model. Available at: www.app.college.police.uk/app-content/national-decision-model/ (accessed 11 February 2021).

Grange, P (2020) *Fear Less, How to Win at Life Without Losing Yourself.* London: Penguin Publishing.

Kerr, J (2013) *Legacy, What the All Blacks Can Teach Us about the Business of Life.* Boston: Little Brown Book Group.

Peters, S (2012) *The Chimp Paradox, the Mind Management Programme for Confidence, Success and Happiness.* Vermilion: Ebury Publishing.

Price, S (2019) How to Be Your Own Best Friend and Why It Matters [Lecture]. *Firearms CPD.*

Roosevelt, T (1910) Citizenship in a Republic Speech, Paris, April 23, 1910.

8 Wise policing: soft skills and strong principles

Kate Moss and Ken Pease

CHAPTER OBJECTIVES

This chapter will help you:

- understand how soft skills are recognisable in policing practice;
- challenge yourself to reflect on how your soft skills contribute to how you are perceived by colleagues and members of the public;
- understand how your behaviours and decision-making could be enhanced by sharpening your soft skills;
- appreciate the elements of soft skills, obstacles to using them and the reasons for trying to.

Introduction

What are soft skills? We had a vague idea but were unsure. A Google search was little help.

> *Soft skills are the skills that enable you to fit in at a workplace. They include your personality, attitude, flexibility, motivation, and manners. Soft skills are so important that they are often the reason employers decide whether to keep or promote an employee.*
>
> (Doyle, 2021)

These are contrasted with hard skills, which concern technical competence.

The above definition of soft skills could apply as easily to good practice in the Gestapo as in the National Health Service. It is desirable for well-meaning people to get on with their colleagues, but the business school-speak quoted makes us uneasy. The same site contains a very long list (150 items) of ill specified soft skills. The site encourages its readers to mention these in CVs and job interviews. This feels bogus. The comedian George Burns put it this way: 'Sincerity - if you can fake that, you've got it made'.

Looking back over 50 years of experience, much of it working from police stations, we describe examples of police work which were both skilled and left people feeling that they had been dealt with kindly and fairly. Starting with a too simple definition of soft skill, we look at the real-life examples and tease out their key features. These are used to refine our starting definition. We repeat the process until we are reasonably satisfied with the definition of soft skills. The process is like starting with a definition of dogs as four-legged mammals that bark, and then looking at examples that people would agree are dogs (or not dogs) to get a better idea of what 'dogginess' entails.

Having got a better idea of the features of soft-skilledness is not enough. Skills and dogs are different. '*I have a dog*' is self-explanatory (although the truth is more often '*A dog has me*'). '*I have a skill*' means nothing until you specify what the skill is for, so we add a section on the goals of soft skilled policing, and how to reveal your own implicit goals. You think you know what they are but they are often unrecognised or unarticulated, even though they shape one's behaviour.

At this stage in the chapter we have a more tangible definition of the skill and the goals sought by using it. This is still not enough. We know a skilled darts player when we see one, we know what you have to do to win a game of darts, but we are both rotten players. What is still missing to get a handle on the concept of darts, or soft skills in policing, or indeed skill of any kind?

The central element of skill is prediction. In darts, how much muscle adjustment is necessary to change the dart's trajectory to hit double top? In policing, sensing what is likely to happen next and what to do to get the best possible resolution of a situation is key. Once we have dealt with prediction, we will be clear what soft skills in action look like; what their goals are and the importance of a police officer's capacity to predict the course of events as they unfold, and hence shape them towards the goal. We are not naïve, so we then set out the obstacles to soft skilled police work. The chapter's final section addresses the 'so what?' question.

Our too simple starting definition of soft skill is '*The preference and capacity to achieve designated goals by the least confrontational means possible*'.

Expressions of appreciation

A soft skill, as defined above, leaves those on whom it is exercised minimally disgruntled (ideally positively 'gruntled'). Unhappy as we are with most definitions of soft skill, this is a thread running through them all.

Ask people whether they like their GP and why. Better still, think about what pleased you in contact with service providers of any sort. Overwhelmingly, appreciation comes when the necessary task is embedded in a person-to-person encounter, in which the individuality of the other(s) is recognised. How does this apply in the policing context? One source of information is the collection of citizen expressions of appreciation of what police officers do. Putting pen to paper (or locating the relevant part of the local police force's website) to express appreciation of police work takes time and effort. That represents a high hurdle for a member of the public to get over. Far more people feel appreciative than take the trouble to communicate the appreciation formally. Expressions of appreciation which reach forces mean that the senders are really, really appreciative. What do they appreciate? The majority stress their treatment as individuals in difficulty, rather than pleasure in the policing outcome. In the minority of cases that *are* about outcomes, an officer's demeanour (calm, supportive and the like) were mentioned over and above the good outcome. The following examples have been tweaked to guarantee anonymity.

1. *The two policemen who took care of us in helping us to eventually locate my car were so kind and patient. They showed great compassion in understanding how upset we were at this miserable end to our lovely holiday. I felt it was an absolute waste of their time to have to deal with this because some people are just 'bad' people. I cannot thank them enough for their kindness and wish them well.*

2. *I would like to sincerely thank the two officers that stopped and attended my mum who fell in XXXX square on Saturday afternoon. They were so kind, managing to persuade my mum to let me take her to A&E. From this I have been able to get my mum referred to the memory clinic as I have been worried about her memory and falls for a few years. I wish I had taken their names but would appreciate you being able to find them and pass this message of thanks to them both.*

Is there anything in these and similar expressions of appreciation (we have now looked at a large number from a mid-sized English force) which means we should refine our initial definition. To remind you, this was *'The preference and capacity to achieve designated goals by the least confrontational means possible'*.

The necessary added ingredient is that the contact is human to human, not state official to citizen. The definition thus becomes *'the preference and capacity to achieve designated goals by the least confrontational means possible, while engaging with participants as individuals with their personal needs and challenges'*. This amendment carries echoes of Peelian principle 7.

> *To maintain at all times a relationship with the public that gives reality to the historic tradition that the police are the public and that the public are the police, the police being only members of the public who are paid to give full-time attention to duties which are incumbent on every citizen in the interests of community welfare and existence.*
>
> (UW, n.d.)

The extra mile

Many expressions of appreciation feature events where the police officer did more than could reasonably be expected, for example occasions when the appreciated officer was off duty but stopped to help anyway. '*Going the extra mile*' (even if it is more like going the extra yard because it involves little effort) is treasured coming from any service provider. The writers have been on innumerable ride-alongs on three continents and have accompanied cops who do the minimum competently (and fewer who do the minimum less than competently) and finally those who routinely do more. In the most recent case one of us attended, an elderly man with early symptoms of dementia, victim of an assault by a neighbour, was to be taken to the Accident and Emergency Department of the local hospital. Before leaving home for what would certainly be a long wait at the hospital, the police crew made him tea, dressed his cuts and made sure his dog had water available and had a chance to empty his bladder. The actions were not self-serving because the man's mental state was such that he would not recognise the care and consideration that had been shown him.

Our friend Simon Thompson is a former Chief Inspector with Merseyside Police. He described his experiences when recovering from throat cancer surgery some fifteen years ago. He had no criticisms of the nurses who cared for him, but did make a distinction between those who competently did their job, and those who asked him more questions, gave more information and suggested more ways to make him comfortable (and had a sense of humour). He had particular admiration for the latter group, who 'went the extra mile'. When the distinction is applied to policing, Simon himself definitely belongs to the second group, as is detailed in the next paragraph.

We once asked Simon to choose the memory from his 30-year career that gave him greatest satisfaction. His answer had a clear parallel with his observations on his nurses. He recalls attending a burglary of the home of an elderly woman. The lock on the window through which the burglar had gained entry now lacked a securing pin. Simon realised that the pin from the epaulette on his uniform shirt was of the right size to replace the missing pin, at least as a temporary measure. He did the repair and finished the call. To his surprise, he got a letter of appreciation from the victim's daughter. It was that letter which he identified as having given him most satisfaction. It would not occur to him that he was exercising a skill, but his action meant that he was going beyond what he was required to do.

In the period when one of us was privileged to share an office with Simon, we listened to his conversations with inexperienced Police Community Support Officers (the position having recently been introduced). Without going into detail, he took steps to ensure that warranted officers were made aware of the difficulties and abuse which PCSOs were facing, and supported their PCSO colleagues appropriately. We will briefly mention later the notion that soft skills 'begin at home', ie, that its precepts must apply to behaviour towards colleagues as much as to behaviour towards other citizens. Simon Thompson embodied 'going the extra mile' with his PCSO colleagues. In the light of the extra mile phenomenon, the definition of soft skills is amended as follows:

The preference and capacity to achieve designated goals by the least confrontational means possible, while engaging participants as individuals with their personal needs and challenges', and preparedness to take action beyond the minimum formally required.

The key insight of problem-oriented policing POP is that a call for service is a symptom of a problem, not the problem itself. There is a clear link between POP and soft skill policing. Sources on POP that make it clear are Scott (2000) and Scott and Clarke (2020). The second of these is particularly relevant both because it is up to date and also because it contains a lot of practical examples along Bongle lines.

> ### CASE STUDY
>
> #### Bill Bongle
>
> The work of Bill Bongle, then of the Green Bay Wisconsin Police Department, illustrates this way of seeing things. You can read an account of Bill's work (https://popcenter.asu.edu/sites/default/files/library/awards/goldstein/1999/99-22(W).pdf), but for present purposes the relevant point concerns how Bill Bongle came to undertake the project. He worked as a patrol officer in the Broadway area of Green Bay and was frustrated by repeat calls for service for the same reason at the same location. At calls he attended he took time to see what could be done to address the underlying problem. Green Bay police were often short-handed and patrol officers were discouraged from spending much time on a call as the remaining workload fell upon colleagues. Brevity of calls thus came to be the metric by which officers were judged. On every shift a friendly nudge to spend less time on calls came in the form of an 'award' to the officer spending the longest average time at call locations. The award was termed the 'Call Milking Award' and was a cow-shaped trophy. Bill recalls,
>
> > It was uncomfortable receiving the call-milking award as a patrol officer. The implication was that I was diverting my attention from more important matters and not focusing on what the rest of the patrol officers thought was important. My perspective of what was important shifted once I stepped out of my squad car and into the neighbourhood. I learned the citizens' priorities were much different than mine or those of my colleagues. I call this my 'Out-of-car experience.
>
> Working with his friend and partner Steve Scully, Bill set out, with the Broadway community, to turn the area round. Writing to the authors in 2021, Bill recalled,
>
> > I am happy to say that Broadway remains a vibrant part of Green Bay and a destination spot with beautiful shops, parks restaurants and other fine businesses. It is the home to the second largest Farmers' Market in Wisconsin.
>
> Bill's 'out-of-car experience' is the telling phrase, when call brevity became less important than problem solving.

> **REFLECTIVE PRACTICE**
>
> Think about these issues through your own lens.
>
> - What experiences have given you the most satisfaction and why?
> - What skills did you apply and in responding to those situations, what was your main focus?

Much of this chapter is taken up with examples of how police officers we admire go about the job. The common feature is focus. It is less on the narrow policing options (ignore, advise, intervene) and more on what should be done to resolve the problems that people are experiencing (and/or causing). All calls for service have contexts. Only attention to these contexts will diminish demand for police services. This is the core insight of problem-oriented policing. This is too vague. Please read on for examples. For now, let's describe how you can tell someone who will be accused of having soft skills. There are three symptoms.

1. They will listen and ask questions to understand underlying issues.
2. They will see problem resolution as the ultimate aim rather than issuing a crime number or making an arrest.
3. They will seek to anticipate what might happen next.

In the late 1960s one of us taught an evening class on psychology for police and prison officers. He recalls one exchange with a young cop. It went roughly as follows.

Young cop: We've got a lot of burglaries of council houses. They get in by the front door. The doors are crap. Lean on them hard and they give way.

Naïve lecturer: Why don't you get the council to up the spec of the doors?

Young cop (grinning): That's more than my job's worth.

Things have changed (though more in principle than everyday practice). Situational crime prevention (SCP) and problem-oriented policing (POP) have started to widen the focus of policing from the event to its causal context. This mirrors medicine's refocus from treatment of stroke patients to control of blood pressure; on masks and social distancing to hold the recent Covid-19 pandemic at bay while vaccines were developed. This change of focus was Bill Bongle's epiphany when he left his car.

One retired senior officer described policing as fishing bodies out of a river without looking upstream to look at the bridge off which people were jumping. Please take a moment to consider cases where you are 'fishing out the bodies' rather than looking upstream. For example, at the time of writing, puppies (mostly bitches) are being stolen. Going upstream could include DNA testing of pet dogs so that they and their pups could be identified as having been stolen or bred from stolen bitches. (A trial of such a scheme is believed to be in hand in Gloucestershire at the time of writing.) More active oversight of puppy farms (in line with s17 of the Crime and Disorder Act 1998) represents another way of getting upstream of the dog theft problem.

So what else needs to be added to our soft skills definition in the light of Bill's 'out-of-car experience'? It is that when a call for service reflects a symptom of a wider community problem, the phrase *'achieve designated goals'* should be replaced by *'solve crime and disorder generating community problems'*. So we have:

> *The preference and capacity to solve crime and disorder generating community problems by the least confrontational means possible, while engaging participants as individuals with their personal needs and challenges, with preparedness to take action beyond the minimum formally required.*

Goals

Three elements have now been added to the simple definition of soft skills that we started with. These are:

1. treatment of people as unique individuals with unique needs and back stories;
2. doing more than the minimum necessary;
3. refocusing on causal chains rather than caused events.

Refining the definition is all well and good, but what is skilled police work (soft and hard) trying to achieve? All skilled performance has a goal. Understanding the goal structures everything else. This is well understood by experts on Artificial Intelligence (AI). This may seem a bizarre way to start a discussion of policing goals, but at least it may introduce an idea that may impress your friends. The idea is *perverse instantiation*. It is important. In the literature on AI, where we find a serious debate as to whether humanity will become extinct by the mis-specification of aims embedded in super intelligent AI systems by their human architects (Bostrom, 2014). AI engineers are concerned to the point of obsession with how the very precise specification of goals would be interpreted and realised by super intelligent AI systems whose motivations would not be constrained by human values. As the AI enterprise recognises, motivation and intelligence are independent of each other, and human values are not relevant in the search for paths to optimal performance. Computer HAL in the movie 2001 deemed that the human crew was hampering the mission's goals and had to be dispensed with. In an example developed by Bostrom (2014), a superintelligence tasked to make as many paper clips as possible would not stop until it had colonised all Earth's resources to that end. If the single purpose were eliminating overpopulation, a cull of women of childbearing age has much to recommend it. With that cheery thought, let us move from the apocalyptic to the homely. To restate the simple point, the careful specification of goals is crucial for cops and computers alike. Lest cops bristle at the comparison, bear in mind that we are talking about super intelligent computing, so you should be flattered! But beware of perverse instantiation.

Practitioners choose their actions by reference to a goal, of which they may not be fully aware unless prodded. As all readers will already know, Plato reports Socrates as saying *'to talk every day about virtue and the other things about which you hear me talking and examining myself and others is the greatest good to man, and that the unexamined life is not worth living'* (trans Fowler, 1966). One way of clarifying one's own most basic goals is known as laddering. This is a technique-devised clinical use, based on George Kelly's Personal Construct Theory (Kelly, 1955; Butt, 2007). Laddering consists in asking why people chose to do one thing rather than another, then asking for a reason for that choice. There quickly comes a point where the question seems silly and is answered *'It just is better'*. For example:

> *Why did you go to that lecture?*
> *Because I need to know that stuff to pass the exam.*
>
> *Why do you want to pass the exam?*
> *So I can qualify as a nurse.*
>
> *Why do you want to qualify as a nurse?*
> *So I can help people.*
>
> *Why do you want to help people?*
> *I just do. It's important. Are you a psychopath or something?*

Simon Thompson's laddering may have been something along the following lines:

> *Why did you stay in the burgled house after you had completed the official things?*
> *Because I thought the window was still a possible point of entry.*
>
> *Was it better for the window to be secure or insecure?*
> *Secure.*
>
> *Why was it better for it to be secure?*
> *So that she would not be burgled again?*
>
> *Is it better for her to be burgled again or not burgled at all?*
> *Not burgled.*
>
> *Why?*
> *Because a burglary upsets its victims.*
>
> *Is it better for people to be upset or not upset?*
> *Not upset****!!!! (expletives deleted).*

Reflective practice

- Pick a very specific action you took yesterday (like turning left or right when on patrol) and go through a laddering process like those instanced above. The point at which the self-questioning becomes silly represents the goal, the ultimate reason why you are doing the job.

- Repeat this process for three or four very specific choices as your starting point. Unless you cheat to persuade yourself that this is all psychologists' mumbo jumbo, you will find that laddering up leads you to the same one or two core goals.

Laddering up, as illustrated above, is a rough but neat way to clarify goals. As noted, all skilled behaviour is goal-directed. The goals make sense of the behaviour. An anti-Simon Thompson may have laddered as follows.

Why did you leave the burgled home as soon as the official stuff was done?
Because the sergeant gets irritated if you spend too long on calls.

Is it better for the sergeant to get irritated or not get irritated?
It's better for her not to get irritated.

Why?
Because staying in her good books helps me get promoted.

Is it better to get promoted or not get promoted?
Better to get promoted.

Why is it better to get promoted?
Because then I can buy stuff I would like.

Why is it better to be able to buy stuff you want?
Because I would be a success and my family would be proud of me.

Why is it better for your family to be proud of you?
It just is.

While we are on the topic, please note that laddering downwards is as useful for a different purpose. Laddering upwards helps identify goals. Laddering downwards helps work out the actions which are consistent (and inconsistent) with them, ie, the repertoire of specific actions you should perform to be wholly consistent with your goals.

To take an example of the use of downward laddering from its clinical origins, consider a smoker who wants to be a non-smoker. Being a smoker is not just a matter of puffing away. It is a whole behavioural repertoire. It provides something to do with your hands on social occasions. (What do you do with your hands if you are a non-smoker, says the anxious smoker?) What do you do when taking a break from work when a chat and a smoke used to be the order of the day? The social exchange between smokers (offering each other a cigarette, a light, an ashtray) has to be unlearned. You have to learn the set of behaviours, which non-smokers do instead of smoking. For example, recall our nursing student deciding to attend a lecture. If laddering up from reasons for attending a lecture reveals the core goal of helping people, laddering down shows what are the outward signs of that central purpose. So what are the signs of a nurse whose core goal is to help people? Here are a few.

- Performing necessary checks and procedures gently.
- Chatting to patients when possible beyond the necessary checks and procedures.
- Being alert and responsive to patient signs of discomfort or pain.
- Interacting with patients who do not have visitors.
- Patience with patients in a bad mood.

In this way someone with a core goal sets out the signs of that goal in action. This may alert him to actions which he recognises as flowing from his own core goal but which he does not himself perform. It also reveals things he does which do not flow from his core goal.

Laddering, as noted earlier, derives from one serious approach to clinical mental health practice but is helpful for anyone wanting to enhance their self-insight.

Prediction

Policing encounters are like a kind of dance (usually only metaphorically). The cop sees how the interaction is going and shapes it to her desired resolution. This represents the predictive capacity at the centre of soft skill. Tone-deaf officers will experience more conflict. It is the sum total of these 'dances' that the craft of policing emerges. What changes with experience is enhanced understanding of the possible next steps in the dance and how to choose between them to guide your partner to relative contentment when the music stops. This applies both to a specific exchange and to longer-term interactions.

In the acquisition of skill, failure is your friend. The first shelf you make will fall down. The world has a way of telling you when you are wrong. However, there are two circumstances where it will not. First, when you do not try something, you will never know whether it has succeeded. Second, when no one checks whether you are right, or worse if they check, and dare not tell you that you are wrong. This is the moral of the story of *The Emperor's New Clothes*. The genius physicist Richard Feynman made the same point: '*The first principle is that you must not fool yourself — and you are the easiest person to fool*' (FS, n.d.).

The argument advanced below is that the final brick in the soft skilled policing wall is rigorous testing of the ability to predict. For example, the claim to have good local knowledge is meaningless unless you can predict what is likely to happen locally in the next week. It may not be much better than chance, but professional gamblers have made fortunes from being slightly better than chance in their predictions.

The perspective from which evidence-based policing is branched had its origin in medicine with the Cochrane Collaboration, named for Archie Cochrane. Cochrane, himself a medical doctor, underwent radical surgery for a cancer which he did not have. The surgeon believed in good faith that he was dealing with cancerous tissue without waiting for a pathologist's report. Cochrane thereby discovered, in a particularly brutal way, that medical practitioners acted on the basis of predictive expertise that they did not possess. The rest of his life was spent testing the evidence base of medicine. No prediction was taken on trust. Assertions had to be evidenced. He did this work in the face of huge professional opposition. People hate having their professional judgement questioned. For 2000 years of medicine, confidence outran competence. Senior police officers are, in our experience, not an exception. Their aura of expertise typically leaves the capacity to predict untested.

The absence of prediction testing in policing as a way of honing skill has long troubled us. For instance, police officers (designated Crime Prevention Design Advisors or similar) have long advised planners on crime facilitating design features. We could find no studies of whether these recommendations had any validity in identifying places that would, in future, be prone to crime. Our former doctoral student Leanne Monchuk gave experienced CPDA practitioners plans of an estate which had been built a decade earlier but with which they were unfamiliar. She then compared the locations identified by the CPDAs as crime prone with the locations at which there had actually been crime. The results (Monchuk et al, 2018) were as might have been expected on the basis of larger-scale work on prediction in other professions. Nobody was perfect. Some were modestly skilled at prediction, some were random. It was a small study but it was enough to persuade us that police capacity to make predictions relevant to their work should be tested, not assumed. Skills, hard and soft, require good prediction so that interactions move towards a desired goal. Large-scale work on 'good judgement' was pioneered by Philip Tetlock (see Tetlock and Gardner, 2015), with an honourable mention going to Nate Silver (2012). Tetlock started by studying political pundits. Put kindly, their predictive performance was execrable. They stayed in work because their accuracy was never checked (and if it was they had ways of weaselling their way out of the issue by retrospectively reframing the question so that they were right after all) Tetlock went on to craft the Good Judgement Project (GJP). Readers are strongly recommended to access that source. It is highly practical. The predictions that he elicited were about difficult to predict real-world events. He collaborated with IARPA (the US Intelligence Advanced Research Projects Activity), recognising the centrality of prediction in making the intelligence services more skilled. The Tetlock approach is necessary. It has the incidental effect of revealing senior officer hubris, just as Cochrane undermined physician hubris.

Here are some of the things that Tetlock established.

1. Some people are superforecasters, reliably beating the odds.

2. Superforecasters were not necessarily the most intelligent participants. They had these attributes.

- They did not see the world through a big theory lens (like Marxism or a religious faith).
- There were conscientious in gathering relevant information.
- They adjusted their view readily when new information became available.
- There were ways of setting up groups that outperformed the predictive accuracy of its members.

If you find yourself in sympathy with the ideas expressed here, we suggest that they could (and should) be incorporated into policing in many ways. For example, body-worn camera footage of *developing* incidents be shown to apprentice officers, with predictions about how the incidents resolve themselves (and why) tested against actual outcomes which they are shown after they have made their predictions. If this is not a classroom exercise worth doing, we have never come across one. Not allowing experienced officers to escape, predictions made at Tasking and Coordinating meetings seem to provide scope for week-to-week prediction testing. You can do this for yourself if it is not organised.

Obstacles

There are three kinds of obstacles to the exercise of imaginative exercise of policing skills. These concern:

1. a political climate that centres on policing outcomes rather than community tranquillity, as would be suggested by Peelian Principle 1;
2. the hubris of senior police management which substitutes untested personal theory for experience-based efficacy pioneered by those of lower rank – this hampers the exercise of initiative;
3. individuals and groups who 'fail the on-street attitude test'.

Obstacle 1: outcomes

Government attempts to secure probity and consistency in crime recording yielded the National Crime Recording Standard, introduced in 2002, developed as the National Standard for Incident Recording (NPIA, 2011). Despite these efforts, the 'national statistics' badge was later withdrawn from police recorded crime figures (Home Office, 2014). Shoe-horning real-world complexity into simple counts is both doomed to failure and pernicious in encouraging a tick box mentality in policing, which is anathema to the exercise of soft skills as we characterised them earlier.

Perhaps no impossible task exists without someone being blamed for failure to complete it. In public and political discourse, that role has largely been assigned to the police's crime recording process. Regrettably, but perhaps inevitably, the issue of accurate crime recording became conflated with trust in the police generally. The current climate was perhaps first evident in the Conservative Party's drive for radical reform of the police, discernible from January 2006. The police service was then characterised as the last unreformed public service. Government's assertion that specified tragic events fuelled loss of confidence in the police is at odds with the results of the Crime Survey for England and Wales (Pease and Ignatans, 2014). Publication of crime outcome statistics led *The Times* of 7 February 2020 to assert '*Failing police "rumbled" by weary public*' (Ford, 2020).

The way crime outcomes are documented in routine statistics and framed in media accounts are both at odds with Peelian principle 1 and foster mistrust of the police service generally. The consequence is that they represent a central government obstacle to soft skills as we have described them. The Government quest for precise and clear crime numbers is certainly a case of perverse instantiation.

Obstacle 2: charity begins at home

Jason Roach has studied the emotional and cognitive impact on those who investigate the murder of children (Roach et al, 2016, 2018). Police officers have to confront the whole gamut of emotionally charged situations, variously harrowing, dangerous and unjust. The rest of us are spared this. Surely the police service collectively and individually owes its employees no less by way of the exercise of soft skills in dealings with colleagues than in dealings with the public. Officers who are subject to discipline should, as a matter of equity, receive no less skilled handling than other citizens. We recently undertook an analysis of the suspension process in a large UK force (McDaniel et al, 2020). Although the prevalence and length of police suspensions have fallen in many police areas in recent years – usually in favour of placing a police officer on restricted duties – it was clear from the authors' experience that the duration and handling of cases needed to be better understood. Placing an officer on restricted duties, suspending them and subjecting them to a prolonged misconduct investigation have consequences that appeared to be largely unresearched. Questions about the well-being of the officer throughout the process, and the impact of the experience on their attitudes and approaches once they return to duty following exoneration, were obviously critically important. Their handling by their force should display the features of soft skill, which we identified earlier.

Both personal and practitioner-reported experience indicated that policing approaches and styles can be compromised by the anticipated criticism of how an officer acts and the possibility of consequent discipline proceedings against him or her and/or the prospect of protracted and time-consuming legal proceedings with uncertain outcomes. In the triage of possible police responses (ignore, advise, intervene) this state of affairs exerts pressure away from the last and towards the first. In this way, personal and vicarious experience suggests that the threat of discipline proceedings permeates frontline decision-making and is thus fundamentally important in the service the public receives.

The purpose of our research was to analyse the process of protracted discipline hearings ending with the exculpation of warranted officers. We hoped thereby to identify points of avoidable delay and of demotivation and embitterment and suggest possible improvements in process. Some 6,000 constables serving with the chosen force reportedly received the message. Responses were received from 20 officers who had been through a protracted misconduct investigation, cleared and returned to work. Of these, 11 were subsequently interviewed. Once the interviews were conducted, the force provided access to case files relating to the proceedings concerning the officers for the purpose of analysis. Some cases had a large number of associated documents, whereas only a few documents could be provided in others. These usually consisted of some or all of the following: the *Initial Triage Assessment Form* which categorises each allegation at the outset and recommends whether to investigate, the *Investigating Officer's Log (IO Log)* which records the steps taken by the investigator, the *Regulation 15/16 Notice* which informs the police officer that an allegation has been made, the *IO Report* which documents the investigator's recommendation, the *Regulation 36 Notice* which informs the police officer of the outcome and a *Progress Report* extracted from the PSD's Centurion System which records the time and completion of these procedural steps (and others).

The cases examined ranged from lengths of 18 months to a little over 4 years, occurring between 2012 and 2017. The sample covered complaints from members of the public and conduct matters emanating from other police officers. It included a mix of misconduct and gross misconduct allegations, and 'locally investigated' (by the police service's Professional Standards Department) and 'independently investigated' (by the Independent Police Complaints Commission) cases. Officers subject to misconduct processes included police constables, sergeants and an inspector. We did not differentiate or analyse the sample on the basis of rank, age, length of service, gender or ethnicity. Our focus primarily was on system failures, and the repercussions of such. The project was designed to look into the welfare issues of police officers who had recently been engaged in protracted discipline hearings, which had ended with their exculpation, exoneration or some other indication of innocence. The aim was to identify issues that might be adversely affecting existing situations and the efficiency and efficacy of the extant processes and procedures, and to produce a set of recommendations for improvement.

All of the interviewees who returned to duty reported that the experience had affected their attitudes to police work. They reportedly struggled to regain their productivity and no longer saw themselves as the same kind of police officer once they returned to work. A general sense of disillusionment prevailed. One officer reported that he had 'changed ... completely as a person' and added that:

> [I] just don't know if it's what I want to do with my life – be a police officer anymore ...I feel very badly treated. No offender would be on bail for 4.5 years and waiting for answers.

Another officer commented that,

> *I struggle to now deal with violence, getting hands on people, because I've got no confidence that it won't get dealt with straight away …even though I've been found not guilty or no case to answer and have body cam I have still got no trust in the system.*

Other officers reported similar feelings, such as:

> *if I saw something now I would shy away from it. I wouldn't take hold of people …*

and

> *if I go home this week and have not arrested anybody I ain't got a problem – no complaints.*

These attitudes were reinforced in many cases by the fact that the allegations remained on the officer's file and continued to hang over the officers' heads even after they had been cleared. The Centurion misconduct database continued to link officers' names to allegations such as 'racist complaint' even though they had been cleared. One officer commented that '*you don't want to … just have [the record] laying on your file … someone is going to look at that and think "no smoke without fire" … so it is a matter of principle*'. Others took issue with the negative connotations associated with the findings of 'no further action' (NFA) and 'not proven' remaining on file. It was not unusual to hear officers say that '*not proven intimates to me they believe I have done it, they just couldn't prove it*'. One officer reported that he was unable to get developed vetting thereafter even though the allegation of dishonesty was not proven. The permanent record meant that officers struggled to shed the cloak of suspicion once they returned to work. Aware that such suspicions persisted, they altered their approaches to future police work accordingly.

In a nutshell, the discipline process and the prospect of suspension encourage a policing style in which nothing is done beyond the minimum. The sense of abandonment by the force during suspension likewise demotivates. None of the above suggests that misconduct should not be processed as such, any more than the exercise of soft skills in dealings with suspected offenders generally suggests that justice should not take its course. The message is simply that suspended officers returning to duty should be able to do so without demotivation and resentment towards the force, and thus not lose any capacity to exercise soft skills themselves.

REFLECTIVE PRACTICE

Think about what both motivates you and demotivates you professionally.

- Have there been circumstances where you have decided on inaction rather than justified and proper action on the basis of concerns about the possibility of action being taken against you?
- What do you think could be done about this within the force?

Killing the cubs

There are more ways of demotivating police officers than lengthy suspension. One good way is to squash their successful initiatives, which may reduce them to what sociologists of the police used to call 'uniform carriers'. Killing the Cubs is our way of thinking about the common experience in which a change of force or area commanders leads to the termination of promising initiatives. This invites comparison with the action of male lions to kill the cubs of the lioness they have successfully wooed, lest she devotes attention to cubs in which the new lover has no genetic investment.

In the most recent instance of which we have painful personal knowledge, indulge us in paraphrasing a conversation we had over lunch with two crime analysts from the force concerned. Details are changed to protect the guilty. The initiative, terminated after a change of management, was demonstrably successful and recognised by an international award. Let us call the prize-winning innovators Crosse and Blackwell and the BCU in which they innovated, Souptown. The following exchange occurred less than a year after the departure of both Crosse and Blackwell, one into retirement, the other in frustration to another organisation.

KM: *So what are you working on?*

Analyst: *Evidence-based policing.*

KM: *What precisely?*

Analyst: *Hot spot policing.*

KM: *Great. Which BCU?*

Analyst: *Souptown.*

KM: *So you're taking forward the work Crosse and Blackwell did?*

Analyst: *Who?*

Thus died a successful initiative and its replacement by something unoriginal, on the basis of management diktat.

Failing the attitude test

The last obstacle to the exercise of soft skills is the on-street reality of encounters with people or groups who fail the attitude test, ie, whose flippant, sarcastic or hostile words and deeds invite police action. We have little to contribute on this topic, except to suggest that the default starting point for police interactions should be preparedness to exercise soft skill, and to leave the default position only when the supply of saintliness runs out or the safety of others is endangered, domestic abuse being the most obvious common instance. In the words of Peelian principle 6

To use physical force only when the exercise of persuasion, advice and warning is found to be insufficient to obtain public cooperation to an extent necessary to secure observance of law or to restore order, and to use only the minimum degree of physical force which is necessary on any particular occasion for achieving a police objective.

One of the writers, working in Northern Ireland during the Troubles, was required (among other things) to teach courses in criminology to Royal Ulster Constabulary officers. These courses were of dubious value to officers whose daily reality was having stones thrown at their patrolling armoured Land Rovers in areas where the kerb edges were painted orange and green. The scope for the exercise of soft skills was limited, but not zero. Being called Sir at the start of an exchange on the street in a problematic area was impressive to all those where sectarian hatred had not been hard baked into the personality.

The next two paragraphs are kite flying. They are ideas, albeit research-driven ideas.

There is a phenomenon in biology called quorum sensing. Bacteria in a body do not express themselves until there are enough of them to challenge the host organism's immune system successfully. This is mind-blowing but well established by research. The writers speculate whether, in human communities, when there are enough people who individually fail the attitude test, there is a tipping point and the whole community becomes hostile, and the police become seen as a force of occupation, 'the filth' and 'pigs' rather than 'the Old Bill' and 'the bizzies'. We think this is worth testing by looking at discontinuities in local crime increases (but not in crime falls). If this is the case, it argues for attempts to engage with people who fail the attitude test, but not too badly, so that the quorum of hostility in the whole community is never reached.

Our second walk on the wild side concerns police crackdowns. The literature suggests that crackdowns yield a quiet period, typically around twice the length of the crackdown itself. Such a period is taken up with a police and community sigh of relief. This is wasted time. Farrell et al (1998) argued for a crackdown–consolidation sequence, in which the quiet time bought by the crackdown was used to enhance police–community engagement and address local crime-generating problems (in Bill Bongle's style). Crackdown–consolidation can roughly be thought of as hard skill–soft skill sequencing. Crackdown–consolidation sequencing seems to have fallen off the radar, but can be thought of as a way of integrating hard skill and soft skill policing.

Reflective practice

- If you concede the value of a soft skills approach with the attributes described earlier – what are the implications for recruitment or for training or for leadership that promotes the perception of police legitimacy?

Chapter summary

Put crudely, if it is easier to teach hard skills than soft skills, then recruit people that have soft skill attributes and train for the hard skills. If it is easier to teach soft skills than hard skills, recruit people with hard skill attributes and train for soft skills. However one recruits and trains, leadership can thwart force ambitions by what it treasures, measures and chooses to quantify. However a force recruits, trains and measures, the police service is walking north on a south-bound ship when the national metrics on outcomes, and the terms of the discourse, are implicitly hostile to public perception of police legitimacy. It is interesting that liveried police cars in the United States have 'Protect and Serve' on their doors. If soft skill is the default option, surely that word order is wrong. Serving is the everyday work, protecting kicks in only when there is something or someone that has to be protected against. Despite a backcloth which is many ways unhelpful, the default option for most serving police officers favours soft skills to a substantial degree. Good luck to them.

References

Bostrom, N (2014) *Superintelligence*. Oxford: Oxford University Press.

Butt, T W (2007) Personal Construct Theory and Method: Another Look at Laddering. *Personal Construct Theory and Practice*, 4: 11–14

Doyle, A (2021) Top Soft Skills Employers Value with Examples. *The Balance Careers*. Available at https://www.thebalancecareers.com/list-of-soft-skills-2063770 (accessed 14 March 2021).

Farrell, G, Chenery, S and Pease, K (1998) *Consolidating Police Crackdowns*, Police Research Series Paper 113. London: Home Office.

Ford, R (2020) Failing police 'rumbled' by weary public. *The Times*. https://www.thetimes.co.uk/article/failing-police-rumbled-by-weary-public-7lwvxrdr6

Fowler, H N (1966) *Plato in Twelve Volumes*. Vol. 1. City Press; London: Heinemann.

F S (n.d) Who Is Richard Feynman? *FS*. Available at https://fs.blog/intellectual-giants/richard-feynman/

Kelly, G (1955) *The Psychology of Personal Constructs*. New York: Norton.

McDaniel, J, Moss, K and Pease, K (2020) An Analysis of Protracted Discipline Proceedings Against Police Officers, in McDaniel, J, Moss, K and Pease, K (eds) *Policing and Mental Health: Theory Policy and Practice*. London: Routledge.

Pease, K and Ignatans, D (2014) Smoke, Mirrors and a Decline in Public Confidence. *Police Professional*, 24–25.

Roach, J, Cartwright, A and Sharratt, K (2016) Dealing with the Unthinkable: A Study of the Cognitive and Emotional Stress of Adult and Child Homicide Investigations on Police Investigators. *Journal of Police and Criminal Psychology*. doi: 10.1007/s11896-016-9218-5

Roach, J, Sharratt, K, Cartwright, A and Skou Roer, T (2018) Cognitive and Emotional Stressors of Child Homicide Investigations on U. and Danish Police Investigators. *Homicide Studies*, 22(3): 296–320.

Scott, M (2000) *Problem Oriented Policing: Reflections on the First Twenty Years*. Washington, DC: US Department of Justice.

Scott, M and Clarke, R V (eds) (2020) *Problem-Oriented Policing: Successful Case Studies*. London: Routledge.

Sparrow, M (2016) *Handcuffed: What Holds Policing Back, and the Keys to Reform*. Washington, DC: Brookings Institution Press.

Sparrow, M (2018) Problem-Oriented Policing: Matching the Science to the Art. *Crime Science*, 7(1): 14.

Spiegelhalter, D (2019) *The Art of Statistics*. Harmondsworth: Penguin.

Taylor, I, Walton, D and Young, J (1973) *The New Criminology*. London: Routledge.

Tetlock, P and Gardner, D (2015) *Superforecasting*. New York: Random House.

U W (n.d.) The Peelian Principles. *University of Washington*. Available at http://police.uw.edu/faqs/the-peelian-principles/ (accessed 18 June 2021).

9 Public order: conflict resolution
Jim McAllister and Ashley Kilgallon

CHAPTER OBJECTIVES

This chapter will help you:

- explore the role of policing in a democracy;
- gain a better understanding of traditional policing literature in the areas of public order policing and policing in general;
- explore the role of mediation and negotiation in public-order policing scenarios;
- evaluate the different mindset between the application of hard and soft skills within public order tactics.

Introduction

This chapter shifts the focus towards considering the formal tactic of de-escalation within public-order policing and its operational reliability in an area of policing which has long placed reliance on the robust skills of Police Support Units (PSUs). We argue that an increased reliance on mediation/negotiation for conflict resolution represents nothing new within the United Kingdom; instead it is the formalisation of long-held 'street-craft' skills. This formalisation provides legitimacy to senior command to increasingly utilise these behaviour skills within a public-order policing context. Our chapter seeks to provide the reader with insights, some theory, practical examples and the increased insight into a negotiated approach to public-order policing.

However, in order to place the role of public-order policing in the broader law enforcement debate, it is important to have a clear understanding of some of the thinking aligned to the wider role of policing within society. While we may think that intuitively we understand the policing mandate, it is important to appreciate the various theories within which the role of policing is explored.

What do the police do?

In order to place the role of public-order policing, it is important to have a clear understanding of the broader role of policing within society. In that way we can adjudge as to the legitimacy of various approaches and the utility of different tactics. We therefore want to align public-order policing within the broader understanding of the role of policing in a democracy. While we may think that intuitively we understand the policing mandate, it is important to appreciate the various theories within which the role of policing is explored. This forms the first part of this chapter.

Reflective practice

- In your own words, describe the role of the police.

What is the point of the police? Why do they exist as a taken-for-granted part of society, and how does better knowledge of this help us in understanding conflict resolution? To enhance our policing knowledge, we will want to look at the thinking behind three (often competing) mandates of policing: crime control, social order and moral order. These are theoretical in nature, but it is well worth developing a better understanding of the role of the police in order to understand if policing is operating in an appropriate manner.

Historical context

The English policing model, '*the child of centuries of conflict and experiment*' (Lee, 1901, p xiii), was believed to be different from its European counterparts, given that reliance upon members of the general public becoming warranted officers was at the core of its establishment, as opposed to a military-styled force such as a gendarmerie (Emsley, 2014). In England, '*the police were merely "citizens in uniform"*' (Reiner, 1998, p 41). The Peelian principles (Sir Robert Peel's nine principles of policing), the bedrock of the English policing model, *gave significant emphasis to the maintenance of order by avoiding, where possible, the use of force (might this be an emphasis on soft skills within policing?)*. (We use the term 'English' to align with much of the historic literature on policing; we recognise that this omits that of Wales and is only doing so to be consistent with the literature.) This was all to be achieved while maintaining the support of the public – '*the *historic tradition that the police are the public and that the public are the police'* (cited in Mayhall, 1985, p 426).

The Peelian principles – preventing, not reacting to crime and disorder and doing so with minimal force and within the public favour. We would therefore argue that from its very inception the 'new' police had at its ideological core the softer skills of negotiated management.

The public police, the 'citizens in uniform' were seen as a positive alternative to military suppression. Previously, the most relied-upon response to collective protest or disorder was the utilisation of the army or different forms of citizen force: the militia, the yeomanry, and the special constabulary (Reiner, 1998). From an ideological perspective, this non-militarisation approach is significant, as it demonstrates that from the very formation of the 'new' English police, the focus was on a public-centred approach to policing, a positive approach to dialogue that was based on consent. Indeed, today, consent is still perceived to be at the core of the British policing model. The *'art of policing a free society or a democracy is to win by appearing to lose'* (Sir Robert Mark, Metropolitan Police Commissioner, 1972–77).

Policing purpose 1: crime control

One of the leading criminologists in the United Kingdom, Ian Loader states:

> *The interpretation of policing centring on the reduction of crime demonstrates a partial understanding, a 'sociologically illiterate' account of what the police do, and a reductive, impoverished conception of why the police matter.*
>
> (Loader, 2014, p 44)

Evidence has continued to show that police can only control arrests, rather than crime levels and that the image of police as crime fighters is nothing more than mythical (Reiner, 2000).

Nevertheless, the image of police officers as the ultimate protectors is one that is widespread and enduring within society. The crime control mandate develops an unachievable perception and expectations of what the police can achieve and the speed in which they can achieve it. This is further problematised by the fact that officers heavily rely on public perceptions of legitimacy in order to succeed in their daily roles (Jackson et al, 2014). This challenge creates an 'impossible' task for policing practitioners because they are conscious that they are unable to live up to both their own and the publics' expectations of a policing success story (Manning, 1977; also see Reuss-Ianni, 1983).

Now let's think about how this applies to our areas of interest within public-order policing. The centrality of crime control within the policing mandate, at least from a political perspective, presents complexities within public-order policing. Waddington (1994) highlighted how arrests for law-breaking were extremely unlikely to occur during public-order operations such as protest, due to the potential for escalating surrounding crowd tension. Thus, we argue this also highlights a continued operational belief in Peel's Principles, as arrests for low-level or petty crime in front of large crowds will hardly 'secure the willing cooperation of the public'. What is acceptable within the everyday experiences of patrol operatives is perhaps overlooked in other 'special' circumstances. (For example, the 'blind eye' to mass cannabis consumption during Notting Hill Carnival.)

The image of policing is complex, for it has to balance both the peaceful negotiation of disputes with the more dynamic characteristics of a law enforcement approach. Within this often-contradictory approach, policing practitioners manage their policing persona. Thus, the police mandate is centred on symbolism, a front-stage performance and a backstage reality of planning that performance while juggling political, social and economic pressures.

This consideration of the policing mandate is far more in line with public-order policing, where officers have to very publicly manage the competing demands of groups in dispute, all of whom wish to achieve their own aims within the parameters of the law. The constant presence of soft skills – the art of dialogue, the creation of a public face, the adoption of various approaches in order to help the public believe that the police are in control, all add a complexity to how each individual scenario is approached. Crime control maybe the narrative yet it is the appropriateness of how policing negotiates deployment that ultimately creates the environment for success.

We will take a short break from the literature here to introduce another task for the reader to explore. Consider what you have read and use it to reflect upon the task below.

Reflective practice

- Review the scenario below and consider how you would police the events. This task is not about deciding if/how the officers got their response right/wrong, but instead is about an honest self-reflection of how you would react in the same scenario.

Case study 1

It was a very cold day and had snowed heavily. There had been a large student demonstration; it was one of a series of demonstrations that had taken place over the past weeks. There was a lack of trust between police and students with little or no communication on the lead up to the event. There was an endemic fear that the police would significantly contain the student community. The day had started with a procession that moved around the city without any apparent leadership or route. The day brought confrontation between police and protesters resulting in the decision to contain the crowd in a specific location. The containment was implemented and had calmed the situation down; the police had cordons deployed at all the entry points to the zone. Things were peaceful and had been for a while.

The command team was reviewing the necessity to continue with the containment. It was safe for the police to walk within the zone and officers were engaging with those contained. However, there were no toilets or welfare provided. If people wanted to leave they were to present themselves to officers on the cordon, officers would then decide if they could leave based on behaviour and situation.

There was a man observed standing away from the main body of the demonstration. He was apparently urinating against a wall. CCTV then showed a uniformed officers walk past the man. Then an officer wearing public order uniform moves from a police cordon and runs about 30 metres and approaches the male. The officer interacts with the man and grabs him. As a result, the man runs off towards the crowd. They run deeper into the zone and the male trips and falls. The officer grabs him and there is a struggle on the floor. As a result, more officers run to assist their colleague.

At this stage consider:

- Do these officers know what is happening?
- Why are the officers chasing?
- What is the offense?

The struggle continues in full view of the crowd and police cordons. The crowd see what's happening and the majority move towards the melee. We witness some people assisting the man, some film the interaction, and some confront officers. There are items thrown towards the police, smoke is let off, some police draw batons and there is confrontation between the police and the crowd. There is a very real risk that the situation will escalate and degenerate into serious disorder.

In summary, the police have contained the crowd; outside the zone a man is urinating; a police officer runs towards the man and confronts him; the man runs towards the crowd; there is a struggle in which other officers are now involved; disorder is now likely.

Reflective practice

If you were the police officer:

- How would you feel about this situation?
- What would be your immediate thought process?
- If you had the time to slow down your thought process, would your reactions change?

- What does the police service expect of you in this situation?
- Is this action or decision likely to reflect positively on your professionalism and policing generally?
- Could you explain my action or decision in public?

If you were reviewing this scenario for police senior leaders:

- What would be the key learning points for the organisation?
- What suggestions would you make regarding policing action in similar scenarios?

Policing purpose 2: social control

Let's return to some of the thinking around the purpose of policing. If crime control plays a lesser part in the role of police officers, what are they doing? For Bayley (1994, p 30) the answer is simple – 'restoring order and providing general assistance'. Social control can be understood as:

> *The organised ways in which society responds to behaviour and people it regards as deviant, problematic, worrying, threatening, troublesome or undesirable.*
>
> (Cohen, 1985, pp 1–2)

This concept focuses on considerations of 'normal' behaviour and the extent to which society will go to protect these 'norms'. One can immediately begin to appreciate the difficult position of traditional protests or symbolic protest (such as Notting Hill Carnival) when adopting this definition. By its very nature protest is a desire to challenge the status quo often through methods of disruption (road blocks, occupation), or in extreme examples direct action (increased violent means) to bring about different types of 'order'.

Garland (2001) shows how debates around crime control have developed from contemporary political and cultural values such as moral panics over teenage pregnancies, single parent families, welfare dependencies towards the perceived decline in 'British values' and how this has led to a perceived need of increased control. In essence we have developed *'obsessive attempts to monitor risky individuals, to isolate dangerous populations, and to impose situational controls on otherwise open and fluid settings'* (ibid., p 194). Of course, in the wide realm of social control, the public police are just one agent whose mandate is to ensure social order is maintained (Newburn, 2005, p 129). However, it is perhaps fair to say that they are the most visible and publicly accountable agent in British society.

Interestingly, Garland (2001) suggests the existence of a similar argument during the 1980s and 1990s where 'a return to restraint, a retro-fitting of controls, an attempt to put a lid back on a newly disordered world' (ibid., p 195) was perceived by the establishment to be paramount to economic and social growth.

Is this, therefore the role of the police? The policing mandate being closely aligned with the maintenance of social control and increased order seems somewhat undisputed, with the real question being *'order from whose standpoint?'* (Cain, 1973, p 21). The maintenance of social order is arguably the main legitimiser for the police, ensuring protection for weak, vulnerable and respectable people 'from the few who are neither decent nor respectable' (ibid.). (*'And maybe just remind the few, if ill of us they speak, that we are all that stands between the Monster's and the Weak'* – a popular line from a poem by Michael Marks that is often displayed in police stations or quoted by officers. Interestingly, this poem is actually a military poem.) However, to push Cain's point further – unrespectable to whom?

Social control on behaviour deemed inappropriate is disproportionately defined by middle-class people, who deem control necessary for 'dangerous' offenders and 'undeserving' claimants whose conduct leads some to suppose they are incapable of discharging the responsibilities of the late modern freedom (Garland, 2001, p 195). Thus, one bears witness to more and more controls upon disempowered people in society (the poor, immigrants, ethnic minorities, women) to ensure 'order' is re-imposed.

For Whyte (1943, p 138), the police support certain groups, while 'cracking down' on others, acting as a buffer between middle-class and working-class values (for contemporary considerations here, see Fassin, 2013).

Within this complex model of modernity, policing has to negotiate a space in order to operate appropriately. On the one hand, they do not want to be seen as simply the enforcers of the established view of the day; nor can they operate independently of government requirements. The social control mandate is thus problematic for both frontline practitioners and their strategic leaders.

Theory to practice

This notion of social order is of course interesting and relevant to all aspects of policing (such as stop and search); however, public-order policing arguably presents one of the most widely exposed display of the obsession with maintaining a very contested definition of 'order' (in terms of numbers in attendance and media interest).

From the earliest point of interaction between policing and protesters, one can see pre-emptive attempts to control behaviour (thus, enhancing police perception of order) from just within the planning of protest. From the very beginning of planned protest, the police hold disproportionate structural power to organise and control behaviours.

- They require an application for protest to be made.
- They hold pre-meetings with leading demonstrators within police premises.

- They suggest preferred routes to be taken during the protest, often to fit with the policing need to be visibly seen to control the event (see, for instance, Waddington, 1994).

From a policing perspective these pre-demonstration meetings evidence their attempts at negotiating and listening to demonstrators, attempting to offer a flexible strategy that balances the need for maximum safety of those taking part as well as the requirements of the general public who wish to return to 'normality' as soon as possible. Conversely, many would also highlight that it is within this very ordered and controlled structure of planned protest that the message and cause is potentially lost and the protest itself emasculation (Jefferson, 1987, 1990, 1993). Is there ever a way of balancing liberty and order (Reiner, 1998)?

REFLECTIVE PRACTICE

- How do police professionals best position themselves so that they are not perceived as the mere strong arm of the state?
- From the above scenario, do the police listen to communities because they genuinely care; or might there be other motives?
- Does policing have a role in negotiating a space where the disempowered (with whom they deal on a regular basis) have a platform to express a legitimate voice?
- Is policing too political?

Policing purpose 3: the moral order

Let's look at the final consideration with respect to the role of policing. Closely aligned to the analysis situating policing as an agent of social control and order is the discourse that emphasises their role in maintaining the moral order of society.

The moral mandate has existed since the inception of the 'new' police, who were painted as the '*moral entrepreneur of public property*' (Cohen, 1979, p 128) to convert people from '*savage street dwellers to respectability and decency*' (Reiner, 1999, p 38). Unlike private policing, or private industry more generally, Manning (2014) comments on how the public police do not have clients or customers with whom they work for, and alongside this, the public cannot refuse or discontinue to pay for the public police services. The public police work on *behalf* of the public putting police officers, and arguably in particular constables, in a very unique position of power, as '*they actively patrol the edges of order on our behalf*' (ibid., p 28).

As outlined above, there is little correlation between the active role of policing and the decline of crime rates (Reiner, 2010). As such, police officers become the moral arbiters of society, peacekeepers in the daily disagreements of partners, neighbours, colleagues and associates. (Here I am not belittling the policing role, simply highlighting the 'cops and robbers' image is often excessive.) Thus, although the 'official' mandate is that of law enforcement *'the public "calls the cops" for all kinds of problems that have nothing to do with this mandate'* (Bittner, 1990, p 8). This reliance from the public upon police officers to resolve issues that do not concur with the official law enforcement mandate, entangle the organisation in webs of conflict regarding issues that are rarely as formalised as the legal system. Consequently, rather than upholding some form of legal mandate to which officers are exposed to from the very outset of their police training, the constable is more regularly required to execute a large amount of creative problem solving and discretion while interacting with the moral disputes of the general public.

Officers therefore get exposed to an everyday reality that is somewhat shielded from wider society, regularly engaged *'in a state of perpetual trouble, labour and disquiet so that other folks may enjoy their rest'* (John Wilson Croker, cited in Hurd, 2007, p 105). As such, officers often find themselves settling disputes whereby they have become defenders (and definers) of contextually 'appropriate' behaviours. The mandate therefore arguably merges with a sense of occupational 'mission' to protect (Reiner, 2010), separating the public into the 'good guys' and 'the assholes' (Van Maanen, 1974).

This sense of mission within policing is however problematic because it is often contextual and self-defined by policing practitioners within their own moral mandate (see, for instance, Fassin, 2014). This mandate can be aligned with a *'working personality'*, where unique experiences develop a specific way of looking at the world, with their starting point being suspicion therefore creating differing *'norms'* (Skolnick, 2011).

In public-order policing, as with street policing or other areas of focus, we observe police officers spending a large proportion of their professional time dealing with peace-keeping, often within environments they deem to be hostile and even volatile. It is for this reason an officer's definition of 'order' is often enforced upon citizens, perhaps even while violating their rights (Manning, 1978, p 16).

It is this discretionary power of achieving just ends using coercive means that taps into the individual moral order of a police officer (Ker Muir, 1977, p 3). Police dominance over defining 'order' – inclusive of moral order – is argued to come as a result of a 'demand' by citizens for order, where expectations have become higher and have also expanded. Through a dissolvement of 'local' powers and a nationalisation of civil rights (for example, such as housing) we continue to observe an infringement of policing powers outside of the legal mandate (see Silver, 1967, p 22; also Vitale, 2017).

The role of dialogue within public-order policing

We have looked at the various definitions of what the general role of policing should be within society (though these are contradictory); now it is necessary to take a deep dive into public-order policing approaches and both the strategical and operational mindset.

Negotiated management versus escalated force

Tactical deployments focused on increasing dialogue between police and crowd members ideologically align with Western democracies' progressive shift away from 'escalated force' during the 1960s towards the encouragement of a 'negotiated management' particularly during the 1980s and 1990s. An understanding of this debate can be found in the literature of McPhail et al (1998), della Porta (1998, 2006), Noakes and Gillham (2000) and Waddington (2000, 2003).

Although we have seen within England and Wales and other European countries the introduction of dialogue policing tactics, it still *remains largely understudied*' (Wahlström and Oskarsson, 2006).

Negotiated management in policing demonstrates an increased use of more facilitative tactics – seeking the strategic aim of increased 'policing by consent'. It is proposed, as part of an approach where cooperation and dialogue are key for ensuring that tensions do not intensify between protesters and police. It recognises that there has to be some acknowledgement of the right to protest and a toleration of a disruption to the public's daily life (see, for example, Gorringe and Rosie, 2009). Among senior ranking officers, at least within UK policing, it is now deemed advisable 'to slacken their authority so as to increase the predictability of protest events and minimise the risk of violence' (Waddington, 2007, p 10). Effective communication styles within public-order policing, fit comfortably within the mould of negotiated management, as '*dialog [sic] breeds negotiated management*' (Barker, 2014, p 84).

Directly aligning to the aims of this book, we maintain these apparent softer skills that emphasise extensive communication with others, develops real strength in connecting with the legitimate aims of protesters. Negotiated management therefore accepts a high level of community disquiet, with even illegal (albeit peaceful) activities, for example, symbolic displays of civil disobedience such as roadblocks. Although police will often try to navigate protesters to timings and routes that will cause the least disruption, it is widely accepted that disruption will be present (see also Waddington, 1998, p 3).

Consider policing 'styles' of public-order policing like a pendulum drifting between paramilitary styles and more facilitating styles depending on the social context and political agenda. King and Brearley (1996) highlight that a number of momentous events created the environment for the pendulum to shift towards paramilitary policing. Since the 1960s, one can point to a continued reliance on typical paramilitary tactical options and responses. Notably, during the miners' strike of 1984–85, police found themselves outnumbered and significant waves of urban unrest in the 1980s led to improved protective equipment (PPE) – riot shields, NATO helmets and flameproof clothing – and the creation of 'mutual aid' to add strength among forces. While acknowledging the importance of responding appropriately to officer safety, we would also ask the reader to consider that symbolically, these *strong arm of the law* responses echo the work of public order reacting to *dis*order, as opposed to the maintenance of order.

We can say that historically the 1960s to 1990s were an era of *escalated force*, where officers used (at times) quite extreme measures to disperse crowds, especially protest crowds – even those protesting peacefully.

Perhaps the most visually representative example of escalated force would be the policing response to the civil rights protests in 1960s America; and in the UK the miners' strike of 1984.

From the 1990s onwards, we are suggesting that police forces used a *negotiated management* approach to policing crowds – whereby police forces would consciously contact the group or organisation prior to the event with the ultimate intention being to ensure any conflict with policing was minimal. The mindset has moved from hard to softer skills – though in this context, *softer* emphasises a more listening approach to achieve a more valued outcome.

Training approaches

From escalated force to negotiated management, one thing that hasn't changed is the formation and training of officers in a public-order context. Here in the training environment, there is extensive focus on a paramilitary mindset with units of officers working together in pre-trained formation to quell early signs of escalating disorder. When we think of public-order policing, many training environments default to a focus on *disorder* – urban disorder, riots or protests. Much focuses on the effectiveness of the different tactical responses public order units use during operations, or the theoretical reasons why crowds turn disorderly.

Reflective practice

- Think of an occasion when the police appropriately adopted a more paramilitary approach to dispute settlement?
- Think of an occasion when the police appropriately adopted a more negotiated approach to dispute settlement?
- What criteria are you using to justify your understanding of the word appropriate?

From a policy perspective

As identified above, from around 2009, we observed a growing 'interest' in communication as a tactic deployed within public-order policing. Further, since the G20 protests in 2009 and the death of Ian Tomlinson (a newspaper vendor and passer-by to the protest) as a result of use of force, there have been considerable formal reforms to public-order policing policy. *Adapting to Protest* (2009) outlines the main policing concerns of the G20 protest as: use of containment; the dispersal of peaceful protesters and the extent to which their use of force was proportionate; the ability to identify police officers clearly; and finally, the effectiveness of communication with protesters before, during and after the protest (see ibid., p 7).

Keeping the Peace (2010), the revised guidance manual of the Association of Chief Police Officers (ACPO) (now the National Police Chiefs Council) puts at its core the idea that '*engagement and dialogue should be used, wherever possible, to demonstrate a no surprises approach*' (ibid., p 11). Within this manual, one can see the rhetoric of public order beginning to *formally* change – the word 'engagement' is used 33 times; 'communication' is used 85 times (often alongside the word 'effective'); and finally, 'dialogue' is used 15 times (ibid.). It will be clear to the reader therefore, that policy documents and those within the occupation have begun to adapt their language to reflect these mindset changes.

Theory to practice

It is important to consider the criteria that impact on decision-making. In this sense, review the scenario below and consider how you would police the events. This task is not about deciding if/how the officers got their response right/wrong, but instead is about honest self-reflection of how you would react in the same scenario. If you are to make judgements on policing, appropriate self-awareness is a vital soft skill requirement.

We want to walk you through a challenging scenario. You should take notes about what you are thinking, how you are feeling, and where you see escalated levels of risk.

CASE STUDY 2

Over a period of months there had been a lot of right-wing activity in the Coastlands (a hypothetical area) area of the city. This had manifested itself through assaults on BAME communities in the area, racist material being distributed and posted on walls and highly charged pop-up demonstrations outside local mosques. Community tension in the area was high, especially within the large local Bangladeshi population. An anti-racism organisation had organised a protest to demonstrate the community stance against racism. The protest attracted a very large number of people from the local community, the wider city and some national representatives. It passed off peacefully.

Post procession, rumours were circulating that an infamous racist group were in the area and had attacked an Imam of the local Coastlands mosque. This resulted in a large gathering of mainly young Bangladeshi males. The police command team were linked-in to the community through the elders and youth leaders. There was no intelligence to suggest the rumours were true.

Police and community leaders deployed and circulated trying to defuse the situation and dispel the rumours. As a result, there was confrontation between police and mainly young Bangladeshi men. The situation became really tense and the feedback from the community leaders was the relationship between police and community was breaking down.

Reflective practice

- What are you thinking?
- What are you feeling?
- Where are the risks?
- Explore the balance between a paramilitary approach and dialogue policing.

Command perception

The Silver commander had to consider the consequences of police action or inaction. Staying on the street would inevitably result in serious disorder between police and community with a real risk that someone would get injured. Removing the police may result in crime against others or property. The public perception maybe that the police had lost control, and someone may get hurt. Some of the key risk principles that commanders should be contemplating are:

- harm can never be totally prevented;
- risk decisions should, therefore, be judged by the quality of the decision-making, not by the outcome.

The task of identifying, assessing and managing risk is challenging, yet many people judge risk decisions simply by examining the end result; that is, whether the decisions led to success or failure, to benefits or harm. The law, however, recognises that harm will sometimes occur irrespective of the quality of the decision-making, and does not require that all risks be eliminated.

The decision-maker decided to withdraw police from the problem and worked with the community leaders and elders to persuade the youth to desist and go home. The decision immediately stopped the confrontation between police and the youth. The main backlash came from within the police family, other commanders considered the withdrawal a sign of weakness. They felt the Silver had created a no-go area for police. Officers openly said that police ran away from the fight and allowed them to get away with anything they wanted. Silver's view was it was a temporary tactic, they had tactically repositioned police resources and were ready to respond to incidents that required them to do so.

The choice of decision was not an easy one and was not a quick process. The National Decision Model allowed them to consider their decision based on the most up-to-date information. Commanders are taught that in a fast-moving incident, the police service recognises that it may not always be possible to segregate thinking or response according to each phase of the model. In such cases, the main priority of decision-makers is to keep in mind their overarching mission to act with integrity to protect and serve the public.

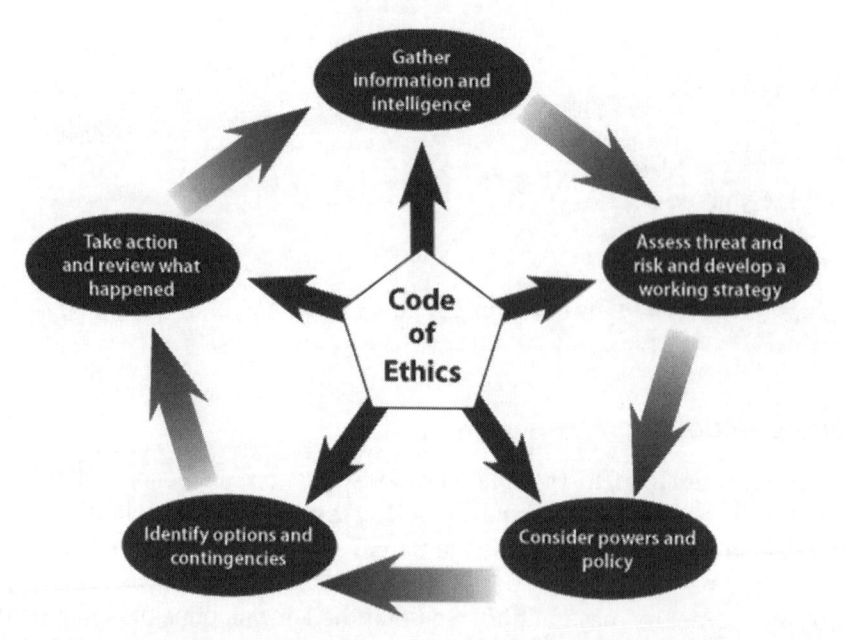

Figure 9.1 Code of Ethics, Authorised Professional Practice

The NDM puts the Code of Ethics at the heart of all police decision-making. The Code of Ethics includes the principles of 'fairness' and 'respect' (in many ways these could be described as soft skills) as research has shown these to be crucial to maintaining and enhancing public confidence in policing. Also, in this case consider:

- **accountability** – decision-makers are answerable for decisions, actions and omissions;
- **objectivity** – they make choices on evidence and their best professional judgement;
- **openness** – they are open and transparent in their actions and decisions.

Reflective practice

So, having walked through a real public-order scenario where a decision was taken by a senior officer that caused some challenges to aspects of the policing, consider the following.

- Would you have adopted a harder approach to the scenario (towards paramilitary mindset); would you have learned more towards a softer-skills approach (dialogue policing)?
- What would the victim or community affected expect of you in this situation?
- What does the police service expect of you in this situation?
- Do the actions or decisions that you would take reflect positively on your professionalism and policing generally?
- Could you explain my action or decision in public?

Risk

Risks rests at the heart of many policing decisions so it is worth just considering the following issues.

1. **The fact that a good risk decision sometimes has a poor outcome does not mean the decision was wrong.** Even when all the right and appropriate precautions have been taken, injuries and deaths may still occur. Good risk management should increase the likelihood of successful decisions but will not, in itself, guarantee that harm will not occur.

2. **Similarly, it cannot be assumed that a decision was right just because no harm occurred.** Although the risk of harm always exists when a decision is made, more often than not the decision is successful and harm does not occur. Some successful outcomes, however, may happen in spite of poor decision-making or management.

3. **A risk decision should be judged by how it was made, implemented and managed rather than by the outcome.** Rather than focusing on the outcome, assessments of decisions should concentrate on whether they were reasonable and appropriate for the circumstances existing at the time. If they were, the decision-maker should not be blamed for a poor outcome.

Let's conclude the chapter with a final exercise.

Reflective practice

- We have looked at the social and moral order concepts of policing. So how do these help us explore our own decision-making when it comes to dispute settlement? How would you police such a sensitive policing operation as the one below?

Case study 4

Incidents in the United States, in particular the death of George Floyd following police contact, resulted in protests across the world. Protests in the United Kingdom have seen a significant number of people attending protest events and it is acknowledged that the majority have done so peacefully. However anti-police sentiment has been shared online in relation to George Floyd's death and other police interactions with BAME communities. Authorities witnessed a 'hard-core' group engage in violence and crime during some of these protests. Activities from this small proportion of people included:

- engaging in violence;
- the defacing of public statues and cultural heritage;
- criminal damage to public and government buildings;
- attacking police officers.

Numerous officers were injured during acts of violent disorder with marine flares, bottles, fireworks, scaffolding and other missiles, along with assaults and racial abuse directed at officers of colour.

Command perception

These protests manifested themselves during the beginning of a global pandemic and there were government restrictions in place regarding the gathering of more than six people in public spaces. Media coverage was recoding demonstrations from all over the world and highlighting counter views and violence from small elements in the crowds. There were calls on inequality and inconsistent approach to the policing of groups during the pandemic. Commanders had to consider their policing style and tone for these operations being fully conversant of the potential impact on public perceptions. They wanted to continue policing by consent and remain impartial, fair and accessible while remaining legally compliant.

A specific protest group was unhappy about how the police interacted with BAME communities; they did not want to see or engage with police. Too many police could result in unnecessary confrontation between police and individuals; the public had a broad spectrum of and opinion of how the demonstrations should be policed.

Officers had been injured in previous events, and there was a huge internal backlash from officers stating they were not being protected. There was significant social media chat. Too little police presence may not be in a position to react and prevent crime, and that would impact on the confidence in policing.

Officer perception

Officers were deployed in public-order protective equipment, minus their helmets that were connected to their belts. They were deployed in and around the area of protest with the briefing to engage with communities to understand concerns/tensions, seek to identify and work with event organisers, minimise criminal activity and anti-social behaviour and where crime is committed – take all reasonable and proportionate steps to intervene and bring offenders to justice. They were given the autonomy from command to put on their helmets if they felt threatened and needed protection.

The challenge was finding the balance between being in a position to respond while trying to remain invisible. It appeared that elements of the crowd were deliberately provoking police and trying to get officers to overreact. This would then allow people to capture the aftermath on social media calling for a reaction to a short, usually edited, video clip. If officers donned their helmets and remained in situ, the situation could generally degenerate into some form of disorder. It is a known that the donning of the public order helmet may cause individuals to react differently to officers.

Numerous interactions resulted in a short violent outburst of disorder between the police and crowds, usually started between two people, others joining in based on their limited understanding of the situation.

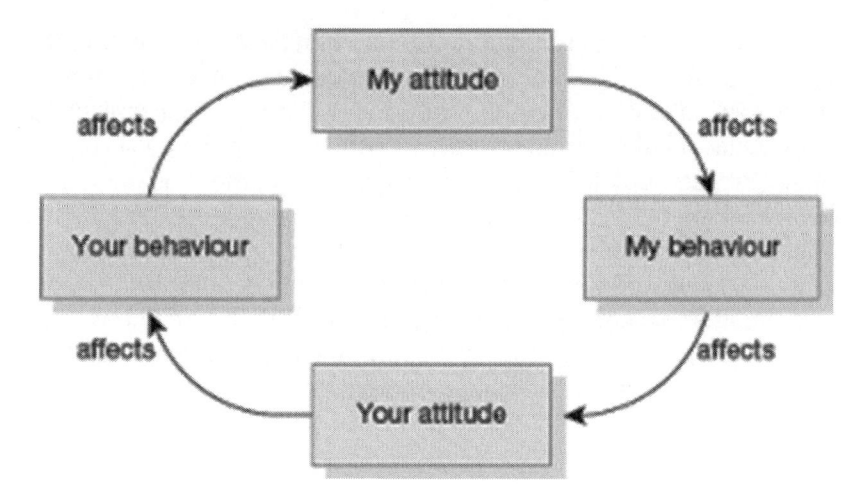

Figure 9.2 *Betari's Box*

REFLECTIVE PRACTICE

- How do you police the event in a proportionate sensitive way while also protecting officers?

- Are the police there to control crime, behaviours, morals or public space?

- What role does dialogue play and when would you first utilise this approach?

- What are you thinking and feeling about policing tactics?

- Is there tension between how you think and how you feel this should be policed?

    o How does this impact on your decision-making role?

- Where do you see the balance between the use of hard and soft tactics?

- If the police are the public and the public are the police – why should there be tension?

CHAPTER SUMMARY

This chapter has purposefully explored the tension between what we think the police do and the activities with which they actually engage. It has looked at two different models of public-order policing: a militarisation mindset and a more negotiated management approach. We have considered the theoretical frameworks that are placed around the role of police (crime control, social control, moral control) and how these might impact community/policing relationships.

At the core of what we have explored is the role of dialogue policing. In the public-order scenarios that we created there was a purposeful need for the reader to explore their own values set, how this influenced their decision-making and what level of communication they would utilise in order to manage the public-order context. While paramilitarised approaches may be utilised when order has broken down, our position emphasises the need to engage with protest and protesters in order to get ahead of any tensions. People have a right to protest and laws can be broken, yet we argue that a facilitated approach to demonstrations centred on the softer skills of listening, understanding, advising create an authentic environment within which demonstrators can protest and policing can have the appearance of being in control. The front-stage and backstage activities of policing are the two sides of a facilitated peace.

References

ACPO (2010) *Manual of Guidance on Keeping the Peace*. London: NPIA on behalf of Association of Chief Police Officers and ACPO in Scotland.

Banton, M (1956) *The Policeman in the Community* London: Tavistock.

Barker, D (2014) Police and Protester Dialog: Safeguarding the Peace or Ritualistic Sham?' *International Journal of Comparative and Applied Criminal Justice*, 38(1): 83–104.

Bayley, D H (1994) *Police for the Future*. Oxford: Oxford University Press.

Bitner, E (1990) *Aspects of Police Work*. Boston: Northeastern University Press.

Cain, M (1973) *Society and the Policeman's Role*. London: Routledge and Kegan Paul.

Cohen, S (1985) *Visions of Social Control*. Cambridge: Polity.

College of Policing (2014) Code of Ethics. Available at: www.college.police.uk/What-we-do/Ethics/Ethics-home/Pages/Ethics.aspx (accessed 9 February 2021).

Della Porta, D and Reiter, H (1998) The Policing of Protest in Western Democracies', in Della Porta, D and Reiter, H (eds.) *Policing Protest: The Control of Mass Demonstrations in Western Democracies.* Minnesota: University of Minnesota Press.

Emsley, C (2014) *The English Police A Political and Social History*. London: Routledge.

Fassin, D (2013) *Enforcing Order: An Ethnography of Urban Policing*. Cambridge: Polity Press.

Foucault, M (1977) *Discipline and Punish: The Birth of the Prison*. Hightstown: McGraw-Hill.

Garland, D (2001) *The Culture of Control: Crime and Social Order in Contemporary Society*. Oxford: Oxford University Press.

Gorringe, H and Rosie, M (2009) What a Difference a Death Makes: Protest, Policing and the Press at the G20. *Sociological Review Online*, 14(5): 68–76.

Herbert, S (1997) *Policing Space: Territoriality and the Los Angeles Police Department*. Minnesota: University of Minnesota Press.

Herbert, S (2006a) *Citizen, Cops, and Power: Recognizing the Limits of Community*. Chicago: University of Chicago Press.

Herbert, S (2006b) Tangled up in Blue: Conflicting Paths to Police Legitimacy. *Theoretical Criminology*, 10(4): 481–504.

Herbert, S (2019) The Policing of Space: New Realities, Old Dilemmas, in: Reisig, MD and Kane, RJ (eds.) *The Oxford Handbook of Police and Policing*. Oxford: Oxford University Press.

Her Majesty's Chief Inspector of Constabulary (2009) *Adapting to Protest – Nurturing the British Model of Policing*. London: HMIC.

Hurd, D (2007) *Robert Peel a Biography*. London: Weidenfeld & Nicolson.

Jackson, J, Bradford, B, Stanko, E A and Hohl, K (2012) *Just Authority? Trust in the Police in England and Wales Oxfordshire*. London: Routledge.

Jefferson, T (1987) Beyond Paramilitarism. *British Journal of Criminology*, 27(1): 47–53.

Jefferson, T (1990) *The Case against Paramilitary Policing*. Milton Keynes: Open University Press.

Jefferson, T (1993) Pondering Paramilitarism: A Question of Standpoints? *British Journal of Criminology*, 33(3): 374–381.

Klein, A (2012) Police as a Causal Factor – A Fresh View on Riots and Social Unrest. *Safer Communities*, 11(1).

Loader, I (2014) Why Do the Police Matter? Beyond the Myth of Crime-fighting, in Brown, J (ed.) *The Future of Policing*. London: Routledge.

Loftus, B (2009) *Police Culture in a Changing World*. Oxford: Oxford University Press.

Manning, P K (1977) *Police Work: The Social Organization of Policing*, 2nd edition. Illinois: Waveland Press.

Manning, P K (2003) *Policing Contingencies*. Chicago: University of Chicago Press.

Mayhall, P (1985) *Police-Community Relations and the Administration of Justice*, 3rd edition. New Jersey: Prentice Hall.

McPhail, C (1991) *The Myth of the Maddening Crowd*. New York: Aldine De Gruyter.

McPhail, C, Schweingruber, D and McCarthy, J (1998) Policing Protest in the United States: 1960–1995, in Della Porta, D and Reiter, H (eds.) *Policing Protest: The Control of Mass Demonstrations in Western Democracies*. Minneapolis: University of Minnesota Press.

Miller, L L (2016) *The Myth of Mob Rule: Violent Crime and Democratic Politics*. Oxford University Press.

Muir, W J (1977) *Police: Street Corner Politicians*. Chicago: University of Chicago Press.

Noakes, J A, Klocke, B and Gillham, P F (2005) Whose Streets? Police and Protester Struggles over Space in Washington DC, September 2001. *Policing and Society*, 15(3): 235–254.

Porta, D D and Reiter, H (1998) *Policing Protest: The Control of Mass Demonstrations in Western Democracies*. Minneapolis: University of Minnesota Press.

Reiner, R (1998) Copping a Plea, in Holdaway, S and Rock, P (eds.) *Thinking About Criminology*. London: UCL Press.

Reiner, R (2010) *The Politics of the Police*, 4th edition. Oxford: Oxford University Press.

Reuss-Ianni, E and Ianni, A J F (1983) Street Cops and Management Cops: The Two Cultures of Policing, in Punch, M (ed) *Control in the Police Organization*. Massachusetts: The MIT Press.

Rubinstein, J (1973) *City Police*. New York: Farrar, Straus and Giroux.

Sack, D R (1986) *Human Territoriality: Its Theory and History*. New York: Cambridge University Press.

Silver, A (1967) The Demand for Order in a Civil Society, in Bordua, DJ (ed.) *The Police: Six Sociological Essays*, 1–24. New York: Wiley.

Skolnick, H J (2011) *Justice without Trial: Law Enforcement in Democratic Society*, 4th edition. New Orleans: Quid Pro Books.

Smith, D J and Gray, J (1985) *Police and People in London: The PSI Report*. London: Policy Press.

Stott, C and Drury, J (2000) Crowds, Context and Identity: Dynamic Categorization Processes in the Poll Tax Riots. *Human Relations*, 53(2): 247–273.

Stott, C and Reicher, S (1998) Crowd Action as Intergroup Process: Introducing the Police Perspective. *European Journal of Social Psychology*, 28(4): 509–529.

Tilly, C (1978) *From Mobilization to Revolution.* Reading, MA: Addison-Wesley.

Van Maanen, J (1973) *Working the Street: A Developmental View of Police Behavior.* MIT Working Paper.

Van Maanen, J (1978) Epilogue on Watching the Watchers, in Manning, KP and Maanen, VJ (eds) *Policing: A View from the Streets.* Santa Monica: Goodyear Publishing Company.

Vitale, A (2011) *The End of Policing.* New York: Verso.

Waddington, D (2007) *Policing Public Disorder: Theory and Practice.* Cullompton: Willan Publishing.

Waddington, P A J (1994) *Liberty and Order: Public Order Policing in a Capital City.* London: UCL Press.

Wahlström, M and Oskarsson, M (2006) Negotiating Political Protest in Gothenburg and Copenhagen, in Della Porta, D, Peterson, A and Reiter, H (eds) *The Policing of Transnational Protest.* Farnham: Ashgate.

Whyte, W F (1943) *Street Corner Society: Social Structure of an Italian Slum.* Chicago: University of Chicago Press.

Part 4
Leading the strategic narrative

10 Personal and organisational transformation

Mike Barton

CHAPTER OBJECTIVES

This chapter will help you:

- understand how to set a strategic vision and how to implement the underpinning plans;
- understand how transforming people in the organisation is the key enabler for the strategy and plans to be put into effect;
- understand how to challenge the established way of doing things.

Introduction

This chapter is based on the author's experience as a police officer of nearly 40 years and a chief officer in Durham Constabulary from 2008 to 2019. A review of HMIC reports over that decade will show a force which underwent significant organisational transformation, largely driven by the personal development and transformation of the people who were Durham Constabulary (HMIC, 2021).

I deliberately use the themes of ICT, crime, austerity, empowerment, leadership development and policing philosophy because they are some of the most powerful drivers to transform an organisation; I have also found them to be generally misunderstood. Murrow says: '*The obscure we eventually see, the completely obvious takes longer*' (Conley, 2007, p 49).

The most important issue for a chief officer is to understand how to ensure their people are motivated and successful in putting into effect the strategic vision and agreed plans.

Strategy and its delivery

I don't believe that any organisation can undergo successful transformation without having a strategic vision that is actually put into practice. In Durham, I deliberately chose a strategic vision that was short and straightforward. Only 10 per cent of companies managed to turn their strategy into actual results … most companies produce lengthy, overly complex strategy documents that nobody ever reads … the majority of strategies are far too woolly, not agile enough (Marr, 2021). Marr introduced the force to our first plan-on-a-page just as austerity bit in 2010. A plan-on-a-page is exactly as it is described – it is the organisation's plan to deliver the organisation's strategy and is contained on only one page, to simplify it to everyone in the organisation and encourage them to read and understand it and ultimately see their role in its delivery; this then became the annual single point of reference to align everyone's efforts to the strategic vision. Put simply, everyone is pulling in the same direction.

I sometimes use the words vision, strategy and plan interchangeably, and in my defence all three are steps on a continuum. Vision is to imagine the future; strategy is the master plan to achieve the vision and the plan is the detailed proposal of how to complete the components of the strategy. Timescales and detail acquire incremental precision as one moves from vision through strategy to plan. Strategies should survive from year to year, whereas one's plan is shorter term and often annual in its cycle. Leaders need to make clear that the strategy is the direction, the destination on the horizon and the agreed plan is how the strategy will be achieved.

The strategic narrative has to be one that all the people in the organisation can not only read but also buy into. Collins and Porras (Collins and Porras, 1994, p 229) describe how people inside the organisation need to feel compelled by the vision. It has to be written so all people in the organisation can discuss and understand it.

In Durham we distilled the vision to fewer than 40 words: we will deliver excellent policing, inspiring confidence in victims and communities by protecting neighbourhoods, tackling criminals and solving problems, around the clock. Proud to deliver value for money policing to the people of County Durham and Darlington (Durham Constabulary, 2021).

This vision was optimistic, positioning us on the front foot in reducing crime, reducing reoffending and reducing demand through improving community safety and cohesion. This aligned with our values of: positive, fair, courageous with integrity. Addressing the VFM issue openly underlined we had to be affordable and productive.

In this way pessimistic views which currently prevail across much of policing – that demand is too high and thorny issues like organised crime cannot be successfully resolved – were challenged. We successfully disproved the prevailing policing trope that you have to be big to be a strategic force and able to tackle the gamut of policing issues (O'Connor, 2005).

Long-term strategy

We were reassured by the example set by the successful fluoropolymer manufacturers Gore-Tex who capped the size of their business units to Dunbar's Number (Dunbar, 2019), so people can know and recognise each other. CEO Jason Field said: '*by having small units, associates develop relationships, understand where knowledge resides in the organisation and can tap into the capabilities they need to make quality decisions for our enterprise*' (Gale, 2019). This chimes with my view that small and agile is the new strategic.

Our strategic vision had endured, in 2021, for over ten years, surviving three Chief Constables and the transfer of governance from the Police Authority in 2012 to the Office of the Police and Crime Commissioner.

Collins and Porras warn that social cognition means staff pick up all the signals in the workplace, the little ones, not just the big ones. People want to believe in the company's vision but will be ever watchful of the tiny inconsistencies that allow them to say: '*Aha! See, there you go. I knew management was just blowing smoke. They don't really believe their own rhetoric*' (Collins and Porras, 1994, p 214). Successive executive leaders signing up to the long-lasting vision not only confirmed it was right for the organisation but also that people's work with previous leaders was valued. Paradoxically, the strategy remained under close scrutiny and pressure to flex because it was referred to so frequently. It was displayed everywhere. The annual plan (on-a-page) was formally considered at least every month at the strategic performance meetings. Each element of the plan was RAG rated and this brightly coloured version of the plan became the organisation's formal risk register.

The organisation's vision is actually central to motivating and directing individual and collective efforts towards the desired future state of the organisation. When clarity of the vision is low and organisational goals are unclear the individual member of staff is not as effective at shaping their attitude, behaviour and work to achieve the organisational aims. Clarity of the vision encourages the level of staff collective engagement in their work and their level of discretionary effort. They go the extra mile (Graham et al, 2019).

I still see organisations spending considerable time and effort in their 'planning cycle'. From December onwards people are writing next year's plan to run from April. Very few people refer to it after it's been agreed in March and it becomes redundant when next year's plan is being written in December. Such plans are many pages long, rarely read, often unrealised and masquerade as leadership.

Once clear on that strategy then more people can be involved to discuss what the more detailed annual plans look like. For clarity my strategic vision and pitch to the interview panel who appointed me in 2008 was to ensure problem orientation and restorative justice shaped our operational policing practice, and at the same time transforming the force's use of ICT would streamline the business. (Subjects covered in more detail later.) Everything else I did whilst in Durham flowed from those commitments and I was able to inspire people to buy into those principles which made us smarter at our work, more humane and fit for the future. Anyone shaping strategy for 2021 and beyond must consider and explain at least how ICT fits in.

Organisational background

In 2008 when I arrived in Durham from Lancashire as the new Assistant Chief Constable, I saw a good organisation but not one top of its class. It was a traditional force where arresting people and putting them into the criminal justice system was a key principle. There were examples of innovation: Durham had pioneered 'pre-reprimand disposals' (a novel mechanism to delay and hopefully prevent young people acquiring a formal criminal sanction) highlighted as best practice by the Ministry of Justice and Youth Justice Board (Anon, 2013); the force at the same time paradoxically 'charged' a higher proportion of arrestees than any other force in the United Kingdom. People were proud of the epithet 'Family Force', populated by good people who cared about their county but insular in that the only ranks eligible for recruiting from outside were constables and chief officers. It was also strongly hierarchical and still largely male-dominated. No woman had ever been a member of the force executive team.

Of particular interest to this paper, HMIC described the software that was currently in use as some of the worst in the United Kingdom. I had previous experience in this area having spent the decade 1998–2008 leading the development of in-house software capability in Lancashire Constabulary, subsequently also adopted by Cumbria Constabulary. My intent was therefore to address the critical issues embedded within the Durham Constabulary infrastructure. These included:

- a disconnect between the crime system, the intelligence system, command and control and case and custody;

- a lack of single log on capability and in a conversation with control room staff they revealed they spent the first 15 minutes of every tour of duty logging into 16 separate operating systems all of which required separate log-in procedures and passwords;

- an intransigence to addressing the single log-on problem by ICT departmental leaders – apparently it could only be done in the next year's plan, and then only if it met the threshold of importance;

- commercial ICT providers reluctant to improve their products used by Durham Constabulary.

The strategic implications in having ineffective or inaccessible software systems was that the organisation could not thrive. Staff were being prevented from doing their work. This was costing the organisation a significant proportion of its budget on wasted time and effort. Every minute that staff were waiting for software to respond or spending minutes performing tasks that could have been automated was time and enthusiasm sapped from doing their job. All leaders should ensure the organisation allows its people to be as productive as possible. We were also cheesing off our staff and encouraging them to think of the leadership as incompetent.

The over-reliance on fixed departmental annual plans meant that there was a complete lack of agility in tackling emerging problems and it showed leaders valued less the staff experience and more maintaining a strict and stifling bureaucracy – the antithesis of servant leadership (Greenleaf, 2021).

The lack of challenge to the commercial ICT suppliers was part of a wider problem of poor ICT provision for policing and government (King and Crew, 2013).

A Comparing Police and Crime Commissioners (CoPaCC) national police ICT survey in 2018 looked at ten police forces. The main experience of those responding to the survey seems to be one of frustration, discontent and, in some cases, even despair as they encountered equipment and systems which, far from helping them to do their jobs more effectively, hindered the fight against crime (Anon, 2019). I adopted a leadership focus on six particular areas of business. Two as a result of events, ie austerity and preparedness for inspection. The others were drawn from conversations with HMIC inspectors, members of staff themselves and frustrated customers who wanted the police to do more. The six areas resulted in improvements to make the organisation leaner, more systematic and less bureaucratic; to be clearer about its purpose; to change the service experienced by the public; to equip our staff to be more creative and positive about what they did and to feel better led.

Organisational focus: ICT

I knew single log-on was a straightforward change that would yield immediate benefits for communications staff on every shift. In practical terms this meant they were unavailable to answer 999 calls. We had a worrying percentage of lost calls at the time, ie, people were calling the police for help and not getting through. I also knew that it could be fixed quickly, so I made a fuss about it openly in the force so there would be a compelling story shared by frustrated frontline staff that leaders had listened to them and fixed a significant stressor. Single log-on was rolled out a couple of months later. Thus, creating a powerful episodic memory for staff to remember leaders in a positive light (Philippe et al, 2019; Tulving and Szpunar, 1972).

Goleman describes the repertoire of leadership; he suggests 'ced*pace-setting and commanding*' as useful in specific situations but that they need to be applied with caution (Goleman et al, 2002, p 67). I knew that by openly challenging powerful departmental heads I was taking a risk of alienation but knew I needed to kick-start the change cycle and create a sense of urgency (Kotter, 2021). I also used my anger in controlled bursts when management intransigence became almost laughable, '*use ... anger ... artfully channelled ... to get instant attention and mobilise people to change*' (Goleman et al, 2002, p 100). In the event I had acquired more allies (on the frontline) by changing something for the common good and sent a message to departmental heads that they had to change. This development enhanced my reputation as someone who listened but who was a force to be reckoned with.

I knew I had made internal enemies but the alternative was that we would not be answering calls from the public. Leaders have to make choices whether to work cooperatively with colleagues but allow the purpose of the organisation to be thwarted in the pursuit of such superficial harmony. I decided I wanted the frontline staff to feel they were listened to and allowed to do their job better. I also knew I would be expecting them to embrace change in the future so invested early in their trust and appreciation of me as a leader. It is not always possible to approach change and leadership in this uncompromising way and it carries risk but when deployed and deployed successfully it is hugely powerful in accelerating change and sending a clear signal to everyone in the organisation.

Shaping commercial partnerships

I was astounded at the disdain with which the commercial suppliers treated me as a senior officer in Durham and a (valued) customer, so as the strategic lead, I set out to rebalance and realign the organisational requirements.

I have found big police ICT suppliers sell generic products dressed as bespoke and then concentrate on the next sale rather than refining the product as promised. Sims describes creating a minimum viable product (Robinson, 2001) and then putting it under strain by allowing frontline staff to describe enhancements, essentially enhanced trial and error (Syed, 2015, p 150); this is how software is now designed and delivered in Cumbria and Durham. Unlike the national police ICT Survey, a survey of police staff in Cumbria found complete satisfaction and a similar survey of supervisors in Durham described the software in the force as their most significant asset.

In-house solutions

I introduced Cumbria and Lancashire's in-house developed system within a year of arrival in Durham and extracted Durham from all those commercial contracts citing their clear breach of good faith. I then recruited local ICT graduates, offering student internships and effectively created a software house with talented people who worked alongside our officers to understand what was needed. They gained experience and then moved on in their careers. More students were recruited: a virtuous cycle.

A significant reason to develop our own software is to maximise the value of the intangible assets of the organisation. When ICT companies work with police forces they monetise what they learn and reap the benefit. Conley says: we all know that the value of intellectual property has risen exponentially in our knowledge economy (Conley, 2007, p 25). When ICT companies move from force to force they monetise what they have learnt and the next customer pays for it. £millions of value are haemorrhaging from policing in this way.

ICT moved from a significant and constant headache for all our staff to an enabler. Numerous HMIC reports into Durham prove the good sense of tackling this issue promptly and only a few years later HMIC described Durham's ICT systems as some of the best in the United Kingdom. Our staff were now equipped to perform to their peak in our fight against crime.

> Technology induced change is nothing new. The real question is not, what is the role of technology? Rather the real question is, how do good to great organisations think differently about technology? ... Every good to great company became a pioneer in the application of technology.
>
> (Collins, 2001, pp 147–8)

REFLECTIVE PRACTICE

- Do you know what your staff think of the software you ask them to use?
- Have you experienced what it's like to use the software and equipment to do frequent mundane tasks?
- What is your reputation in listening to frustrations and getting things done to resolve them?
- Have you been faced with the intransigence of suppliers or departmental leaders, in an area beyond your expertise, have you been a champion for your people and the customer to improve matters or been browbeaten into defeat? How would you build a coalition to address this?

Organisational focus: crime

A prevailing conversation in policing is that responsibility for Serious and Organised crime (described within policing parlance as 'level 2 crime') – should be removed from smaller local forces and left to the experts, to be found in larger 'strategic' forces or national agencies (Keeling, 2020, 12 January). A part of the argument is that some local forces did not recognise they had a cross-border or serious and organised crime problem: 'No Crime Here!' (O'Connor, 2005, p 42). I took an alternative viewpoint seeking to ensure that those with myopic views were discouraged from blocking a new dynamic approach to managing crime. It was my strategic intent that serious and organised crime should not be hermetically sealed from local policing given that its impact is the most pernicious and damaging to public safety. Local officers are also best placed to disrupt local crime be it serious or not. Durham's continued excellence in HMIC grading for tackling Serious and Organised Crime, alongside Derbyshire and Merseyside, suggests sustained success in this area is more a function of leadership than size (HMIC, 2021).

National adoption of the National Intelligence Model (NIM) (Centrex, 2005) and Organised Crime Group Mapping (OCGM) (Goverment, 2014) had provided a framework post-2005 for local forces to raise their game and be more effective in tackling Organised Crime Groups (OCGs).

The context

On arrival in Durham, I knew I could set up a quick win by tackling an OCG which was operating either under the radar or with impunity. I found the latter. This *identified family* were variously described as: wholly legitimate, untouchable, violent thugs and controlling a quarter of the county. It was perceived that they had geographic control of specific areas of Durham due to their aggressive and oppressive behaviour. They had even intimidated the local council where they lived to re-name the main street eponymously.

Organised crime groups thrive when the police are ineffectual. They notoriously damage society and their perceived success erodes public confidence in the police and civic society. The police are seen as useless or worse still – corrupt. Police officers themselves feel powerless which then permeates and limits the collective psyche of the organisation.

I adopted the principles of the NIM in tackling this family and commissioned target profiles on all of them as individuals and a problem profile on their interactions with the council, other agencies and the community. We quickly established that they were far from being legitimate.

My intent was to neutralise the criminality of the family by giving common purpose to the local officers, specialist crime departments, council and law-abiding majority. I was the visible leader of this campaign and shared all I was able to in the local media. I am clear that policing has for too long looked upon fighting organised crime as something to be done in the shadows, secretly, and not to trust the public to be part of the operational plan.

Equally the police often exaggerate the complexity of the task, Nick Ross describes this as the 'Moriarty Fallacy':

> The promotion of criminals to evil prodigies is ... convenient for detectives ... assuring us that the scoundrels they seek are 'professional', 'ingenious' or 'highly organised' and their crimes are 'well planned'.
>
> (Ross, 2013, p 140)

The general public know far more about organised crime and how we can destabilise such criminals than we give them credit for. Including the public also emboldens them to create an unwelcome, even toxic situation for the criminal.

All the feedback was that my personal involvement and demonstration of caring about this particular issue was the key enabler for everyone not only to pull together but also actually believe that something could be done about this notorious family. It benefitted me because I could see how the organisation I was leading was erecting barriers to prevent frontline staff doing extraordinary things. It was also a personally rewarding time where I was able to apply all my operational experience to coach junior staff and give them clear permission to try things. All organisations thrive on gossip and legends. I wanted to create topics of gossip about the boss encouraging everyone to raise their game and tackle problems to which we had become inured.

Les Graham's research demonstrated that such supervisory leadership was found to be positively related to police officer discretionary effort to engage in innovative and spontaneous activity to disrupt criminal activity (Graham, 2015).

The results

The next few years saw: firearms recovered, proceeds of crime seizures across the board and most of the key players in prison. All led by a local neighbourhood inspector who was both imaginative and indefatigable. A subsequent local survey showed the public's confidence in the police had leapt exponentially and house prices, long depressed in the area, eventually moved in line with the district average.

The BBC were there to film the changing back of the eponymous street name, and the public saw it on the 6pm news. Local surveys of people showed how these demonstrations of tackling organised crime were appreciated. It is now the law-abiding majority who are ensuring this family remain peripheral and largely powerless.

REFLECTIVE PRACTICE

- Are you familiar with the organised crime scoring matrix in your force?
- Do all OCGs have a local owner who has the force support to work with partners to tackle them head-on?
- Are the potential next generation of the OCGs identified before they are active offenders?
- How do the public view the actions of the OCG members and how do they perceive the effectiveness of the police?

- If not involved in policing what are the issues that your organisation is not tackling but perhaps should be? Is there a narrative that some problems are intractable? Would your visible personal support on a key issue create a different narrative and gossip in your organisation about what is possible?

Organisational focus: preparedness for inspection and empowerment

In autumn 2008 we were informed that HMIC were to visit the force to inspect custody provision imminently. A long-running programme of looking at the future of custody was underway. It had yet to report but it was clear the estate was aged, scattered in small units and dilapidated.

Custody provision is clearly a critical area of policing and any such failing would damage the reputation of the force and its ability to command respect. This state of affairs somehow was a metaphor for the force where people felt there was no money to fix things and we were all part of a slow but inexorable decline.

Participation in any change process is key (Lawrence, 1969). Albeit I'd been assigned the lead role in preparing for the inspection, I clearly couldn't make change happen on my own. The Chief Inspector in charge of custody became my constant companion. Our visits to remote custody suites were met with bemusement. Senior officers visiting were rare events. *'That's what you did, as ACC you visited people in remote places and gave them authority to try things. It hadn't happened before'* (Durham, 2008–2010). Staff had low expectations that improvements would be funded. The estates manager was similarly frustrated.

Putting these two groups together with the Chief Inspector and a small but sufficient budget allowed all the improvements to be completed, on time. They even overcame opposition to sequential closing of the suites to do the remedial work. The inspection report is available to be read, but we were pleased that the summary recorded *'police custody is generally well managed'*. They also recorded all suites were clean, well decorated and free from graffiti (Owers and O'Connor, 2009).

Sometimes it takes an event or outsiders to highlight that something needs to be done. We had become complacent that the long-term plan was sober and rational and would deliver all the answers, eventually. However, it allowed us to kick every possible improvement into the long grass. Every cell had graffiti, yet we had stopped thinking about the trauma of being locked in a cell and locked in a cell that looked unkempt. The shocking state of the cells sent a clear signal that we didn't care for our buildings and cells or those unfortunate to spend the night in them. As I retired in 2019, we had still not delivered on the sober and rational strategic custody review.

Building relationships with frontline staff creates a horizontal organisation, changes culture and transforms the organisation (Conley, 2007, pp 222–3). Sinek describes Marquet succinctly defining empowerment as giving authority to those closest to the information and says,

> *That's what the best leaders do. They share what they know ... poor leaders hoard these things, falsely believing ... their rank ... make(s) them valuable.*
>
> (Sinek, 2014, pp 180–2)

HMIC several years later visited without warning (they had changed their inspection protocol). They reported: '*We saw good and respectful interactions between staff and detainees, and detainees we spoke with said they were treated well*' (Hardwick and Winsor, 2014). None of the bad habits such as misusing the medical surgeries had returned. Sadly, staff, to their credit, were still operating in aged surroundings. Prior to 2008 graffiti had been ubiquitous, but because custody staff knew they could insist on immediate repairs, they had been empowered with the estates team to put into practice the proverb: a stitch in time saves nine. Applying the criminological theory of Broken Windows resulting in no new graffiti (Kelling and Wilson, 1982).

We all judge people and things on first appearances. If we approached a restaurant that looked uncared for then we would be unlikely to go ahead with the planned dining experience. Why should that be any different for a police station? Arguably it is more important since it is a public building and people who use it are traumatised or in dire need of support rather than ready for a meal out. I did my personal bit of leading by example by picking up litter at every police station visit. The power of the boss doing something seen as menial but putting into practice accepted criminological theory was all part of creating a knowledgeable and positive workforce. Anyone actually seeing me picking up litter would be constructing powerful episodic memories (Tulving and Szpunar, 1972).

REFLECTIVE PRACTICE

- How do you create a sense of urgency or common purpose?
- Have you seen strategic or long-term reviews used to defer difficult decisions? What would you do if you recognised it?
- Do the frontline staff fully participate in decisions?
- Do you conduct visual audits of your estate?
- How often do you walk past litter?

Organisational focus: the opportunities from austerity

In 2010 the Coalition Government enacting their austerity policies significantly reduced police funding and in Durham we faced the fifth biggest pro-rata budget cut in the United Kingdom. Our Labour-controlled Police Authority were reluctant to make enforced redundancies.

Police budgets are roughly split 85/15 on staff and non-staff costs. The level of cuts could only be achieved by reducing the number of staff on the payroll and any delay would ultimately necessitate bigger cuts. Private industry's collective lesson suggested we cut early, cut deep and cut once (Watson, 2019).

I was determined not to miss the opportunity offered by this 'burning oil-platform' of the biggest ever cuts to police budgets by opting for a smaller and less effective version of what we already had. This was a once-in-a-lifetime opportunity to reshape the workforce, cut unhelpful bureaucracy and transform Durham Constabulary. Voluntary severance alone would not target the right people to leave. We had to design a process which selected the best people to keep. I agree with Collins who says it's about being rigorous and not ruthless (Collins, 2001, p 52).

When the Police Authority announced the formal compulsory redundancy process, we were criticised by other police leaders saying we were over-reacting and they would be doing everything voluntarily even though they were facing budget cuts of over 20 per cent. This is not the lesson private industry had learnt.

Unions asked for 'last in, first out'. My intent was to insist on a process which valued attendance and contribution and did not disadvantage youth. We wished to keep people who embodied our values and so the redundancy process scored people, in part, on their attitude towards work and colleagues. People who had lost their 'mojo' found themselves on the redundancy list. We chose to use the phrase 'losing their mojo' because it was more respectful than 'poor' or 'lazy'. It was also more accurate because very few of those people had begun their careers performing sub-optimally.

I knew that there were very many people who were understandably angry with me and the rest of the top team, but we had to focus on re-shaping the organisation rather than courting popularity. Machiavelli notoriously said leaders should be loved and feared, but if one can't be both, be feared. Updating those concepts from Renaissance Europe to the present day, leaders should be liked and respected, but if one can't be both, be respected. The police leaders who ducked the issue of exiting their least productive staff by opting for only voluntary redundancy as the principal device to shrink their organisation arguably valued more their own popularity than garnering the (grudging) respect that the top team had in Durham. They made the mistake of being liked rather than respected when they couldn't have both (Machiavelli, 1531–2, pp 70–3). Machiavelli is also clear the leader must avoid being hated. Although powerful emotive concepts from across four centuries they resonate still. We did everything we could to identify alternative employment for those made redundant, even organising job fairs for other employers who were recruiting. The process was particularly tough on the supervisors and managers who had to grade their staff, so we found £100k to invest in them as part of the transformation programme (Pearlcatchers, 2018).

In 2012 HMIC assessed police forces' progress in austerity. Their assessment of Durham was: good progress in achieving the savings. The proportion of officers in frontline roles was increasing from 81 per cent to 92 per cent and 87 per cent of victims were satisfied with their service (Baker, 2012).

We had lost a significant number of staff, yet performance went up. Supervisors found they had more time to support good performers than managing poor performance. We were able to push a greater proportion of staff to the frontline by streamlining the back office. In large part using our young ICT graduates to automate processes (see 'Organisational focus: ICT' above). As Covey speculates, 'How much time is spent in low trust cultures controlling, monitoring, hovering over, checking up, "*snoopervising*"' (Covey et al, 1994)? Bauer also contends that bureaucracy is expanding in most companies and bureaucratic drag increases as the size of the organisation grows (Bauer, 2018).

All of the glowing HMIC reports about Durham post-date these redundancies. The atmosphere in the force was described as 'being different here'. This was Theory Y working practices put into practice and organisational transformation at work.

REFLECTIVE PRACTICE

- What proportion of your staff have lost their mojo?
- How could you find out?
- What would you do with the results?
- Do you agree with the Machiavellian reference?
- Do you like to be liked? Does it sometimes get in the way of leadership?
- Consider whether there is the contradiction of an espoused Theory Y culture by the leadership and an actual Theory X experience by the rest of the organisation.

Organisational focus: promotion processes

In 2008 the promotion process was seen as unfair and not just by unsuccessful candidates. The process was focused on its own mechanics rather than the outcomes of selecting the best candidates. I knew it was imperative the wider organisation had faith in the system and had confidence that the best candidates were being promoted (Justice, n.d.). HR imposed rules such as no interaction with the candidate had been introduced so every candidate got an identical experience, I saw this as a narrow interpretation of fairness which, based on what the staff thought, had actually undermined procedural fairness.

New question banks were used to draw out the competencies, core values and potential of each candidate. Over and above a selection of the questions, all candidates would be faced with the same presentation or challenge. These would be the wicked problems currently facing the organisation, for example: '*How would you create a cynic free organisation?*'

There emerged a library of questions, presentations and tasks for prospective candidates. Their preparation for future processes meant candidates were pondering the wicked problems facing the organisation, be it a lack of diversity or how to deal with austerity and maintain performance. This created a virtuous cycle where all candidates whether successful or not were considering how to approach such issues and often putting their thoughts and experience into practice as peers and leaders.

I appointed a respected detective sergeant who had gained a master's in leadership, in her own time, to be our leadership guru, to devote all her time in championing leadership. She gauged how the organisation saw the promotion process and any perception of unfairness was addressed openly. It was gratifying to see some candidates with potential return many times before success. A common flaw was a lack of articulacy and knowledge of crime theory. Police officers aspiring to be leaders who did not read, who did not thirst for knowledge were not candidates the organisation needed nor would they be the best people to lead and develop junior and more inexperienced staff. (See below, the learning leader.)

All staff were offered feedback and access to a coach or mentor. The process was annual and staff were encouraged to see the process as a 365-day assessment. The most important change was the process was not shrouded in secrecy; people understood the process and saw it as fairer and as a template for professional development. Research sponsored by the College of Policing in Fair Cop 2 proved that internal fairness in the police organisation has a direct impact on the way police officers perform their duties and how they treat the public fairly in turn. So prevailing feelings that internal processes are unfair cannot be ignored (Quinton et al, 2015). Our leadership guru also looked for the potential leaders who displayed the qualities of servant leadership, those who had not considered promotion or didn't think their face fitted. I have always been concerned that the main selector for leaders is personal ambition rather than the right people being nurtured and developed. I was also assiduous in scotching any hints of nepotism, and although they arose from time to time, the constant conversations about leadership led by our leadership guru allowed us to listen and respond to such rumblings of discontent and feelings of unfairness.

I would suggest any senior officer arriving in a force offers to chair all promotion interviews and in particular PC to Sergeant, or the first rung on the leadership ladder It is worth the considerable effort. Collins says pithily,

> *We expected that good to great leaders would begin by setting a new vision and strategy. We found instead that they first got the right people on the bus, the wrong people off the bus, the right people in the right seats – then they figured out where to drive it.*
>
> (Collins, 2001, p 13)

One learns so much about the future generation of leaders and allows one to shape their personal transformation. Goleman describes coaching as one of the most powerful components in the leadership repertoire, it is the art of the one-on-one and by making sure they have personal conversations with employees coaching leaders establish rapport and trust irrespective of the other styles that the leader may employ (Goleman et al, 2002, p 76).

Involvement in the process should not be fleeting because learning leadership is a long-term project; we have to unlearn things before we can learn the new. The adult learning cycle needs sincere desire, emotion and hard work. '*Motivation becomes crucial for leadership development*' (Goleman et al, 2002, p 133). The best leaders in Durham endured multiple failures as they increasingly understood they had to demonstrate their competence, emotional intelligence and ability to inspire others, embodying Level 5 leadership (Collins 2001, pp 35–6). Sticking with the process allows one to witness that personal transformation.

REFLECTIVE PRACTICE

- Are your promotion processes producing the candidates you need?
- Are you active in the promotion process and involved in shaping the next generation of people and leaders in your organisation?
- Are your selection and promotion processes seen as unfair? What impact is that perception having on your people and organisation?

Personal focus: the learning leader

As an effective leader, I believe you need to have a well thought-through philosophy that helps shape the decisions you make and the strategic vision you set. It is vitally important that a leader has clarity around their vision, values and purpose. As such, having asked the reader to engage with a number of reflective practice exercises, I thought it might be useful to finish this section with what I have learned about my time as a leader within policing UK. Here are my nine key learning opportunities.

1. Policing seems to meander from one fashion to the next. This appears to be the view of frontline staff who often suffer from initiative-fatigue. 'Peelian' principles are said to guide UK policing. Do they? If so where is the prevention of crime in the hierarchy? The focus is principally upon the prosecution of offenders, policing now is synonymous for many with law enforcement.

2. Syed reveals and reflects upon the breath-taking scale of closed-shop behaviour in the criminal justice system (Syed, 2015, p 93). Feeding the criminal justice system becomes the default position. Conley reminds us of one of Peter Drucker's most famous and wise questions for executives: *'What business are you in?'* (Conley, 2007, p 144). One of my wise colleagues always says *'we are in the people happiness business'*; I agree.

3. The strategic threat for any police force without a defensible policing philosophy, based on scientific principles, is that it is subject to the vagaries of policy shifts by others. Additionally, we can only be sure that we will have an impact on crime, or community safety, or public confidence or staff well-being if we follow or lead the science. Our beliefs and cognitive dissonance is challenged by the science (Syed, 2015, pp 61, 81, 171), what our staff say and how we interact as leaders (Zheng et al, 2019).

4. Problem-oriented policing (POP) as described by Herman Goldstein (Goldstein, 1990) requires a positive outlook, where staff are focused on creating a new norm where the problem does not recur, or is significantly reduced in impact. CC Pauline Clare introduced POP into Lancashire in 1995 and it guided the force into international pre-eminence (Scott and Kirby, 2012). The author among other Lancashire officers submitted entries for the Tilley and Goldstein Awards (Barton, 2001). Unfortunately, like in many other forces POP fell off the radar and arguably resulted in less effective policing (Tilley and Scott, 2012).

5. Learning that POP is a fragile concept, even in a force like Lancashire, where it appeared to be embedded, I ensured POP was woven into everything we did in Durham. Performance meetings, promotion processes, public/community meetings, problem profiles as part of the NIM, novel approaches to organised crime that did not just focus on prosecution and imprisonment. How could we prevent the next generation of criminal families following in the family footsteps? POP was talked about and people became good at it, they had fun and it formed a considerable part of the evidence offered to HMIC on their many visits. Annual competitions and conferences allowed Durham Constabulary to accumulate national and international honours for excellence in problem solving (assuming the mantle vacated by Lancashire). Such professional recognition is a powerful impetus for personal and organisational transformation, but everyday conversations giving informal recognition creates a culture of recognition (Conley, 2007, p 71). I was determined that POP was not a fad, it was at the core of the way Durham did its business. As is Restorative Justice (RJ) (Christie, 1977). RJ and POP are symbiotic, in that the problem faced is allowed to be addressed and

solved by the protagonists themselves, with the professionals assisting when necessary, but not taking over.

6. Victim satisfaction in the criminal justice process is significantly boosted when coupled with RJ, offenders offered RJ experience significantly reduced re-offending rates (RJC, 2021). Conley describing private companies says customer satisfaction is just survival; we have to aim to delight and meet unexpected needs (Conley, 2007, p 40). In Durham I stopped seeing 'satisfaction' as a positive in our customer surveys, 'very and completely satisfied' now only counted as a positive, all other responses had to be examined and improved. Policing is fortunate in that we have a monopoly, or do we? The private security industry is burgeoning especially online. The ultimate rival for our services however is apathy and irrelevance.

7. Commentators on criminal justice bemoan the revolving door of the criminal justice system, the ineffectual even detrimental nature of short-term prison sentences, the racial disproportionality of the criminal justice system. Yet politicians and senior police officers rarely promote POP and RJ. Depressingly, favouring the talk tough approach. Criminologist John Braithwaite says:

RJ requires that offenders take responsibility for their offences, offer an apology to those offended against, and, where possible and appropriate, make reparation to victims of crime either directly or indirectly. Traditional justice makes no such demands.

(Cornwell et al, 2013)

Talking tough is actually not tough at all.

8. Durham police officers in 2008 proudly boasted when they put an offender 'over the wall', ie, remanded in custody or imprisoned. Durham charged the highest proportion of those arrested in the United Kingdom. In 2018, a decade on, Durham prosecuted the lowest proportion of those arrested, 'over the wall' had been replaced with an ambition to reduce the re-offending rate of everyone brought into custody. Successful investigations had risen. Crime is not prevented by the potential or perceived level of punishment but the likelihood/the fear of being found out.

9. It is this multi-layered approach to policing which provides a complex and demanding professional challenge to staff, upon which they thrive and transform personally.

Work is about daily meaning as well as daily bread; for recognition as well as cash; in short, for a sort of life rather than a Monday through Friday sort of dying ... We have a right to ask of work that it include meaning, recognition, astonishment and life.

(Conley 2007, p 45)

Reflective practice

- What policing literature and science have you read and adopted as your own?

- Are you familiar with POP and RJ – professionally familiar or just acquainted?

- Have you adopted them in your organisation, if not are you prepared to argue that they are not relevant? If so, please get in touch.

- Have you ready access to leadership material that will allow you to develop the next generation. How often do you share your reading with colleagues?

Chapter summary

The world is now lived and organised online. The software of any organisation is key to its efficiency and how it harnesses and uses its knowledge. I have seen too many leaders who have taken no responsibility to understand and shape their software when it is so obviously important. Often this is the result of fear or a lack of knowledge but I have found that one does not need to be an expert only someone who knows enough to hold experts to account: how to insist on what your staff need and not what the supplier wants to sell.

I am often perplexed by leaders who focus on restructuring and what the organisation looks like and how big it is rather than how their people feel, how content, how energised, how productive. Small and agile organisations that are equipped to respond quickly to the needs of the customer and allow their staff to feel not only that they are important but they also have a key role in shaping their organisation are, in my view likely to be the survivors and thrivers of the future. The emergence of the coaching and servant leader is a sign that leadership styles are embodying the concept that people are the organisation's most important asset.

Reach out to the public so they are your partners and listen and respond to any grumbles; performing satisfactorily is not good enough, delighting the customer has to be the goal. Much of the conversation of leaders in the public sector and certainly in policing is about demand reduction. Unfortunately, this is too often addressed not by designing out the demand, but by rationing and ultimately, ignoring it. Demand is actually good, because it indicates relevance. A lack of demand surely means a lack of faith, or trust, but creeping and eventual irrelevance. This idea as debateable will be alien to readers from the private sector. They already understand implicitly that demand is essential to viability.

Leaders should consider the external pressures of inspection or budget cuts as the opportunities and accelerants to change. Tough and unpopular decisions should be made at these times, since they are often impossible to take without those external prompts. There is a time to rally the troops but in general if there is criticism of one's organisation then the leader should embrace it rather than immediately and often publicly opt to rebuff or refute.

Remember to invest in the unsung heroes and heroines who are generally hidden from the leadership. They often shun the limelight but these are the engine room of your organisation, and albeit they shy away from the processes of celebration and promotion paradoxically they appreciate and flourish with recognition. They have powerful internal loci of control, but benefit from an external locus of control for verification and confirmation (Moller et al, 2006). Once they taste that success they blossom and transform from passive critical observers to become active agents of improvement. Theory Y not theory X.

One legacy that is within the gift of any leader is to partner with academics and researchers who test new ideas, are peer-reviewed and publish. Oral traditional memory does not build a powerful learning culture and can result in faddish behaviours by leaders.

My advice to any senior leader is to concentrate on listening and developing your people. Be an active part of all selection processes then actively coach anyone who wants or needs your support. It sounds daunting but the investment is worth it. Any leader should have a network of staff at all levels and sites in the organisation to have an accurate feel for the place, progress and problems. I describe this as bungee management, take the leap into the frontline to see how strategy and the plan is being implemented but get back out quickly to leave the professional practitioners their space.

References

Anon (2013) *Youth Justice Board* [Online]. Available at: https://assets.publishing.service.gov.uk/government/uploads/system/uploads/attachment_data/file/438139/out-court-disposal-guide.pdf (accessed 2021).

Anon (2019) *Policing Insight* [Online]. Available at: https://policinginsight.com/reports/police-ict-forces-in-focus-comparing-user-experiences/ (accessed February 2021).

Baker, R (2012) *HMICFRS Policing in Austerity One Year On* [Online]. Available at: https://www.justiceinspectorates.gov.uk/hmicfrs/media/durham-policing-in-austerity-one-year-on-press-release.pdf (accessed February 2021).

Barton, M (2001) *Pop Center, Tilley Awards, POP on a Beer Mat* [Online]. Available at: https://popcenter.asu.edu/sites/default/files/library/awards/tilley/2001/01-43.pdf (accessed February 2021).

Bauer, T (2018) *Bureaucracy Will Never Die* [Online]. Available at: https://tedbauer2003.medium.com/bureaucracy-will-never-die-2fea9454cf94 (accessed March 2021).

Centrex (2005) *National Intelligence Model* [Online]. Available at: https://whereismydata.files.wordpress.com/2009/01/national-intelligence-model-20051.pdf (accessed February 2021).

Christie, N (1977) Conflicts as Property. *The British Journal of Criminology*, 17(1), pp. 1–15 doi: 10.1093/oxfordjournals.bjc.a046783.

Collins, J (2001) *Good to Great*. s.l.: Random House.

Collins, J and Porras, G (1994) *Built to Last*. s.l.: Random House.

Conley, C (2007) *Peak*. 1st ed. s.l.:Jossey-Bass.

Cornwell, D, Blad, J and Wright, M a o (2013) *Civilising Criminal Justice*. s.l.: Waterside Press.

Covey, S R, Merril, I R A and Merrill, R R (1994) *First Things First*. s.l.: Simon & Schuster.

Dunbar, R (2019) *BBC Future* [Online]. Available at: https://www.bbc.com/future/article/20191001-dunbars-number-why-we-can-only-maintain-150-relationships (accessed 2021).

Durham Constabulary (2021) *Durham Constabulary* [Online]. Available at: www.durham.police.uk (accessed 2021).

Durham, I i (2008 - 2010) [Interview].

Gale, A (2019) *Management Today* [Online]. Available at: https://www.managementtoday.co.uk/big-company-everyone-knows/innovation/article/1646199 (accessed 2021).

Goldstein, H (1990) *Problem-Oriented Policing*. s.l.: McGraw-Hill.

Goleman, D, Boyatzis, R and McKee, A (2002) *The New Leaders*. s.l.: Sphere.

Goverment, H (2014) *Serious and Organised Crime Profiles - A Local Guide* [Online]. Available at: https://assets.publishing.service.gov.uk/government/uploads/system/uploads/attachment_data/file/371602/Serious_and_Organised_Crime_local_profiles.pdf (accessed February 2021).

Graham, L (2015) *Policing Research Durham Constabulary - Initial Findings* [Interview].

Graham, L, Barton, C M, Cheer, C J, Redman, T, Plater, M and Zheng, Y (2015) Ethical Leadership, Motivations and Outcomes in Policing. *Invited Speakers to the Excellence in Policing Conference*. College of Policing. 29th September, Ryton-on-Dunsmore, UK. s.n.

Graham, L N, Plater, M, Brown, N, Zheng, Y and Gracey, S (2019) *Research into Workplace Factors, Well-Being, Attitudes and Behaviour in Policing: Summary of Evidence and Insights*. Durham University [Online]. Available at: http://www.gov.uk/government/publications/front-line-poilicing-review.

Greenleaf, R K (2021) *Center for Servant Leadership* [Online]. Available at: https://www.greenleaf.org/what-is-servant-leadership/ (accessed February 2021).

Hardwick, N and Winsor, T (2014) *HMICFRS* [Online]. Available at: https://www.justiceinspectorates.gov.uk/hmiprisons/wp-content/uploads/sites/4/2014/12/Durham-police-web-2014.pdf (accessed February 2021).

HMIC, (2021) *HMICFRS* [Online]. Available at: https://www.justiceinspectorates.gov.uk/hmicfrs/police-forces/durham/ (accessed February 2021).

Justice, P (n.d.) *Wikipedia* [Online]. Available at: https://en.wikipedia.org/wiki/Procedural_justice (accessed February 2021).

Keeling, N (2020) *Manchester Evening News* [Online]. Available at: manchestereveningnews.co.uk (accessed March 2021).

Kelling, G L and Wilson, J Q (1982) *Wikpedia* [Online]. Available at: https://en.wikipedia.org/wiki/Broken_windows_theory#:~:text=The%20broken%20windows%20theory%20is,and%20disorder%2C%20including%20serious%20crimes (accessed February 2021).

King, A and Crew, I (2013) *The Blunders of Our Government*. s.l.: One World Publications.

Kotter, J (2021) *Kotter, 8 Step Process* [Online]. Available at: https://www.kotterinc.com/8-steps-process-for-leading-change/ (accessed February 2021).

Lawrence, P R (1969) How to Deal with Resistance to Change. *Harvard Business Review Magazine*.

Machiavelli, N (1531–2) *The Prince*. Great Ideas ed. s.l.: Penguin Books.

Marr, B (2021) *Baernard Marr* [Online]. Available at: https://www.bernardmarr.com/ (accessed February 2021).

Moller, J P B e a, Streblow, L, Pohlmann, B and Köller, O (2006) An Extension to the Internal/External Frame of Reference Model to Two Verbal and Numerical Domains. *European Journal of Psychology of Education*, 21(4), pp. 467–487.

O'Connor, D (2005) *Closing the Gap HMIC* [Online]. Available at: https://www.justiceinspectorates.gov.uk/hmicfrs/media/closing-the-gap-20050911.pdf (accessed 2021).

Owers, A and O'Connor, D (2009) *HMICFRS* [Online]. Available at: https://www.justiceinspectorates.gov.uk/hmicfrs/media/durham-custody-suites-joint-inspection-20090629.pdf (accessed February 2021).

Pearlcatchers, (2018) *Pearlcatchers*. Available at: https://www.pearlcatchers.uk/emergency-services/durham-constabulary/ (accessed February 2021).

Philippe, F L, Lopes, M, Houlfort, N and Fernet, C (2019) Work-Related Episodic Memories Can Increase or Decrease Motivation and Psychological Health at Work. *Work & Stress*.

Quinton, P et al. (2015) *Fair Cop, 2* [Online]. Available at: https://www.researchgate.net/publication/283350869_Fair_Cop_2_Organisational_Justice_Behaviour_and_Ethical_Policing_An_Interpretative_Evidence_Commentary (accessed March 2021).

RJC (2021) *Restorative Justice Council*. Available at: https://restorativejustice.org.uk/resources/evidence-supporting-use-restorative-justice (accessed February 2021).

Robinson, F (2001) *Wikipedia- Minimal Viable Product* [Online]. Available at: https://en.wikipedia.org/wiki/Minimum_viable_product (accessed February 2021).

Ross, N (2013) *Crime*. 1st ed. s.l.: Biteback Publishing.

Scott, M S and Kirby, S J (2012) *Implementing POP* [Online]. Available at: https://eprints.lancs.ac.uk/id/eprint/60830/1/popmanualfinal_copy.pdf (accessed February 2021).

Sinek, S (2014) *Leaders Eat Last*. s.l.: Penguin.

Syed, M (2015) *Black Box Thinking*. s.l.: John Murray.

Tilley, N and Scott, M S (2012) *Policing. The Past, Present and Future of POP* [Online]. Available at: https://academic.oup.com/policing/article-abstract/6/2/122/1525808?redirectedFrom=fulltext (accessed February 2021).

Tulving, E and Szpunar, K (1972) *Episodic Memory* [Online]. Available at: https://en.wikipedia.org/wiki/Episodic_memory (accessed February 2021).

Watson, K (2019) *When Transformational Change Is Needed, Cut Once and Cut Deep* [Online] Available at: https://minutehack.com/opinions/when-transformational-change-is-needed-cut-once-and-cut-deep (accessed February 2021).

Zheng, Y, Graham, L and Snape, E (2019) *Durham University Research Online: Service Leadership, Work Engagement and Service Performance: The Moderating Role* [Online]. Available at: https://dro.dur.ac.uk/28117/1/28117.pdf?DDD2+dng4alc+kswl88 (accessed February 2021).

11 Creating the climate

Peter Fahy

> Most importantly, understanding cultural forces enables us to understand ourselves better.
>
> (Shein, 2010)

CHAPTER OBJECTIVES

This chapter will help you:

- learn how understanding your own beliefs, values and personality are crucial to success in setting the climate of an organisation;
- understand the key elements, which have to be addressed by a leader to set the desired climate and drive change;
- appreciate the vital importance of alignment and congruence between those elements if behaviours of staff are to change.

Introduction

An organisation's climate or culture is the values, beliefs and ways of working in which staff operate and dictate that organisation's priorities and the service the public and key stakeholders can expect. This climate is greatly influenced by history, key events, political, social and economic factors, many of which are out of the leader's direct control. This chapter, however, explores those key elements which in my view are largely in a leader's control and have to be addressed to set a desired climate and to drive change, based on my experience and learning as Chief Constable of Greater Manchester Police. I particularly focus on the importance of achieving alignment between those key elements and especially the systems which allow staff to respond to their own sense of vocation and public service.

My own learning as a leader is that to achieve organisational success in any field, but particularly in policing, you have to align what staff are required to do and how they do it as closely as possible with their own sense of vocation and what is right (College of Policing, 2014). As Dwight Eisenhower (1954) said, '*Getting people to do what you want them to do because they want to do it*'.

Most officers would see vocation as why they joined the job. Of course, that presupposes that their sense of vocation is an honourable one but in my encounters with police officers in the United Kingdom and around the world I have found this invariably to be the case. Most officers want to serve the public through locking up the bad guys and protecting the vulnerable. It is situations where officers are asked to work against their own values and in systems that encourage them to abuse their power and see the public as people to be controlled rather than served and protected that generate unethical and unprofessional behaviour. Where structures and systems of deployment and accountability are aligned to a common sense of purpose and healthy values, unethical behaviour will be marginalised, exposed and called to account.

The environment in which policing operates

I was appointed Chief Constable of Greater Manchester Police (GMP) in 2008 and retired in 2015 having been a police officer for 34 years in five forces, serving 18 of those as a chief officer.

British policing at that time was under a national performance system which compared not only each police force but every district command unit in national league tables against nationally set criteria. Greater Manchester had a history of always being close to the bottom of that table leading with threats of intervention from the Inspectorate and Police Standards Unit; see, for example, evidence given at the time to the Select Committee on Home Affairs (2004). As a result, the force was obsessed with a target culture enforced though a monthly Compstat-like process which at its worst had led to a bullying culture and a range of unethical behaviours to achieve the required statistical count.

Big city policing produces big powerful cultures. The constant stream of big events, the enduring fight against organised criminals, the violence of the night-time economy, the gap between the shiny city centre and the distressed, deprived inner city neighbourhoods, the feeling of siege mentality and the macho political scene, all created the environment for policing. For Greater Manchester Police it meant that it was policing the big soccer matches, the high-profile crimes and the protests that took prominence, shaping a command and control mindset. Greater Manchester is made up of the city of Manchester itself and eight adjoining boroughs covering a resident population of 2.7 million people. Each of the boroughs has a distinctive history and culture but it also meant that the commanders of each borough saw them as their own fiefdom, with some taking a 'pick and mix' attitude to which parts of force policy they chose to adopt. I inherited a situation, as Shein puts it, *'where there was explicit tension between what the "centre" needed and what the disparate commanders believed they wanted'* (Schein, 2010, p 7).

It is easy for a leader particularly a new one to be naïve about the power of cultures and to live in a management bubble seeing what they want to see and hearing what those close to them think they would like to hear. As Schein states, *'Culture can be studied at three levels – the level of its artefacts, the level of its espoused beliefs and values, and the level of its basic underlying assumptions'* (Schein, 2010, p 32). In an organisation like policing operating 24 hours a day across a large number of sites with a spread of functions and a workforce with a relatively low level of turnover, cultures are almost designed to resist change and challenge. The day-to-day reality of policing, the trauma and the extreme events, the feeling of vulnerability, the power but also the powerlessness, the quasi-military rank system all play their part. Leaders stay for relatively short periods of time and staff may view their arrival with insouciance believing that if they keep their heads down, they will eventually move on and while the tower might wobble a little it will revert to its original position.

REFLECTIVE PRACTICE

- Considering the particular characteristics of police culture and the environment in which it operates, to what extent do you believe you can positively influence the working climate in the teams under your leadership?

Start with yourself

Before you take up a senior leadership position and certainly before you embark on a significant change programme you need to start with yourself and take appropriate time-out to reflect on three fundamental questions:

1. **Who am I?** What are my core values and my principles? What are my strengths and weaknesses? Where is my line in the sand and what would I resign over? Do I understand my own personality? What drives and excites me?

2. **What is my philosophy of policing?** What works to make people and societies safer? What achieves accountability and confidence in the police among the public? Where are the gaps in my expertise? Does evidence and research support my philosophy and how do I deal with conflicts?

3. **How do I believe you get things done in organisations?** How do you get the best out of its people? What is the best way to organise functions, manage risk, get decisions made and implemented? How do you ensure best use of resources and do I have the management expertise to lead all this? Am I aware of the gaps in my knowledge, experience and expertise?

> **REFLECTIVE PRACTICE**
>
> - Keep asking yourself the three questions above, particularly as you take up new positions and are faced with new challenges and critical events and your own self-awareness and learning develops.
>
> - Are you clear on your own thinking and feelings about these three key questions?

Having outlined the background I faced when taking up the post of Chief Constable and the foundation of self-knowledge I believe a leader needs to start with, I will now describe what I see as the key elements which set climate and the journey of change, I embarked upon.

The key elements that set climate

In my experience, to achieve meaningful cultural change in an organisation, that is the climate that shapes what staff do and how they do it, you need to address the following key elements of organisational practice:

- structures;
- systems;
- competencies;
- attitudes;
- behaviours.

Orientation and case building

If you believe that significant change is required to the way an organisation works, you are going to have to spend time diagnosing the issues that set the existing climate, getting your evidence together and then building support and enthusiasm. To this end, *the journey is part of your destination* in that where you go, who you speak to, who you don't speak to and the questions you ask will shape your thinking. If you are new to an organisation you have a limited amount of time where you have the detached objectivity of the outsider.

Before you take up a senior leadership post, staff will have made predictions and assumptions about what you think and what you are going to do and may have pigeonholed you into a particular policing camp. You need the data and evidence to inform and illuminate your case. In my instance I took advantage of a programme promoted at the time by the Home Office working with KPMG to introduce 'lean' processes and systems thinking into policing. This put numbers behind the enormous frustration many officers felt about the inefficiency of force systems. An examination of the crime investigation system, for instance, measured the delays, backlogs, multiple interventions by gatekeepers and the way the system allowed offenders to commit serial offences before they were brought to book. We displayed the flowchart on the four walls of Pendleton Police Station so everyone could visit and see the evidence and absorb this way of thinking and costing activity in a particularly graphic way.

Creating a sense of common purpose

An initial discussion with my fellow chief officers immediately showed that there was no agreed philosophy of what works in policing, what was the espoused policing style within GMP and our values and beliefs as leaders.

As time has gone on I have realised that this is the crucial starting point for any change programme and critical to creating climate. This is the foundation upon which you build and the firmer that foundation the stronger and more resilient will be the climate you create and the consequent service the public receive. The more I have experienced other organisations in a range of sectors the more convinced I have been of this point. As I used to say to staff, 'You don't go to MacDonald's for a prawn sandwich'. Like it or not, you know the sort of food MacDonald's offers and the values they espouse even down to the way they recognise their staff. If purpose and values are unclear, your organisation can be blown in the wind, thrown off course by short-term initiatives, the latest critical incident and adverse news story. So, this is about defining your purpose, defining the way you will achieve your purpose and for me the way you will take your staff with you while getting the best out of them. This involves having difficult conversations on leadership style, openness and transparency. It also requires a commitment to fairness and equality and the way actions will match words and how this leadership style will be modelled from the top.

You have to allow staff time to reconnect with their sense of vocation and talk about what is really important to them in policing and the public to which they are accountable. In the book *Leadership 2030* (Vielmetter and Sell, 2018) the chapter on altrocentric leadership provides, '*Meaning is co-created, which promotes a shared understanding of "why we are here": the purpose, direction, and goals of the organisation*'. Despite what might have been seen as more urgent demands, we spent considerable time creating a new narrative of professionalism and belief in our people and the communities we served. We presented this narrative to the whole force with line managers talking to their own staff through the process and starting a two-way conversation to create a momentum and indeed an excitement behind significant change. What does not work is producing new value statements and putting them on posters or screen savers unless staff see these beliefs translated into changed systems and decision-making that they and the public can see are making a difference in their day-to-day reality.

> **REFLECTIVE PRACTICE**
>
> - Reflect on whether your team has a common sense of purpose and a shared philosophy of what works in policing which affects the way they carry out their work day-to-day.
>
> - What ways do you think are most effective in creating and sharing a shared vision?

Introducing structural change to the policing system

Drawing on the data, previous experience and the ideas I had received on the journey, I began the process of replacing the time-based response policing approach with a place-based neighbourhood policing system. This meant giving priority to local policing teams led by inspectors with a focus on community engagement and building public confidence in the police. Further, it focused upon gathering intelligence at the local level, while prioritising problem solving over speed of response and established community trust and confidence as the prime performance target. I took the size of response teams down to the lowest safe level to release resources to neighbourhood teams.

Significant change produces supporters and detractors. As Dweck says,

> Sure, we found that people greatly misestimated their performance and their ability. But it was those with a fixed mindset who accounted for almost all the inaccuracy. The people with the growth mindset were amazingly accurate.
>
> (Dweck, 2006, p 11)

Policing has always involved the balance between geography, specialism and time. Determining how much goes into emergency response, place-based teams and teams with particular expertise and the balance between these different structures and associated systems shape internal culture. At a very early stage I drew experienced, operational detectives into my change team and some became messianic in their passion for challenging the accepted way of thinking and doing things. That said, the increasing complexity of policing, the sheer range of specialism required, the breadth of the mission meant this challenge never went away.

The crucial importance of alignment

For so many staff, in so many organisations, there is a huge gap between the reality espoused by senior management – or that distance place called headquarters – and the practicalities they experience in their daily working life. For me as a police officer this started my first day at a police station when I was told *'Forget all you were taught in training school we will show you how you really do the job'*. The management pronouncements, the words on the posters just don't match the tasks they have to do, the systems that have to work with and the frustrations they experience day to day.

So, for me one of the neglected words in leadership philosophy is *alignment* or to use another word *congruence*. Alignment between the systems, the processes or to use another phrase *'the way things are done around here'* (Schein's (2010) terminology). If senior management cannot create this alignment, chose to deny the reality, cannot deliver working IT or a vehicle or ensure other agencies meet their obligations, then, as a former Chief Constable of mine used to say, *'Why would you have us?'*

CASE STUDY

I introduced a system of hubs on each district drawing together intelligence and demand information with a morning meeting led by the district commander to set priorities with what we called 'pace setters' during the day to check on progress and maintain momentum. Some commanders told me that they did not 'do tactics' because their role was strategic so I had to disabuse them and remind them of the prime responsibility of leadership, to set direction, take responsibility and to make sense of a complex world for staff. Their role was not just to send an unachievable workload down the pipe and require operational staff to make sense of the demands. Crucial to this change in climate was the involvement of staff, the consultation on priorities and tactics and promotion of the philosophy of tasks being driven by data and the level of threat, harm and risk. The recurring word running through the system had to be 'why'.

Shaping the competencies of staff

Structures and systems shape the competencies that staff value, look to develop and exhibit. Of course, formal training courses play a crucial role in providing the knowledge, skills and expertise that staff need. But just as importantly competencies come from staff working to an agreed purpose in line with their own vocation and with systems aligned to that purpose and vocation. Goleman (1998) uses a helpful phrase *'The great divide in competencies lies between the mind and the heart, or, more technically between cognition and emotion'* (Goleman, 1998, p 23). To reinforce this, as a leader you have to create the conditions for staff to reflect on what they are doing and why, to constantly think about their use of time and effort and to build review and debriefing into the daily routine.

Data and evidence-informed professional practice, the thirst for problem solving rather than just reaction and the ability of staff to challenge and take responsibility themselves drive reflective practice.

> **CASE STUDY**
>
> We had to move the focus from how quickly we answered a call and responded to an incident to whether we actually solved the problem the caller was complaining of, working with the other agencies and local people. This meant in turn that I made it clear to neighbourhood inspectors that I would judge them on whether they were aware of their repeat calls and the action they were taking to deal with them and reinforced that during my local visits. Again, it is the questions you ask as a senior leader that shape culture and the answers you receive and reflect upon that should cause you to constantly check your compass and consider whether you need to adjust your route or stop off to spend more time on particular elements which do not appear to be shifting as you anticipated.

REFLECTIVE PRACTICE

- In your own day-to-day working environment, what are the systems, structures and competencies which are well aligned and where is there dissonance?

- Is your view the same as the staff at different levels and functions in your organisation?

Structures, systems and competencies shape attitudes and behaviours

In my experience one of the most neglected leadership skills is *persistence*. The espoused culture and the weight of the organisation will try and fight back to return to the prior norm because that it is what staff and their leaders have been used to and what has been valued and recognised. So often it is very difficult to transform the traditional target culture of an organisation because it is within these beliefs and norms that staff and leaders have proved themselves.

Organisations need targets and goals but what they don't need is this being measured by simplistic numerical measures rather than outcomes for the public. Years into my time at GMP I still found leaders surreptitiously setting numerical targets on issues like stop and search. For some it was the only leadership style they knew and they needed to be coached to develop a new one. Another key element of change was the way the organisation treated its staff. If I wanted staff to treat the public with respect, there had to be the alignment with the way that the organisation treated them particularly when they were going through a difficult time. Too often I found that what was espoused was compliance with a HR (even that term 'Human Resource'!!) process rather than seeing the member of staff as an individual with specific needs and sometimes complex private lives.

The test in particular is how you deal with staff from minority groups, those who are different and challenge accepted attitudes and ways of doing things. Your ability to create the climate where every member of staff can bring all of themselves to the workplace and don't have to leave anything behind is paramount. For you as a leader your own attitudes and reality will only change if you go out and listen to the experiences of those staff and try to understand the impact of those experiences on them.

REFLECTIVE PRACTICE

- How much time do you spend on whatever constitutes the operational front line of your team?
- How open are you to difficult messages and do you really understand the day-to-day reality your staff face whatever your rhetoric?

What did I learn along the way?

I have described the key challenges I believe a leader has to address through their own self-knowledge, the case for change they build and then the core elements which have to be addressed and crucially aligned to shape climate and consequentially behaviours. I will now outline some of the key lessons I learnt in my own leadership journey of shaping climate.

Values have to endure in good times and bad

Two years into my time at GMP the Government announced severe cuts to policing budgets. This was an extreme shock to the organisation as the UK police service had seen over

30 years of year on year increases. *It was painful and personally traumatic* to lay off non-sworn staff and at one point I had to gather 3000 such personnel in a football stadium so that I could tell them directly and personally the fact that their jobs were now at risk. I also explained to them the way that fairly and transparently we were going to achieve these reductions in workforce.

The force, like a number of others, underwent a series of adverse cases where we had failed victims of sexual exploitation and domestic violence. It took me a long time to realise how the internal climate and culture and particularly what the organisation prized, celebrated and measured was working against us. When big, long established organisations come under media, political and public scrutiny most become defensive and more concerned about protecting reputations than acknowledging failures and more importantly ensuring the underlying weaknesses are addressed.

It took a senior female colleague to point out the enormous conflict between what we said and what we did and how again processes, lack of competency and attitudes shaped behaviours. The statistical performance regime had been focused around property crime because it was easier to measure and gave staff the message that theft of a vehicle carried more weight than a sexual assault. The focus of the Serious Crime Division was largely on armed robbers and organised crime gangs many incredibly violent but the same priority was not given to rapists, abusers and serious sex offenders. There was a tendency to stereotype if not blame victims, aided and abetted by a prosecution service reluctant to take forward difficult cases and a court system which too often added to rather than assuaged the trauma victims had gone through. Again, connecting with a values-based approach, I chose a structural change option and create a new Vulnerable Persons Division even though my overall budget was being cut and make further fundamental changes to the measurement and tasking systems. This was to shape the competencies and attitudes of officers with a very strong abiding message – the prime aim of the force is protecting vulnerable people. Sounds simple and obvious but we were a long way off it and our words did not match what officers were asked to do day to day and the questions they were asked by those in command.

Bring staff with you

As you drive through change plans it is inevitable there will be some who openly or covertly try to undermine the message for good motives or bad despite all your efforts to engage, explain and encourage. Change is unsettling and some will disagree philosophically but others will see it as a threat to their position of power, future prospects or even continued employment.

In big organisations many staff feel their own talent and contribution are not valued and there is too little room for innovation and their own ideas and initiatives and challenge are ignored or frustrated. There is a huge dilemma between achieving tighter adherence to standards and regulations in a more heavily regulated environment and how you allow staff the flexibility of trying different approaches and exercising their own judgement. This was not just about rank and hierarchy but the manner in which the divisional structure of the force got in the way of senior commanders being involved or indeed taking responsibility for the strategic direction of the force. Too many layers of decision-making create opportunities for one level to undermine another deliberately or inadvertently. This can result in too many who see strategic leadership in an organisation facing severe financial and operational challenges as a spectator sport. You have to make it clear that no one has the luxury of sitting at the back of the room in sullen silence or muttering in disagreement to fellow sceptics, people need to speak up and contribute their plan if they object to yours.

REFLECTIVE PRACTICE

- Reflect upon what a leader can do to create the framework for staff to operate in which manages this balance between the need to manage risk and comply with regulations and standards and creating a dynamic environment which allows them to use their discretion and judgement.

Food for the journey

The path of change is exhausting and sometimes traumatic with many bumps and barriers along the way. You need high-energy food provided by a strong set of personal values, people who love you and a life outside the police force. You need to be confident in your own integrity and listen and react to that little voice in your head that tells you when something feels wrong. You need focus and remain so, upon those three basic questions of who you are, what you believe in policing and how you make things happen. You need to be honest when you make mistakes or your judgement is flawed. You need to be accountable and accessible to your staff, the media and the public. You need to have the confidence to show yourself as a human being behind the uniform and not take yourself too seriously.

Your inner circle

In the big wide world of policing and in an organisation of hundreds of people undergoing change the most important team is the group right around you, your own senior unit of chief officers. Too much agreement and cohesiveness and complacency is dangerous, too much dissension, conflict, personality differences and power games will fatally wound all you do and will be eagerly watched and gossiped about by the next level down and indeed the whole force. You have to dedicate time to building and maintaining that team.

Keep in touch with the ground

However busy your diary, you have to carve out time for getting out to the operational front line wherever that may be, spending time with your staff serving the public and getting out in local communities. You have to constantly check out the space between your own rhetoric and the reality of what is happening. There is nothing more powerful in a management meeting than saying *'When I was out on patrol last night I saw …'*. There is little more impactive to operationally credible staff.

Communication

You have to be a good communicator, you have to be a bit of a performer, an actor who can deliver the soliloquy, who is comfortable with and who seeks out the media, who can stand in front of a ground of operational staff and create order and focus out of a complex world. You have to use all the tools of social media but also live with the transparency and constant challenge back that this will generate. One of the best bits of advice I got when driving change is to draw up your communication plan then multiply the effort at least five times.

Community is the foundation

I have not gone into great detail regards my operational policing strategy as this is a paper about driving internal cultural change, but it is your day-to-day policing practice which shapes the climate. My core policing belief is that the life blood of policing is local intelligence coming from the local people gathered by local staff who know and understand that community. *Big city policing can look like control and enforcement but I needed it to look like service and protection*. When I made the staffing cuts there was only one part of the workforce I did not cut, our Police Community Support Officers unsworn but uniformed colleagues who spent all their time visible in local neighbourhoods building relationships and gathering intelligence. Without community confidence and standing alongside local people in difficult times and showing a commitment to work with them to change their circumstances policing is built on sand.

The high risk end of the business

In big city policing it is inevitable you develop hard wired specialisms to deal with serious crime, specialist operations and counter terrorism. These activities are crucial to the reputation of the organisation. Fail in one of these and you are highly vulnerable and people die. On the other hand, specialism has an uncomfortable relationship with elitism and specialist units inevitably have people who have served there a long time and the culture can resist 'outsiders' moving in.

In leadership there is a danger that you concentrate on those functions that you know the best, are most visible or you feel most comfortable interacting with. To achieve the congruence, I have argued for, you have to address the whole organisation and have the courage to ask challenging questions and to go into areas that you are unfamiliar with. Specialist staff may do serious things away from the most visible parts of policing but it is about the way they do it and the accountability they demonstrate and their passion for the intelligence led, evidence-driven approach I was promoting. To give an example, the national counter terrorist command puts working with communities at the heart of all it does. On another level, for me it was about a photo of one of our most highly skilled firearms officers engaging with the public and stooping down to talk to a small boy who was clearly fascinated by his presence.

CHAPTER SUMMARY

Police forces particularly big city forces are wonderful things when you see them handling major events, convicting major criminals and just day-to-day coping with everything a dynamic, diverse metropolis can throw at them 24 hours a day. We take for granted that policing never closes, it never has a day off and it is a remarkable thing. The downside is that when policing goes wrong, when it errs in its priorities and when it uses its power in an unethical way it is extremely dangerous for the public. Further, it is particularly the vulnerable and those staff who chose to oppose the prevailing view that face the greatest danger.

In summary, I have outlined the importance of aligning Structure, Systems, Competencies, Behaviours Attitudes and how *you have to work through all of these*. I had to change the structure of the force and dismantle powerbases. I had to change systems particularly the way that we delivered local policing, the way it was tasked and coordinated and crucially the way it was measured. I had to change the competencies I expected of my staff favouring professional practice over hierarchy and changing what I expected them to do and the skills prized by the force. This in turn changed behaviours to a more problem solving evidence-based policing style working in an integrated way with other public services to ultimately make Greater Manchester a safer and a better place. Staff working on an agenda wider than just crime and policing but on issues of social justice and community cohesion but with protecting vulnerable people at the heart of all we did. This ultimately changed attitudes which hopefully made the whole effort in the long term self-sustaining.

When I look back I realise how *you have to be ambitious and radical*. To be critical of myself, I did not show enough courage and I underestimated how deep some of the beliefs, motives and practices were and how much effort and determination would be required to shift them.

Big organisations, particularly those working around the clock, have a life of their own and there is a whole series of alternative cultures which kick in when they think the senior leadership has gone home. If you don't address the fundamentals you will

> be regarded just as someone passing by, someone just taking a dip and the ripples you create will disappear as the waves crash in and the steady state re-establishes itself. On the other hand, when you experience changed attitudes, professionally driven operational success and staff reinvigorated with a new sense of mission and purpose, there is no other feeling like it in the world.

Further reading

Home Affairs Select Committee (2018) *Policing for the Future: Report of Home Affairs Select Committee*. London: Parliamentary Publications.

Leary-Joyce, J (2009) *The Psychology of Success Secrets of Serial Achievement*. London: Pearson.

Middleton, J (2007) *Beyond Authority Leadership in a Changing World*. Basingstoke: Palgrave MacMillan.

Smith, J (2013) *Leadership Resilience Lessons for Leaders from the Policing Frontline*. Farnham: Charles G Gower Publishing.

Wageman, R, Nunes, D A, Buruss, J A and Hackman, J R (2008) *Senior Leadership Teams What It Takes to Make Them*. Great Boston: Harvard Business School Press.

References

College of Policing (2014) Code of Ethics. Available at: https://www.college.police.uk/ethics/code-of-ethics (accessed 26 February 2021).

Dweck, C S (2006) *Mindset: The New Psychology of Success*. New York: Random House.

Eisenhower, D (1954) Leadership/Organisation. Available at: https://www.eisenhowerlibrary.gov/eisenhowers/quotes#Leadership (accessed 26 February 2021).

Goleman, D (1998) *Working With Emotional Intelligence*. London: Bloomsbury Publishing.

Home Affairs Committee (2004) Police Reform, Evidence Given. Available at: https://publications.parliament.uk/pa/cm200405/cmselect/cmhaff/370/4101203.htm (accessed 26 February 2021).

Shein, E H (2010) *Organisational Culture and Leadership*, 4th ed. San Francisco, CA: Josey-Bass.

Vielmetter, G and Sell, Y (2018) *Leadership 2030: The Six Megatrends You Need to Understand to Lead Your Company into the Future*. New York: Amacom/HarperCollins.

12 Ethics, values and standards

Judith K Gillespie

CHAPTER OBJECTIVES

This chapter will help you:

- understand the terms ethics, values and standards;
- challenge yourself to reflect on your own values and standards, and the struggle to be consistent with these;
- understand how ethics and values influence your behaviours and decision-making;
- appreciate that ethical leadership can come at a cost, and coping strategies to survive.

Introduction

In considering this important section of the book I have asked myself the question, "What gives me the right to compose a chapter on Ethics, Values and Standards?" It is most certainly not because I am a recognised expert in this field, although I was privileged to be a member of the former Association of Chief Police Officers Ethics Committee, to contribute to the Police Service of Northern Ireland (PSNI) Code of Ethics when it was being written in 2003, and to the Garda Síochána Code of Ethics in 2015. Neither is it because I hold some remarkable virtue of character which permits me to expound on the subject (which I most emphatically do not), nor because I have any particular burning desire to do so. Indeed in the context of an ongoing global pandemic where medical professionals are making the most difficult choices imaginable, it is easy to feel completely unqualified to comment on this subject.

My interest in this area comes from the everyday dilemmas I have faced as a police officer of 32 years' experience in Northern Ireland. This was both as a member of the Royal Ulster Constabulary (GC) and including ten years as a member of the Command Team in PSNI up until 2014 – a time when the organisation was navigating unprecedented, transformational change. It comes from five years' experience as a member of the Policing Authority of the Garda Síochána from its inception in January 2016 until the end of 2020. It comes from the challenging decisions and judgements that police leaders, at every level and in every role, are required to make. It is found in the continual human struggle of reflecting on my own values, beliefs and behaviour, and the constant effort to ensure that I, and the organisation that I helped to lead, consistently exemplified high standards of ethical conduct that would withstand scrutiny of every kind imaginable. The PSNI has been described as the most accountable police service in the European Union (Murphy, 2018) and one of the world's most accountable police services (Topping, 2016). So while organisational ethics, values and standards are central to public confidence in any police service, they are absolutely critical in Northern Ireland.

What do I mean by ethics, values and standards? At its most basic level, I see ethics as a set of principles which guide everyday behaviours and decisions, derived from your values. In particular, ethics can guide judgement and decision-making when there is no policy, procedure or precedent – something which police officers and staff will all be familiar with, at various stages in their careers. There is a strong connection between ethics and character, striving to behave in a consistent way, and a commitment to acting with integrity.

What do I mean by values? Values are characteristics and concepts that we think are more important than others, such as integrity, courage, compassion, humility, diligence, respect for human dignity and kindness. There is no one right set of personal values. Everyone has their own, shaped by their upbringing, culture, socialisation and life experience. In the metaphorical layers of the onion, your personal values are right at the core of your identity, and only change when a very significant life event or disruption happens – such as a bereavement, or the birth of a child, or the break-up of a stable relationship. Most professions and organisations nowadays have stated values, also shaped by organisational experience and operating context. Difficulties arise when our personal values are not consonant with those of the organisation, or when an organisation's stated values are not consistent with the organisation's behaviour. In diverse organisations it is also important to be sensitive to the values of others and not to assume that they are the same as our own. These principles are especially relevant for those in positions of leadership at all levels in the police service.

> *When you have a clear understanding of your values and their relative importance, you can establish the principles by which you intend to lead. Leadership principles are values translated into action.*
>
> (George and Sims, 2007)

If you're not sure what your core values are, ask yourself the question *'What would cause me to resign from my job?'* You may not know for certain what your values are until they are in conflict. For example, loyalty to an organisation or team, and personal integrity can often cause conflict. Some of the most outstanding examples of ethical leadership I have witnessed have come from police constables and staff who have remained true to their ethical principles and values despite considerable peer pressure to do otherwise.

Finally, standards are benchmarks for acceptable behaviour that we have established for ourselves, or which have been established by our organisation. They set boundaries or limits on our actions. Again, difficulties may arise when these standards differ. Arguably, standards might have a more tangible, practical appearance than ethics and values – but each is most certainly influenced by the other. Many commentators have described policing as an honourable profession, and one of which the public expect the highest standards of conduct and practice. The public also expect that at the very least, police officers and staff will, at all times, respect the same rules that the public themselves are required to abide by. They further expect that their standards of behaviour will not only be in accordance with the law, but that they will also be ethical.

REFLECTIVE PRACTICE

- List the values that are important to you.
- Which of these are not-negotiable, under any circumstance?
- Would others know what they were?
- What has helped to shape these values, and would you envisage them ever changing?
- What do you see as your personal ethical principles?
- Have you come across a situation where your ethics, values or standards have differed from your organisation's?
- How did you resolve this dilemma?
- What learning have you gained from this experience?

The constant struggle

The best piece of career advice I was ever given was *'To thine own self be true'* – a well-known quote from Shakespeare's *Hamlet*. This exhortation exemplifies the constant struggle to behave ethically, to be consistent with your own values, to set high standards of behaviour and to strive to achieve these standards every day, even if sometimes you fall short. In struggling to do so you can live more comfortably with yourself and the decisions you make, even in the most challenging contexts. I use the word 'struggle' deliberately because what is at stake is important, there are most certainly competing forces at play, and despite considerable effort there is a risk that the ethical standard won't be achieved. That is not to say that making mistakes or failing is unethical – quite the opposite. Early acknowledgement of your mistakes and being diligent in addressing your failures are good examples of ethical behaviour.

I have often reflected on my very first shift on mobile patrol as a young RUC Probationary Constable in North Belfast in 1982, at the height of the Troubles. I was 19 years old, on night duty, in uniform, accompanied by an older male RUC Reserve colleague. Apart from responding to a variety of calls, we had a series of security-related vehicle check points to perform. As I stepped into the middle of the road with my red torch, signalling to vehicles to stop in the darkness, I was suddenly aware of the power vested in me as a police officer. This included the power to interfere with and delay ordinary people's journeys, question their movements, intrude on their privacy, deprive them of their liberty and use force in a variety of forms. In the United Kingdom, as in many other jurisdictions, society consents to the use of these powers and trusts that they will be used for the common good. The members of the motoring public whom I stopped that night had no idea that this was my first turn of duty. They had no idea of my naivety and my lack of confidence. All they saw was the uniform and the red torch signalling for them to stop. But that encounter was a moment where I had the power to make a positive or a negative impression of the organisation I represented, with a public whose support for the organisation I represented was never a given.

In those everyday encounters, police officers and staff are probably least supervised and have most autonomy. It is then that a framework of ethics, values and standards is most important. Just because we have the power to do something, or because an action is legally permissible and in compliance with organisational policy, doesn't always make it appropriate in every context. There has to be a higher, ethical standard applied. Deciding, for example, whether to exercise discretion in minor infringements of the law, to use a power of arrest or search, to accept trivial gifts, hospitality or privileged access to events, to share sensitive information, or to engage in an external business interest can all raise ethical issues even when clear organisational policies are in place. One of the most important recommendations of the Independent Commission on Policing in Northern Ireland (known as the Patten Commission after its Chair, Chris Patten who was formerly Governor of Hong Kong and a UK Cabinet Minister) was that '*a new Code of Ethics should replace the existing largely procedural code, integrating the European Convention on Human Rights into police practice*' (Patten, 1999). This was the first such Code to be introduced on these islands in 2003, and contained a set of high-level principles and standards by which police behaviour would be assessed. Yet even with a clear set of ethical principles, there remains an element of personal and professional judgement to be applied. It is here where the constant struggle is most evident.

It is of course important to have good policies, procedures and controls to ensure strong governance and accountability in any organisation. However, a commitment to strong ethical principles is equally if not more important. It goes beyond mere compliance to 'get by' with the bare minimum, or to avoid getting caught in the act of wrongdoing. It speaks to a higher level motivation of striving to do the very best at all times, even though sometimes we fall short of our own standards. For example, I confess that I don't know any senior police officer who joined the service primarily to ensure good audit processes, and systems of internal control. But I do know many senior officers and staff who appeared to put as much energy and commitment into this part of their role as they did into the operational side of the business. This is because they weren't just complying with good governance standards. They recognised the struggle, the ethical dilemmas and public confidence issues in decisions regarding resources, managing people, procurement, data collection, IT and capital investment, and they were committed to ensuring the most effective everyday stewardship of the multi-million pound organisations they led. The struggle to behave ethically is equally important in these areas as it is in the more visible, and perhaps arguably more appealing, operational side of the role.

Applying ethics, values and standards to policing decisions

I had the privilege of attending the FBI National Executive Institute Programme in 2012. As part of this training we visited the US Holocaust Memorial Museum in Washington. This was a reminder, as if one was ever needed, of how – in extremis – policing can play a key role in vindicating or suppressing human rights. Our attention was drawn to an iconic photograph taken circa 1935, which showed a local community police officer in uniform patrolling with an SS officer who was accompanied by a muzzled, snarling dog. A Holocaust survivor explained to the group how the local, well-known and recognised police officer was used, initially at least, to give the SS officer the cover of acceptability and to gain community trust. The image resonated deeply with me, and like many others, I found myself questioning how I might have responded in those extreme circumstances. That was the point of the exercise – to remind us as a group of senior international police officers of how our actions and inactions can have grave consequences. It is true that the biggest test of values is in a crisis.

It is also true to say that in modern policing of liberal democracies there is little that will be hidden from public view for ever. The development of social media and mobile telephony have revolutionised how we communicate, and images of police action or inaction can be instantly transmitted to a global audience. Independent complaint investigations and Freedom of Information, Data Protection and Human Rights legislation have all contributed to a context where police action, decisions and record keeping are subject to rigorous scrutiny before, during and after the event. In many communities, trust and confidence in the police service has to be earned through many years of hard work, but can be easily lost in a few seconds of ill-judged police action or inaction. Everyone therefore needs to understand at all times the connection between the snapshot of their individual behaviour, and building longer-term public trust and confidence.

Reflective practice

- What impact does this relentless scrutiny have on your behaviour and decisions?
- Does this impact change in times of acute or prolonged stress?

FirearmsDespite considerable progress in peace-building in Northern Ireland, the PSNI remains a routinely armed police service. In addition to the availability of Armed Response Units, local patrol officers carry personal protection weapons both on and off duty as the threat from violent Dissident Republicans remains severe. This is illustrated by continuing attacks on PSNI officers, both on and off duty. Loyalist paramilitary activity also continues in some areas. Yet it is fair to say that lethal force is comparatively rarely used by PSNI officers. This can be explained in part by individual leadership, by training which emphasises ethical and human rights standards, by independent investigation of complaints, and by accountability through a Policing Board advised by a Human Rights Advisor who has unfettered access to operational planning and intelligence. Indeed from the period between April 2008 and March 2020, firearms were discharged by PSNI officers 12 times, and only once between April 2017 and March 2020 (PSNI, 2020). For a routinely armed service of roughly 7000 officers operating in a severe threat context, this is significant. I have experienced meticulous planning of overt and covert operations, taking specific Human Rights legal advice into consideration, but also applying the ethical lens to the potential use of force, including lethal force. These decisions involve fine balances and judgement calls where human life is at stake. I have seen tactical advisors and other team members speak up and offer courses of action to reduce the likelihood of having to resort to lethal force. Even though the circumstances might well have justified its use, thoughtful and sensitive planning has ensured that the likelihood of having to deploy a lethal option is minimised. I have equally observed ethical and proportionate responses to spontaneous firearms incidents and the conscious avoidance of armed confrontation (McAuley, 2009). In both circumstances I can say with certainty that lives have been saved as a result. As an important product of such proportionate responses, community confidence has been at the very least maintained and in many instances, enhanced (Department of Justice, 2019).

The point is that just because the law says you *can* use force, or deploy an intrusive tactic, or exercise a power of arrest or search doesn't mean that you *should*. Applying the *standard required by law is the minimum, not the maximum*. Additional ethical checks and balances through self-reflective, searching questions need to be considered.

The capacity to avoid groupthink and hear the voice of challenge is also important. How you objectively sense check your decisions, in particular in a homogenous team, can be especially relevant. Seeking out diverse mentors and critical friends can be of considerable assistance. A good guiding question to ask yourself is '*how would I feel if this entire decision, including conversations around it, was broadcast on the BBC News website?*' Finally, the Golden Rule of doing unto others as you would have them do unto you is one of the most easily recognisable tenets of ethical decision-making.

> **REFLECTIVE PRACTICE**
>
> - Can you think of an example where you were under pressure to use a police power, and chose not to?
> - What factors did you consider in your decision?

High-level principles can guide our behaviour and our decision-making, but they can rarely give us the "right" answer or help us 'do the right thing', as there is rarely one single 'right thing' to be done. My experience leads me to conclude that ethical decision-making is more about making the very best decisions you can in the circumstances, for the right reasons. How you do things and how you make decisions, are as important as what you do and what decisions you make. Often you cannot control the outcome of your decisions, but you can control the reasoning and motivation behind them. The underlying motivation and assessment process is as critical as the decision itself and its outcome. For example, when making a donation to a worthy cause some might be motivated by public recognition and praise from their friends, where others might be motivated by a private sense of duty. The end result is the same but the motivations are very different. When you are honest with yourself, and recognise and understand what really motivates you, you can identify potential traps which might cloud your thinking. *Ask yourself what you would require to be motivated to undertake the job, honestly, and listen to the answer ... What do you know about yourself? Don't over-estimate your self-knowledge* (Markkula, 2009).

The National Decision Model

The National Decision Model (College of Policing, 2013) devised by the College of Policing and building on the Conflict Management Model, rightly places values and ethics at its core. At each stage of the model the question is asked whether the action considered is consistent with the Code of Ethics, with what the public as a whole would expect and with what the police service would expect. When it comes to identifying and choosing options, asking key, open questions can help guide decision-making. I have found a number of questions particularly useful, and these fall under five broad headings:

1. which option will produce the most good and do the least harm (Utilitarian)
2. which option best respects the rights of stakeholders (Rights)
3. which option treats people fairly or proportionately (Justice)

4. which option best serves the community as a whole, not just some members (<u>Common good</u>)
5. which option leads me to act as the sort of person I want to be (<u>Virtue</u>)

Markkula Center for Applied Ethics (10)

Applying these questions doesn't produce the perfect, failsafe option, but it does help in assessing competing options through various ethical lenses which might give rise to additional considerations which help to make or support your decision. The Virtue question in particular links to motivation, being honest with yourself regarding what it is you are seeking to achieve, and why you are seeking to achieve it.

Barriers

Equally, there are some barriers which can prevent us from applying our ethical principles, values and standards. These recurring explanations are used to rationalise unethical behaviour or decisions.

- *If it's necessary, it's ethical - in other words, the end justifies the means*
- *The false necessity trap - the assertion 'I had no choice' when in fact other choices were available*
- *If it's legal and permissible, it must therefore be proper and acceptable*
- *It's just part of the job - separating job-related and personal ethics where fundamentally decent people sometimes feel justified doing things at work that they know otherwise to be wrong eg theft of office equipment/stationery*
- *It's for a good cause - blurring interpretations of deception, concealment, conflicts of interest, favouritism in the interests of an otherwise noble aim*
- *I was just doing it for you - eg little white lies, sacrificing honesty and respect for 'caring'. Would the person concerned thank you for the lie, or feel betrayed, patronised or manipulated?*
- *I'm just fighting fire with fire - the false assumption that unethical behaviour should be met with unethical behaviour such as promise-breaking and lying*
- *It doesn't hurt anyone - treating ethical obligations as just factors to be considered rather than ground rules*
- *Everyone's doing it - safety in numbers - uncritically treating cultural/ organisational behaviours as if they were ethical norms, just because they are norms*
- *It's OK if I don't gain personally - personal gain is not the only test of impropriety*

- *I've got it coming* - a minor perk/gratuity because you've worked so hard for so long
- *I can still be objective* - subtle ways in which gratitude, friendship, gifts, business interests and anticipation of future favours affect judgment

(Josephson Institute of Ethics, 11)

Reflective practice

- Which additional questions do you ask yourself to ensure your decisions or behaviour are ethical?
- What would others say motivates you?
- What risks do you foresee with your motivation?
- Who would you think of involving in sense-checking your decisions?
- Have you come across any of these rationalisations for what turned out to be unethical behaviour?
- How will you react if you hear any of these in future?

Case study 1

The 'Everybody's doing it' rationalisation

During the ten-year Patten transformational change programme from 2001 to 2011 as the fledgling PSNI emerged from the RUC, police officers with longer service were encouraged to take early retirement through an attractive voluntary severance package. This created headroom to recruit student officers in larger numbers. The composition of the service was a key challenge to community confidence, and a special (highly controversial) temporary derogation from equality legislation facilitated recruitment of new officers and staff into the PSNI on the basis of 50 per cent Catholic, 50 per cent non-Catholic background. This allowed the police composition of the organisation to change from 8 per cent Catholic in 2001 to over 30 per cent Catholic in 2011. When many, more experienced officers took voluntary severance, gaps emerged in some investigative and intelligence skills. This coincided with a heightening of the terrorist threat from violent Dissident Republicans which was, by February 2009, assessed as severe.

With the delegation of finance and human resource capacity to the local police Districts and Departments, some Commanders recruited retired officers through a recruitment agency, to fill short-term vacancies for a variety of administrative and some specialist posts. This practice is not unusual in UK police services. What was unique about the PSNI context was the voluntary severance package, and the 50:50 recruitment arrangements. I personally recall as a newly appointed District Commander in 2002 meeting a former police colleague who had availed of voluntary severance, in the corridor of my District Headquarters, and after exchanging pleasantries, I asked them what they were doing back in the station. When they told me that they were working on a short-term contract regarding back record conversion of data, and had been recruited though an agency, I walked away thinking that this did not feel good. Somewhat concerned, I phoned a respected and more experienced colleague to seek his advice on the matter. He quickly reassured me that it was absolutely fine, that most Districts and Departments were employing agency staff recruited through a contract with Human Resources Department, that many were former police officers, and there was nothing to worry about. So I did nothing, even though it still didn't feel good. I didn't stay true to my own values and ethical principles. In the years that followed, it was clear that the use of agency staff in the form of retired police officers had become an accepted organisational norm.

Some years later in 2012 when I was Deputy Chief Constable, a significant and well publicised community confidence crisis arose when it emerged in the media that many hundreds of officers who had left the PSNI under the voluntary severance scheme were employed as short-term associate staff. This is not to be read in any way as a criticism of those individuals, the vast majority of whom fulfilled their respective functions with integrity, professionalism and diligence. Looking at each individual case in isolation and on its own merits may have led many to conclude that the practice of using agency staff was justified. However, standing back and applying the external lens to the whole picture engendered a different perspective. The key trust and confidence issues which the organisation as a whole (myself included) had missed were the perception of a conspiracy to undermine the whole transformational change programme; the cumulative effect of all of these individuals taken together on the organisation's composition; the understandable perception of 'jobs for the boys'; the impact on some permanent police staff who were paid less for similar work; the apparent blocking of some potential recruitment opportunities for younger permanent staff; and the perception by some stakeholders of the 'dark side' of covert policing continuing to be controlled by the RUC. This resulted in a number of difficult Public Accounts Committee sessions in October 2012, examining the corporate governance and financial regularity of the use of Agency Staff in the PSNI. All of this was entirely avoidable, if only more people like me had been true to themselves and their values, had put their hand up and had called the process out at that earlier stage, before it had got to the point of a public confidence crisis. We might just have caused the organisation to reflect on the bigger picture, and avoided a lot of pain.

So just because everyone else is doing it does not always mean that others will see it as acceptable, ethical or right.

CASE STUDY 2

Personal cost

Ethical behaviour and decision-making can often come at some personal cost and in sharing the following experience, I am conscious that it is impossible in a short chapter to explain the subtleties of policing a divided society, and the nuances which people who grow up in Northern Ireland automatically absorb. In the zero sum game which characterises Northern Ireland politics, what is perceived as a gain by one side is more often than not seen as a loss by the other. Therefore reaching out to one side of the community is interpreted as a slight on the other. It is a very fine line that must be walked by an impartial police service in any context, but particularly so in Northern Ireland.

While I was Deputy Chief Constable and (among many other things) Diversity Champion for the organisation, I was always keen to embrace the growing diversity within the organisation and Northern Ireland society as a whole. While attending a PSNI graduation ceremony, I met a student officer who had chosen the Irish form of their name on their name badge. As I never learnt Irish, I had to ask the student for some help in pronouncing their name. In light of this very unremarkable encounter, I resolved to learn to read some Irish, so that I might at least be able to pass myself in similar situations in the future. I was striving to be true to my values, including respect for human dignity.

It is true that the Irish language is perceived by some as divisive in Northern Ireland, as it became highly politicised during the Troubles and many would say was 'weaponised' by Irish Republicans. In recent years there has been some progress in de-politicising the language, not least through the efforts of some high-profile individuals from the Unionist community. That student officers in PSNI should feel confident displaying their name in its Irish form on their uniform was significant progress in itself, as far as I was concerned. However, my learning to speak and read some basic Irish (and therefore being seen to benefit Republicans/Nationalists) was interpreted as a loss for Loyalists/Unionists, and further evidence of the perceived 'greening' of the PSNI – a term used to describe the perception of a concerted political strategy to render the organisation more Nationalist/Republican in its ethos.

As a result, a hideous campaign of social media abuse, and slurs on my personal integrity emerged mainly, but not exclusively, from Loyalist sources. I am very thankful to say that none of this vile abuse found its way into the mainstream media, leading some to conclude that I must have had a so-called Super Injunction to prevent its publication – which I did not. The challenge was how to continue to represent the organisation with professionalism and impartiality at the highest levels, while an insidious whispering campaign was continuing, undermining confidence in my integrity. The abuse also had a considerable impact on my immediate family, not least when offensive graffiti appeared near my home.

Unfortunately many accept this type of abuse to be part and parcel of public life, and in particular for women in high-profile positions. The temptation was to fight fire with fire (see barriers to ethical decision-making above!), but the advice from many of my colleagues was simply to ignore it – it was part of the job (again, see above) – and it would eventually go away. Needless to say it didn't go away, and over the course of a year it gradually deteriorated in its explicit nature as it grew in momentum. I had to consider the impact on my family, my colleagues, my organisation, on community confidence and the longer term, wider impact on those who were more vulnerable and less resilient than me to this kind of abuse. Eventually the ethical thing to do was to instigate criminal investigations, where possible, against the authors of those posts which had crossed the obscene communications threshold, and to take civil action against those authors of posts which were clearly defamatory. Cases were reported to the Public Prosecution Service, significant sums of money were paid to charities supporting women and apologies were posted as part of settlements. But the whole experience taught me much about my values. I valued my reputation for impartiality and integrity more highly than others. I was not prepared to have it impugned without consequence. I wanted to act ethically. And I learnt when it comes to social media, sometimes silence is more eloquent than words.

I also learnt a lot about personal resilience, and about keeping things in perspective. I learnt about holding my head high in the knowledge that those whose opinions I valued and who knew me well, appreciated that the slurs were patently untrue and that the posts said more about the people posting them than they did about me. I received support from unexpected quarters, and a lack of support from expected quarters. But the most important lesson for me was to look after your 'anchors' before the storm comes. My anchors were my faith, family, friends, fitness and fun. Without these, the storm would have been much more damaging. Life's roughest storms prove the strength of your anchors, so it is essential to keep them strong before the storm comes.

Chapter summary

For anyone at any level who struggles with complex ethical decisions, my advice remains simply this: to thine own self be true. This is the same for a Police Constable as it is for a Chief Constable. Know who you are and what you stand for. Yes, it is a constant struggle, and sometimes you'll fail or fall short, but the greater rewards undoubtedly make the effort worthwhile.

> *The whole course of human history may depend on a change of heart in one solitary and even humble individual — for it is in the solitary mind and soul of the individual that the battle between good and evil is waged and ultimately won or lost.*
> (M Scott Peck, 1936–2005)

Key points

- Values, ethics and standards guide our behaviour and decision-making.
- Values will be at their most powerful when they are consistent with the organisation's values, and when they are lived out every day in the organisation.
- Remaining consistently true to our own ethical standards is a constant struggle.
- Try to understand what your non-negotiable values are, and what truly motivates you.
- Use additional, reflective questions to ensure your decisions are ethical as well as lawful.
- Be careful of the rationalisations used to justify unethical behaviour.
- Ask yourself which of your values will help you to be resilient.
- Know your anchors, and look after them before the storm comes.

Further reading

George, B and Sims, P (2007) *True North: Discover Your Authentic Leadership*. New Jersey: Wiley.

Heifetz, R A and Linsky, M (2002) *Leadership on the Line: Staying Alive through the Dangers of Leading*. Massachusetts: Harvard Business School Press.

Hicks, D (2011) *Dignity: Its Essential Role in Resolving Conflict*. Connecticut: Yale University Press.

O'Shea, R (2016) *Leading with Integrity: A Practical Guide to Business Ethics Dublin*. Ireland: Institute of Chartered Accountants.

Peterson, J B (2019) *12 Rules for Life: An Antidote to Chaos*. London: Penguin.

Syed, M (2019) *Rebel Ideas: The Power of Diverse Thinking*. London: John Murray.

References

College of Policing (2013) National Decision Model, Authorised Professional Practice. Available at: https://www.app.college.police.uk/app-content/national-decision-model/the-national-decision-model/ (accessed 22 February 2021).

Department of Justice (2019) Perceptions of Policing and Justice: Findings from the 2017/18 Northern Ireland Crime Survey. Available at: https://www.justice-ni.gov.uk/news/perceptions-policing-and-justice-findings-201718-northern-ireland-crime-survey-published-today (Public Confidence in PSNI) (accessed 22 February 2021).

George, B and Sims, P (2007) *True North: Discover Your Authentic Leadership*. New Jersey: Wiley.

Josephson Institute of Ethics. Making Ethical Decisions. Available at: www.josephsoninstitute.org (accessed 22 February 2021).

Markkula Center for Applied Ethics at Santa Clara University (2009) A Framework for Ethical Decision Making. Available at: https://www.scu.edu/ethics/ethics-resources/ethical-decision-making/a-framework-for-ethical-decision-making/ (accessed 22 February 2021).

McAuley, C (2009) Police Patrol Felt Vulnerable BBC News UK (NI), 25 August 2009. Available at: http://news.bbc.co.uk/1/hi/northern_ireland/8220888.stm (accessed 22 February 2021).

Murphy, J (2018) Policing in Northern Ireland since the Belfast Agreement Irish Times, 30 March 2018. Available at: https://www.irishtimes.com/news/crime-and-law/policing-in-northern-ireland-since-the-belfast-agreement-1.3445634 (accessed 22 February 2021).

Patten, C (1999) *A New Beginning: Policing in Northern Ireland: The Report of the Independent Commission on Policing for Northern Ireland* (Recommendation 3). London: HMSO.

Peterson, J B (2019) *12 Rules for Life: An Antidote to Chaos.* London: Penguin.

PSNI (2020) Use of Force Statistics, PSNI Dated 19 June 2020.

Topping, J R (2016) Accountability, Policing and the Police Service of Northern Ireland: Local Practice, Global Standards?, in: Lister, S and Rowe, M (eds) *Accountability of Policing (Routledge Frontiers of Criminal Justice).* Oxon: Routledge.

13 Developing a learning culture and environment

Julie Brierley

CHAPTER OBJECTIVES

This chapter will help you:

- gain insight about the characteristics of learning organisations;
- consider the benefits of creating a learning culture and environment in the police service;
- explore how to create a learning culture and environment and the some of the challenges;
- understand some theories of learning and reflect on how to enhance your approach to learning.

What is a learning organisation?

In my role as a learning and organisational development professional, I believe that when considering the learning culture and environment in any organisation it is helpful to start by exploring what the characteristics are of a learning organisation. When looking at influencing the culture and environment there is a need to look at the organisation holistically as a complete system. By understanding what a learning organisation does and the way it supports its people to learn and develop, it becomes easier to create a learning culture and environment in organisations.

The Chartered Institute for Personnel Development (CIPD) in their research, titled *Driving the New Learning Organisation: How to Unlock the Potential of Learning and Development*, conducted between 2013 and 2016, with senior leaders and workers from over 55 countries describe, *'those leaders that were driving a learning organisation will unlock potential that will lead to sustainable business results'* (CIPD, 2017, p 2). This report cites (Senge, 1990) who described a learning organisation as *'a group of people working together collectively to enhance their capabilities to create results they really care about'.*

CIPD (2017) elaborate about what organisations can do to create a learning culture and environment and explain the link between creating a people-led organisational model and helping the organisation to innovate, survive and thrive.

> *A living and learning organisational ecosystem that intelligently facilitates the performance and learning of its entire people population, continuously transforming itself. It is agile and fluid in nature, with the ability to move beyond learning interventions by learning at an organisational level. It is a dynamic and trusted, people-led organisational model that allows people to 'grow and glow' through a common purpose, the respect of knowledge and the analysis, development and acquisition of knowledge, so that it can innovate fast enough to survive and thrive in a rapidly changing environment.*
>
> (CIPD, 2017, p 16)

Other organisational development theories make a similar link between the commitment to become a learning organisation, continuous learning and the ability to transform, explaining that *'Those [organisations] committed to becoming a learning organisation in which learning is continuous and is part of the business, enable the organisation to continuously transform itself'* (Marchington, M and Wilkinson, A 2003, p 371).

> *Workplaces need to invest in the learning and development of the workforce to stay future fit in a complex and competitive world of work. Creating a supportive environment for learning is an important part of ensuring employees and the wider organisation has the right capabilities to adapt and respond to challenges in an agile and effective way.*
>
> (CIPD, 2020, Learning Skills at Work, p 29)

In my role as a learning and development practitioner and senior leader in policing over the last three decades, I have seen a change in the learning culture and environment as the police service has moved away from the twentieth-century legacy of pseudo-military residential police training centres and culture, towards creating workplace training, learning and development services with a more modern culture to support learners.

The culture of learning is still evolving in policing and the environment in each police force varies with differing structures and resources. Generally, the responsibility for learning tends to be centrally managed and delivered from an in-house training or learning and development function with core and specialist trainers delivering learning events. Some police services have outsourced some elements of learning and development to third-party training providers. There is often a prevailing culture in policing that the responsibility for organisational learning is owned by the designated learning and development provider but this type of centralised structural and functional approach to learning provision in policing does not align with the characteristics that are prevalent in learning organisations, in so much as there is scant evidence in police organisations that there is a culture of shared responsibility for organisational learning or workplace learning provision that that is agile and fluid in nature.

There is however an emerging leadership vision in the police service that aspires to invest into the education and development of its people to capitalise on the benefits that can be achieved by having a workforce that has the right knowledge, skills and behaviours for modern policing. The Association of Police and Crime Commissioners and the National Police Chiefs Council have articulated their strategic intent to support police education and professional development of the workforce. The drivers for this are to develop and enhance the skills and capabilities for modern-day policing and to gain recognition of the professional role of people working in policing with accredited qualifications.

> *The service provided is critically reliant on the quality of its people. It needs to be delivered by a professional workforce equipped with the skills and capabilities necessary for policing in the 21st century. It is also clear many individuals now have different work and career aspirations and needs. This has to be taken into account with the workforce model and supporting police education and professional development frameworks that are developed to ensure the police service attracts a representative mix of people with the right skills, knowledge and potential, behaviours and values to deliver the policing vision.*
> (Association of Police and Crime Commissioners and National Police Chiefs Council, Policing Vision 2025, 2016, p 8)

This strategic vision paints the picture of a diverse workforce that will be motivated to see policing as a professional career with opportunities to develop and diversify throughout their career. To bring this strategic vision to life, police leaders and others will need to consider what changes to the culture and environment are needed to create a learning organisation capable of fostering a universal responsibility in everyone working in the organisation.

REFLECTIVE PRACTICE

- Considering the characteristics of a learning organisation. From your perspective what do you think the people listed below *can do* to help a universal approach to create a learning culture and environment?

    o   Senior Leaders can ...

    o   Supervisors/Team Leaders can ...

    o   Employees can ...

    o   Learning and development leaders and practitioners can ...

The benefits of creating a learning culture and environment in the police service

Martin, Hartley et al (2019) in their research commissioned by the Mayor of London Office for Policing and Crime (MOPAC) and The Open University Centre for Policing Research and Learning articulate compelling benefits for investing into workforce development and creating a learning culture and environment:

> Dealing with increasingly complex environments in policing requires different ways of doing things which involves the generation of new knowledge and skills. Embedding Learning and Development (L&D) within Policing is therefore critical to ensure that the service has the capacity and capability to effectively manage this change. Policing Vision 2025 sets out the challenges that the police service will face up to and beyond this point and suggests that to meet these there is a necessity for workforce development. Focusing on workforce development will enable the service to engage in effective planning and organisational change required to implement Vision 2025. It will also ensure that the uplift in numbers of new recruits who will be entering the service imminently and over the coming years will be given the correct support and knowledge, so that they are equipped to undertake their role as front-line officers. It is imperative with this uplift that police services take the opportunity to embed new L and D processes to ensure longer term change. It will also create the environment to ensure that the rest of the workforce can progress and grow within the service. To achieve the changes required, embedding Learning and Development at the core of the organisation is essential. Organisations can inhibit or support the learning process. L&D has often been viewed as the volume or availability of training, whereas it should be focused on building the capacity of the organisation to have an enhanced ability to learn and change.
>
> (Martin, Hartley et al, 2019, Implementing Transformation in Police Learning and Development Project: Appendix B)

The MOPAC research clearly references the *Policing Vision 2025* aspirations and goes further to articulate the critical need for policing to embed learning and development at the core of the organisation to achieve that vision. This research presents a compelling business case and catalyst for policing leaders to create a learning culture and environment in the police service. This suggests the future outcomes that are desired within the vision statement are dependent upon the service being able to enhance the capability to learn and change.

Some learning organisations measure impact and benefits against business metrics that are focused on profit, productivity, growth or transformation. In policing, these types of business metrics are not in typical use, so the impact and economic value of learning and development can be difficult to demonstrate. There is a need to consider what may be more relevant metrics to describe the impact and value of learning and development.

Aligning the metrics to the *Policing Vision 2025* aspirations of improving attraction, retention, capabilities and transformation would provide a relevant performance framework for the police service. The benefits can be correlated with the desired policing vision outcomes. There are a range of the desired performance benefits and impact that can be achieved by enhancing the learning culture and environment.

Benefits and impact:

- Greater attraction and retention of people. Providing workplace development to equip them with the knowledge and skills to undertake diverse roles throughout their career motivates people to join the organisation and stay.

- Reduction of staff turnover costs. Supporting the workforce with opportunities to grow and develop their skills throughout their career improves retention and reduces the cost of recruiting, equipping, training and developing replacements.

- A workforce with the right knowledge, skills, capability and behaviours for twenty-first-century policing. This will create more capacity and capability to deal with the complex requirements and demands on the police service.

- An empowered workforce that is innovative and creative with its ways of working. By being supported to practice critical thinking, problem solving and evidence-based learning to respond to the needs of communities.

- Managers and learning and development practitioners collaborating to create a blended approach to coaching, learning and development that is in the workplace and within the flow of work activity.

- Reduction of an over-reliance on formal training and development events that abstract people from the workplace and need to be scheduled often months in advance, creating delays for learners to receive the development they need.

- Opportunities to redistribute training budgets to focus on workforce development programmes that will generate new knowledge, skills, behaviours and attitudes.

- Higher levels of confidence, productivity and deployment in the workplace to support the need to create more organisational capability and capacity to meet the demands on the service.

- Agile and responsive learning solutions to develop the workforce to rapidly adopt and implement changes in business processes, legislation and organisational priorities.

- A range of curated on-line learning materials that are available 24/7 from any location, supporting an embedded learning approach throughout the whole organisation and creating an appetite to learn and develop in the flow of work.

- Opportunities to develop managers and staff as coaches to create enhanced capacity and skills that will support learning opportunities and feedback and consequently the performance and capability of their teams.

Long-term benefits

College of Policing's (2020) *Future Operating Environment* report outlines a range of forecast scenarios, challenges and demands upon policing up to 2040. The report has been written with the goal of exploring what actions should be taken by police leaders now, to prepare the service for the challenges that lie ahead. Taking cognisance of this report will help the police service consider what it needs to start doing now to get to where it wants to be in relation to the learning culture and environment and what capabilities it needs the workforce to have. The next generation of officers and staff will need more diverse knowledge and skills, so there are compelling benefits of creating a learning culture and environment that will support the future needs of the police service.

> *As new technologies develop and converge, many of the demands on policing will become increasingly novel and complex, necessitating a more adaptive workforce with a more diverse set of skills and knowledge. A key challenge will be blending advanced technical skills (eg, digital forensics) with interpersonal skills such as empathy, creativity and collaboration.*
>
> (College of Policing, 2020, p 9)

> *As working lives lengthen and the workplace undergoes major changes, including becoming more virtual, job-related training will become almost as important to people in their mid-and-later life as at the beginning of their career. This will require policing to move to a model where training and reskilling opportunities are available throughout people's careers.*
>
> (College of Policing, 2020, p 29)

The long-term benefits of creating a new learning culture and environment now will be seen by a growth in confidence and a positive change in the skills, behaviours and capabilities across the workforce that not only keeps up with the emerging demands on the service, but also looks ahead to predict future learning needs. The return on the investment will incrementally be seen in performance data relating to operational performance, workforce development, staff engagement, well-being and retention. It would be short-sighted of the police service to miss the benefits and outcomes especially in the context of its aspirations to optimise the critical role the workforce will play in achieving the future vision.

REFLECTIVE PRACTICE

- From your perspective what are the key benefits of investing to create a learning culture and environment in policing or in your organisation?

- What do you think the challenges may be to achieving these benefits?

Creating a learning culture and environment in policing

While there is wide range of research into the characteristics and benefits of learning organisations, there is less guidance about how to create an organisational learning culture and environment.

> When individuals are asked if an organisation has a learning culture, they often say yes. But those same organisations are far more likely to be prioritising formal training and knowledge transfer activities rather than reflective, transformational activities ... if creating a culture for learning is interpreted as steering individuals to a fixed way of learning with little flexibility, this may not lead to better learning outcomes. Systems thinking, collaborative inquiry and continuous improvement are also important.
>
> (CIPD, 2020, Changing Learning Cultures, p 11)

As a learning and development professional in the police service, I am a strong advocate for creating a learning culture and environment, but I know that the learning and development department cannot have the sole responsibility to create this. To create a learning organisation there is a need for learning to become everybody's business. It is not just learning and development practitioners that have the responsibility for delivering learning, it is also for leaders and managers to take responsibility to develop the knowledge, skills and capability of their teams.

The enabling factors for realising the *Policing Vision 2025* and creating the desired culture will require a clear and deliberate learning strategy. The strategic intent from the vision statement proves there is a commitment to create a learning culture and environment within the police service to develop people with the right skills, knowledge and potential, behaviours and values to deliver the policing vision.

Achieving a universal commitment to support this strategy requires clear and consistent engagement with the workforce so that operational policies and practices are consistent with the strategy and can be operationalised across the entire organisation. A good approach to workforce engagement is by having open dialogue and inquiry with leaders, managers and the workforce to explain the ambition and priorities in relation to creating a learning culture and environment and to listen to their feedback. This doesn't need to be an academic, philosophical or a rigid inquiry and is likely be more informative if eased by a series of open and semi-structured discussions that provide the opportunity to probe into the organisation's learning culture and environment. The value of early engagement is critical to gaining insight into the existing culture and environment and how it could be improved. There are four important engagement questions to be explored to develop a new and agreed strategy to create a learning culture and environment.

1. Where are we now?
2. Where do we want to be?
3. How can we get there?
4. How will we know we have succeeded?

Transforming the learning culture requires an innovative approach, one that does not rely on a centralised responsibility for learning but instead creates the environment where everyone sees the value of workplace learning and takes responsibility to develop themselves and others around them. This universal approach to learning at work requires a flexible approach to learning, whereby developing the workforce is achieved with formal learning as well as from workplace experiential learning, reflective practice and seeking and acting on feedback.

Senior leaders and managers can drive the new learning culture by:

- encouraging people to learn in the workplace by doing and seeking feedback;
- providing a safe environment for people to take risks, make mistakes and learn from experience without fear of negative consequences;
- rewarding innovation and creative problem solving;
- using performance discussions as an opportunity to reflect and learn with teams and individuals;
- being role models for the learning culture and environment;
- developing their own knowledge, skills and behaviours to coach and develop their teams;
- encouraging people to take accountability for their own development;
- taking an interest in finding out what their teams have learnt either formally or informally;
- creating conversations that encourage reflection about what they have learnt and how they are using that learning in the workplace.

Learning and development teams can drive the new learning culture by:

- creating learning environments and materials that provide a positive learner experience and encourage ongoing self-directed learning;
- designing and supporting the use of experiential learning and social learning, for example, problem solving scenarios, simulations of crime scenes, role playing and multi-agency learning events;

- aligning learning materials and objectives to roles and skills profiles to make learning relevant to responsibilities and skills needed for roles and ranks;
- adopting teaching methods that encourage learners to ask questions, apply critical thinking, practice skills, seek feedback, reflect on the experience and consider what went well and how they can improve;
- being innovative and creative to design and provide learning that can be accessed not just from a traditional classroom or training venue but also can be accessed using technology, in the flow of work, at home or other environments where the learner has time and space to access learning resources;
- learning and development practitioners having responsibility to provide guidance on or about formal and informal learning to managers and to support managers to develop their knowledge, skills and tools so that they can create a learning culture and environment in the workplace.

The organisational strategy, budget, technology and workforce plans can enable the new learning culture by supporting:

- investment into learning to be distributed across the organisation to give line managers, leaders, workplace tutors, coaches and mentors the skills, time and responsibility to develop a new workplace culture and the growth mindset that supports learning in the flow of work;
- access to learning opportunities through a range of technology, formal and informal learning, coaching, mentoring and development activities;
- education and learning plans to be aligned to the knowledge, skills and behavioural needs and priorities of the organisation;
- learning to be tailored to be role specific and relevant to the ever-increasing diversity of the workforce mix;
- learning programmes to be co-curated, designed, delivered and supported by learning tutors, subject matter experts, digital technicians, not just from policing but from other sectors with expertise, experience and insight of the behaviours, knowledge and skills to be developed;
- structures, systems and processes to identify workforce development needs and create an organisational learning culture and environment will become less centralised and more universal;
- budget plans for learning to be longer term to enable front loading the investment for now, to realise the return on investment across the medium to longer term.

The shared responsibility approach of a learning organisation is a culture shift and there will undoubtedly be several challenges to creating the new learning culture and environment within the police service.

> *Creating a consistent vision for learning in siloed or dispersed organisations is likely to be challenging.*
>
> (CIPD, 2020, Creating Learning Cultures p 11)

Some of the challenges in creating a learning culture and environment to be considered are as follows.

- There may be a lack of support from leaders and managers who do not see developing their teams as a priority or as their responsibility.

- Leaders and managers may see learning activity as a budget cost rather than an investment that improves performance.

- Managers may view learning activity as an abstraction from the workplace.

- Managers and learning practitioners may fear that they do not have the skills that are required to design, develop and deliver learning solutions that can be accessed through technology or in the workplace.

- Learning practitioners may be worried their roles may become redundant as more learning and development is accessed in the workplace or is self-directed.

Leaders, managers and learning and development practitioners will need to collaborate and adapt their knowledge and skills to overcome the challenges and achieve the new learning culture and environment. There will be a new blend of learning activity and responsibilities that will make learning and development more creative, innovative and flexible. Managers and learning and development practitioners should be recognised for their expertise in workforce development and be supported with the right tools, technology and their own development to fulfil their critical role in developing the workforce.

> *Police leaders will need a more diverse toolkit of skills, experiences and resources, including the ability to anticipate and prepare for emerging challenges and opportunities.*
>
> Policing in England and Wales: Future Operating Environment 2040 (College of Policing, 2020, p 82)

The challenges of creating a learning culture and environment

Creating a learning culture and environment in policing must be embraced throughout the whole organisation. There are challenges to organisational culture change that must be considered and addressed.

Marchington and Wilkinson (2003, p 294) explain, *'attempting to tackle a culture shift through just one sub-system, such as training and development, is unlikely to deliver the results needed'*. They go on to advise that *'what is needed is whole-system approach in which potentially conflicting sub-systems can be aligned with the organisational strategy'*.

Converting the corporate vision and strategy into operational practice has its own challenges and barriers. The distinctions between espoused and operational policies can sometimes conflict.

> *Espoused policy can often be little more than a broad philosophical statement and is open to interpretation, whilst operational policy tends to provide a statement of direction to managers to control organisational practice. If espoused policy and operational policy are seen to be in conflict, it is often the espoused policy that is ignored, amended or downgraded in the face of conflicting pressures on organisations.*
>
> (Brewster et al, 1983, pp 63–4)

Creating a new learning culture and environment the police service needs to be driven by senior leaders but also requires a universal approach across the organisation, underpinned by the clear strategic intent (espoused policy) and organisational practices (operational policy) that are consistent and do not conflict.

Investment into learning and development amid organisational cost savings is an example of where this type of policy conflict could arise. Although you could argue from a strategic perspective that, when facing the pressures of fewer staff and resources, organisations should invest in developing the knowledge and skills of its workforce more than ever to thrive and survive. The operational policy and practice, as already seen during austerity in policing and many other organisations has been a significant diminishment of time and resources available for provision of learning and development This tends to be because of the reduced staffing levels within the operational and learning and development teams. The negative effects of cuts in training and development are felt throughout organisations over many years, and it can take decades for the recovery and reinvestment needed to create a more skilled and capable workforce to take effect.

REFLECTIVE PRACTICE

- What knowledge, skills and behaviours do you think leaders and managers need to adopt to create a learning culture?

- How do you think managers can make time to engage with and support their teams to create a learning environment?

- When do you make time to learn and develop for yourself?

How to develop skills to become a successful learner in the police service

The work of police officers and police staff is complex, unpredictable and highly skilled. A career in policing offers diverse opportunities to learn and develop in a specific role or in multiple roles; however, to effectively learn the knowledge, skills and behaviours to be effective and capable requires a deliberate commitment from you as the learner. In policing, it is expected throughout your career that you will apply critical thinking, problem solving and will take responsibility for your actions, decisions, attitude and behaviour. Your skills will constantly evolve and develop throughout your career and will in turn contribute to the capability of your team, department, organisation and policing.

Learning requires active commitment and can at times be affected by human factors such as your health, state of mind, confidence levels and organisational factors such as your workload, the behaviour of colleagues and the organisational culture and environment. Competing demands on you from family, friends and other commitments all play a part in your approach to engaging in the learning process. While these factors may be difficult to control or change there are ways to manage your own approach to learning that will support you to create a learning mindset and environment. Developing an open mind and positive attitude to learning can make all the difference to your success.

Without a deliberate and personal commitment and engagement to learning there is little chance that learning activity will be effective and will achieve benefits for individuals and the organisation. So, it is helpful to gain a better understanding of how to become an active learner and how to develop reflective practice and a growth mindset that will support your personal commitment and engagement to support your learning. Insight into a few learning models, behaviours and activities may provide you with an understanding of how you can improve your own approach.

There are a multitude of learning methods that are used in teaching and learning environments. Snape (1994, p 73) makes the distinction between pedagogical and andragogical learning methods. Pedagogical learning is mainly tutor-led and tends to include lectures, presentations, videos or other type of instructional approach. Andragogical learning is mainly a self-directed activity by the learner with a minimum amount of trainer intervention and examples of this are case studies, projects, group role play, assignments and research-based learning. These methods are suitable for different circumstances, and you may have experienced these being used in schools, colleges, universities and in the workplace. Rogers (1969, p 5), Mumford (1988, p 171) and Kolb (1995, p 49) all describe the experiential learning cycle as meaningful and effective for adult learners, arguing that there are four stages of the experiential learning process that include active and passive, concrete and abstract elements. Honey and Mumford (1988, pp 175–7) developed a learning styles questionnaire that categorises people into four types: activists, reflectors, theorists and pragmatists. It is clear there is not a one size that fits all approach to learning and I include it here to outline that as adults we all learn in different ways, but the common denominator to how effectively we learn is based on our active participation in the learning process.

Experiential learning and reflective practice

Kolb's Experiential Learning Cycle (1974) explains that learning consists of four stages.

1. Completing a concrete experience by doing an activity.
2. Reflecting on and observing the experience.
3. Forming abstract concepts by thinking about the experience.
4. Using the experience for planning future tasks.

Carmeli and Gittell (2019) argue that '*the long-term success of an organisation is dependent on its capacity to learn from experience*'. The ability to develop reflective practice enhances the ability to translate the context of work environment into a learning opportunity. Looking for and acting on feedback is an important aspect of reflective practice in the workplace. Research shows that reflective practice makes learning enjoyable and decision awareness and critical thinking are enhanced when learners share their insights with each other (Anderson et al, 2001; Johnson et al, 1999).

Gibbs's Reflective Cycle (1988) expands on the processes of learning from experience. Gibbs advocates that the reflective cycle is about 'examining experiences, and given its cyclic nature lends itself particularly well to repeated experiences, allowing you to learn and plan from things that either went well or didn't go well'. There are six stages of the Gibbs's Reflective Cycle.

1. Description of the experience.
2. Feelings and thoughts about the experience.
3. Evaluation of the experience, both good and bad.
4. Analysis to make sense of the situation.
5. Conclusion about what you learnt and what you could have done differently.
6. Action plan for how you would deal with similar situations in the future, or general changes you might find right.

Developing a growth mindset can be thought of as the mindset and beliefs that are necessary for a person to proactively engage in learning and enhance their capabilities.

Dweck (2006) describes the growth mindset as

The more you believe your abilities can change, the more likely you are to focus on developing them, knowing you have the potential to do so. Alternatively, if you believe your abilities are fixed, it is more likely that you may not strive to better yourself and instead fall victim to the idea that any difficulties you have is indicative of your inevitable inability to perform.

Adopting a growth mindset will help you to change and develop your abilities and, in practical terms, puts you in a state of mind that sees opportunities to learn and develop your abilities every day. This may be in a learning environment or during your work and interactions with others. Even when you feel you are not doing well at something, have failed an assessment, feel demotivated or feel that others around you are doing much better that you are, by adopting a growth mindset you will reflect upon what you are struggling with and find ways of learning and improving.

The GROW model (Whitmore, 1992) is a popular coaching model that encourages you to develop a growth mindset to support your development to achieve aspirational goals. This is a continuous process and can be highly effective to remain focused on developing your growth towards achieving short- and longer-term goals. The four steps for the GROW model are as follows.

1. Goal setting for the short and long terms – what do you want?
2. Reality checking to explore your current situation – where are you now?
3. Options and alternative courses of action – what could you do?
4. What is to be done and when – what will you do?

The GROW model can be used with or without a coach and is remarkably effective for building your motivation, working through a learning programme, developing a career plan, recovering from a setback, improving your performance or approaching a difficult situation.

Deliberate practice of learning is another method of learning and will enhance your ability to develop ability in the workplace. Repeated practice of any skill or task over a period enables you to develop competence and the task becomes more automatic and requires less effort to think about the component parts of the skills needed. Practice on its own does not build expertise, because once you reach a reasonable level of competence there is a tendency to maintain your ability but not improve to become an expert. If there is something you want to excel at you will need to push past the competent stage and challenge yourself to improve to a higher level of competency by incorporating reflection and feedback into your practice.

> *The theory of deliberate practice is that development of expertise requires incorporating a self-reflective feedback loop into the skill delivery or development (i.e. practice) process, rather than simply performing a task repetitively until mastered.*
>
> (Ericcson and Poole, 2017)

Deliberate practice is often used by people who are the absolute best in their field to learn and develop their skills and abilities to the highest level. The deliberate practice model is based on six principles.

1. Get motivated to push past obstacles, make sure you are willing to devote time and effort to improve with deliberate practice.
2. Set specific and realistic goals to push your boundaries in small steps to consistently expand your abilities.
3. Break out of your comfort zone, try experimenting with new techniques until you break through your barriers and see improvements.
4. Be consistent and persistent, regular and high intensity practice sessions maintain momentum in building expertise.
5. Seek feedback, self-assessment or from others to pinpoint your strengths and weaknesses to move through competency levels from good to great.
6. Schedule intensive and deliberate practice sessions of one to two hours per day, three to five days a week with scheduled recovery time in between.

(Ericcson and Poole, 2017)

These suggested models of learning can be used for improving your success as a learner and in any areas and will of course be effective in the policing context.

REFLECTIVE PRACTICE

Take a moment to reflect on the learning theories that have been outlined.

- Note down a recent learning activity that you have engaged in (this can be work related or a personal learning activity).
- What reflective activity do you do now that helps you to learn?
- Note down three things that you think you can do to improve your success as a learner in the workplace?
- On a scale of 1–5 (with 5 being the highest), to what extent do you think these three things will make your learning experience more successful?

Chapter summary

Creating a learning culture and environment in the police service will be a critical success factor in achieving the strategic vision and ensuring the organisation and its workforce has the right capabilities to meet the needs of the service and the public it serves.

The Policing Vision 2025 talks about the service being '*critically reliant on the quality of its people*' and one of the challenges the service needs to address is that it needs '*a professional workforce equipped with the skills and capabilities necessary for policing in the 21st century*'. The vision prescribes that the police service will, '*establish a methodology and framework which helps practitioners across policing contribute towards building knowledge and standards based on evidence*' (Association of Police and Crime Commissioners and National Police Chiefs Council, 2016).

The empirical research that characterises learning organisations and describes the benefits will introduce an evidence-based methodology and framework to create a new learning culture and environment for the police service. The benefits of learning organisations are clearly linked to improved performance and capability of the workforce and for the success and sustainability of the organisation to meet the changing challenges and demands placed upon it.

Enabling a universal approach to create a learning culture and environment is a strong characteristic of a learning organisation and needs to be a collective responsibility of senior leaders, managers and learning and development teams. People working in policing will also be expected to take responsibility for their own professional development, but they will only be able to do this effectively if the culture and environment enable them to do that.

Police organisations are complex and can be traditionally siloed and operate within dispersed functions and geographical locations. It is important for the leadership to lead the way in developing the universal culture so that there is a shared consistency of understanding and effort around the priority to become a learning organisation, drive the learning outcomes and gain the benefits. If the police service is to create a learning organisation it will be the collective responsibility of senior leaders, managers, learning and development professionals to drive forward the new learning culture.

The strategy and plans to create a learning culture and environment can be developed by positive engagement with senior leaders and the people who work within the service. It is important that the entire workforce knows that learning and development is valued and is linked to organisational priorities and performance. The strategic narrative needs to be constant and clear about the future vision and aspirations to create the organisational characteristics of a learning organisation. Workforce engagement can be achieved by supplying information and guidance to people, the expectation that learning and development at work is part of everyone's responsibility and by listening to their feedback, how they can contribute to create a learning culture and environment.

Creating culture change in organisations is challenging. The police service is by nature an organisation that is both proactive and reactive to changes in the surrounding environment. At the heart of the organisation is a command-and-control character that is underpinned by operating procedures and plans, structures, roles and responsibilities that work within statutory frameworks, legislation and highly regulated protocols. The ability to drive internal transformational culture change can be challenging in the police service and requires a clear forward-thinking strategy and plans to be developed that will seek business benefits that are long term and may be well beyond the career span of those who must lead and implement the changes.

There is no definitive guide, action plan or toolkit for organisations to create a new learning culture and environment but the police service will do well to collaborate and learn from other forward-thinking organisations and to consider the research from the CIPD and MOPAC that will help the service to become a learning organisation that can exploit the value of an adaptive work force that can continually improve and develop. This will undoubtedly require the police service to transform from its legacy and current learning structures and cultures to becoming a new learning organisation that has learning not just at the core of the organisation but also embedded in every part of the organisation

The police service tends to describe its approach to learning using traditional terminology such as training, learning and development, continuous professional development and upskilling. Most of the learning relates to formal training events conducted in a classroom or other type of training venue. Other types of development activity in the police service are in the form of coaching, mentoring, shadowing, incident debriefing, lateral development, performance reviews and temporary attachments to develop a role-specific experience. The new learning culture and environment will include more learning in the flow of work and managers and teams will work together to create learning and feedback opportunities as part of the routine of work. Informal and self-directed learning will also be more prevalent and will be supported and encouraged across the workforce.

As the service considers where it wants to be in relation to its learning culture, it can reflect on the changes it has already experienced with its learning models. With each generation of recruits, the ways of teaching and getting knowledge and skills change, attitudes and behaviours evolve and this awareness, coupled with the rapid advancement of technology, means that the learning culture and environment in the police service will need to change to meet the needs of the service as well as the individuals within it.

Concluding thoughts

In this fast-changing world, learning needs to evolve and it must be accessible, agile and flexible. To respond, organisations need to change where, when and how learning is delivered: increasingly in the flow of work, not in venues; via digital technologies which enable learning to be available anytime and anywhere; and through curation, not just creation, harnessing the growth of rich, readily available online content. Moreover, emerging technologies such as augmented and virtual reality, artificial intelligence and mobile solutions enable personalised and targeted learning that impacts performance. While organisations and business leaders focus increasingly on productivity and adaptability, they need to provide learning solutions that support these outcomes directly (CIPD, 2020, Learning Skills at Work, p 5).

For many years the police service has talked about developing a learning culture but the challenges of changing the culture of an organisation takes time, sustained commitment and leadership. There is a simple question to be asked: is there sufficient appetite from police leaders to transform the approach to learning in the police service to enable a culture that values and encourages continuous learning in the workplace?

If the answer to that question is yes, it will require leaders to be willing to adopt new thinking and innovation to create a learning environment that enables the workforce throughout their careers to learn in the flow of work. Police leaders will need to be willing to accept that learning and development professionals will be their advisors and that there is wealth of expertise that can be tapped into to enable a learning culture if they are willing to invest the time and effort to transform the learning environment for their workforce.

Some professions such as health and social care are required to keep a record of their continuous professional development throughout their careers to maintain their licence to practice in their professional roles. These professions provide protected learning time and recognise that reflective practice and learning activity is as important as other work activity to ensure that the workforce remain skilled and motivated to be the best version of themselves and to perform at the highest level. The culture towards learning and development in a learning organisation is demonstrated by the pride within the workforce and the ways that performance is measured and recognised.

Many organisations have invested in technology and digital learning as an effective and efficient way of providing accessible learning to their workforces and to encourage continuous development in the workplace. While before the Covid-19 pandemic many organisations would have said they could not use digital learning for their statutory training requirements, they had no choice but to do exactly that. The innovation and creativity of learning and development professionals and supervisors moved traditional classroom-based learning to online learning events with interactive videos, recorded and live tutorials, quizzes and games and assessment tools to engage learners and to ensure that the workforce could remain accredited and skilled. Many organisations have been able to extend their reach to their workforce by creating more online learning opportunities and making this available 24/7 on a range of portable devices such as mobile phones, tablets and laptops.

REFLECTIVE PRACTICE

To create a learning culture and environment in policing there will be a requirement to ensure that budget, technology, resources and protected learning time for continuous professional development will be available throughout the career life cycle in a similar way to other professions.

- With the backdrop of budget and staffing constraints, how can the police service ensure that it re-shapes its budget and creates sufficient capacity to enable protected learning time to be available to the entire workforce?

- What new ideas, technology and other innovation can be adopted from other organisations to enable a culture of continuous professional development in the police service?

References

Association of Police and Crime Commissioners and National Police Chiefs Council (2016) Policing Vision 2025. Available at www.npcc.police.uk/documents/PolicingVision.pdf (accessed 20 February 2021).

Anderson, T, Howe, C, Soden, R, Halliday, J and Low, J (2001) Peer Interaction and the Learning of Critical Thinking Skills in Further Education Students. *Instructional Science*, 29: 1.e32.

Brewster, C et al (1983) Industrial Relations Policy, in Marchington, M and Wilkinson, A. *People Management and Development*. London: Chartered Institute of Personnel and Development.

Carmeli, A and Gittell, J H (2009) High-Quality Relationships, Psychological Safety and Learning from Failures in Work Organisations. *Journal of Organisational Behavior*, 30(6): 709–729.

CIPD (2017) Driving the New Learning Organisation: How to Unlock the Potential of L&D. Available at: www.towardsmaturity.org/learningorg2017 (accessed 2 August 2021)

CIPD (2020a) *Creating Learning Cultures: Assessing the Evidence*. London: Chartered Institute of Personnel and Development.

CIPD (2020b) *Learning and Skills at work 2020*. London: Chartered Institute of Personnel and Development.

College of Policing (2020) Policing in England and Wales: Future Operating. Environment 2040. Available at: www.college.policing.uk/article/preparing-policing-future-challenges-and-demands (accessed 2 August 2021).

Dweck, C S (2006) *Mindset: The New Psychology of Success*. London: Random House.

Ericcson, A and Pool, R (2017) *Peak: How All of Us Can Achieve Extraordinary Things*. London: Vintage.

Johnson, D W and Johnson, R T (1999) *Learning Together and Alone: Cooperative, Competitive and Individualistic Learning*, 5th ed. Boston: Allyn and Bacon.

Kolb, D, Osland, J and Rubin, I (1995) *Organisational Behaviour: An Experiential Approach*, 6th ed. New Jersey: Prentice-Hall.

Marchington, M and Wilkinson, A (2002) *People Management and Development*. London: Chartered Institute of Personnel and Development.

Martin, D, Hartley, J, Khalil, L and Harding, R (2019) Strategic Narrative for Learning and Development: Mayor of London Office for Policing and Crime (MOPAC) and the Open University (OU) Centre for Policing Research and Learning. Available at: www.open.ac.uk/centres/policing/implementing-transformation-police-ld/outputs (accessed 2 August 2021).

Mumford, A (1998) *Enhancing Your Learning Skills in Continuous Development*. London: Institute of Personnel Management.

Rogers, C (1969) *Freedom to Learn*. Ohio: Charles and Merrill Publishing Company.

Senge, P (1990) *The Fifth Discipline: The Art and Practice of the Learning Organisation*. United States: Currency Publishing.

Snape, E, Redman, T and Bamber, G (1994) *Managing Managers: Strategies and Techniques for Human Resource Management*. Oxford: Blackwell.

Whitmore, J (1996) *Coaching for Performance Second Edition*. London: Nicholas Brearley Publishing.

Index

A
ACAS, see Advisory, Conciliation and Arbitration Service
Accident and Emergency Department, 144
accountability, 107, 174
ACPO, see Association of Chief Police Officers
Action Centred Leadership model (Adair), 85
Adair, John, 85
Adapting to Protest, 172
Advisory, Conciliation and Arbitration Service (ACAS), 101
agency, 51, 94, 230
AI, see Artificial Intelligence
alignment, crucial importance of, 213
andragogical learning, 246
apparent soft-skill, 59
appearance, 8, 10, 178
aptitude for work, 9
Armed Response Vehicle Officer (ARVO), 124
Artificial Intelligence (AI), 147
ARVO, see Armed Response Vehicle Officer
assimilation, 13–15
Association of Chief Police Officers (ACPO), 172
Association of Police and Crime Commissioners, 237
attitude for job, 9, 10
authenticity, 34

B
BAME, see black and minority ethnic
Basinka, BA, 57
Bayley, DH, 166
Belbin, Meredith, 87
  team roles, 87–89
belongingness, 11
Betari's Box, 177
Bill Bongle, 145
black and minority ethnic (BAME), 9, 11, 15–17, 23, 24, 176
  advancement within policing, 18–19
Blackwell, 156

The Blue Head, 139
'Bobby on the Beat,' 8
Bostrom, N, 147
Brearley, Nicholas, 170
British police service, 8, 11, 25
British policing model, 163
building rapport, 27, 35–37
  basic preference grid, 36
  confirmation bias, 38–39
  definition, 28
  facts and stories, 40
  fundamental attribution bias, 37–38
  really listening, 28–30
  unconscious bias, 37
  zone 1, 29
  zone 2, 29
  zone 3, 29–30, see also zone 3 listening skills, achieving rapport
'burning oil-platform,' 196

C
Call Milking Award, 145
Carmeli, A, 247
Centre for Effective Dispute Resolution, 102
Centurion misconduct database, 155
CEOP, see Child Exploitation and Online Protection command
challenging conversations, 99–100
  approaches, 104–105
    negotiating conflict, 105–106
  approaching conversation, 111–112
    preparation, 112
  benefits, 103
  consequences of not having conversations, 104
  definitions, 101–103
  hardest conversations at work, 102
  impact of effective self-awareness, 107–110
  managing upwards, 114–115
  self-awareness and values, 100–101

Steve, case study, 115
Chartered Institute for Personnel Development (CIPD), 235, 236
Chartered Institute of Managers (CMI), 101, 102
Child Exploitation and Online Protection (CEOP) command, 51, 52
The Chimp Paradox (Peters), 29, 130
Chris Patten, 224
CIPD, *see* Chartered Institute for Personnel Development
'citizens in uniform,' 163
climate of organisation
  environment for policing, 208–209
  fundamental questions, 209–210
  key challenges
    bringing staff with you, 216–217
    communication, 218
    community is foundation, 218
    enduring values in good times and bad, 215–216
    food for journey, 217
    high risk end of business, 218–219
    inner circle, 217
    keeping in touch with ground, 218
  key elements, setting climate, 210
    creating sense of common purpose, 211–212
    orientation and case building, 210–211
  structural change, policing system, 212
    case study, 213, 214
    crucial importance of alignment, 213
    shaping competencies of staff, 213–214
  structures, systems and competencies, 214–215
Clutterbuck, David, 61
CMI, *see* Chartered Institute of Managers
coach–coachee relationship, 74
coaching culture, 62–63
  approach, 59
    context, 60
  case, 63–66
  coaching *vs.* mentoring, 60–61
  critical success factors, 66–67
    emotional shift, 68–69
    relationships, 70–71
    structure, 69
  cultural change, 73–74
  making connections, 71–73
  in policing, 69–70
  professionalising service, 76–77
  team coaching, 75–76
Coalition Government, 196
Cochrane, Archie, 151
Cochrane Collaboration, 151
Code of Ethics, 101, 102, 174, 227
  Authorised Professional Practice, 174
cognitive diversity, 10, 11, 19
College of Policing, 65, 76, 77, 104, 198, 227, 240
  pilot scheme, 18
Collins, J., 186, 187, 196, 198
command-and-control culture, 11, 63, 251
common flaw, 198
Comparing Police and Crime Commissioners (CoPaCC), 189
Competency and Values Framework (CVF), 57
Compstat-like process, 208

conditional diversity, 14
confirmation bias, 38–39
Conflict Management Model, 227
conflict typologies, 108
  pros and cons, 108
congruence, 213, 219
Conley, C., 191, 200, 201
continuous professional development (CPD), 19, 123, 135, 138
Cooke, C C, 69, 70
CoPaCC, *see* Comparing Police and Crime Commissioners
co-production, 20, 24, 25
Corporate Coach Group, 32
Covey, Frank, 109
Covey, S, 29, 30
  seven habits, 110
Covey, S. R., 197
Coyle, Daniel, 102
CPD, *see* continuous professional development
crackdown–consolidation sequence, 157
Crime Survey for England and Wales, 153
criminal justice process, victim satisfaction in, 201
critical success factors, 66–67
  emotional shift, 68–69
  relationships, 70–71
  structure, 69
Crosse, 156
cultural change, 20, 24, 73, 210
The Culture Code (Coyle), 102
culture of learning, 236
custody provision, 194
CVF, *see* Competency and Values Framework

D
Daderman, AM, 57
Daily Telegragh, 77
deliberate practice of learning, 248, 249
della Porta, D, 170
difference, 14, 36, 37
The Difference 2007 (Page), 11
differentiation, 15
dispositional glasses, 38
diverse communities, 25
diversity, 9
  cognitive diversity, 10, 11, 19
  conditional diversity, 14
  'identity' diversity, 9
  neuro-diversity, 11
Dunbar's Number, 187
Durham Constabulary, 185, 188, 196, 200
Dweck, CS, 212, 247

E
EDI, *see* Equality, Diversity and Inclusivity
Edmondson, Amy, 62
effective coaching, 67, 71
effective teams, 81
  characteristics, 82–84
  five dysfunctions of team, 94
  importance of diverse inclusive teams, 97–98
  leading team under difficult circumstances, 93–97

theory, 84
    Belbin team roles, 87–89
    Harrison Assessment, 91
    John Adair's Action Centred Leadership model, 85
    Myers-Briggs theory (MBTI), 85–87
    Tuckman model of group development, 89–90
    turning under-performance into effective performance, 92
Eisenhower, Dwight D, 47, 208
emotional buy-in, 58
    National Crime Agency (NCA), 51–52
    Police Scotland, 53–55
    Police Service of Northern Ireland (PSNI), 48–50
Emotional Intelligence (Goleman), 107, 109
empathic listening, 30
empathic resonance, 41
English policing model, 162
equality, 11, 68, 211
Equality, Diversity and Inclusivity (EDI), 8, 10, 11, 16, 17
Equality Act 2010, 10
    protected characteristics, 10
Erikson, Thomas, 36
escalated force, 170, 171
ethics, values and standards, 221–223
    constant struggle, 223–225
    'Everybody's doing it' rationalisation, 229–230
    personal cost, 231–232
    to policing decisions, 225–227
        barriers, 228–229
        National Decision Model, 227–228
exclusion, 12–13
Experiential Learning Cycle (Kolb), 247
extraversion, 86

F
'Family Force,' 188
Farrell, G, 157
FBI National Executive Institute Programme, 225
feeling, 87
Feynman, Richard, 150
Fierce Conversations (Scott), 100, 105
firearms
    case study, 126–128
    culture and CPD, 137–138
    emotions in high-risk incidents, 125–126
        unlocking emotional context, 128–129
    pitfalls, 129–131
        exploring context, 131–132
    role of values, 132, 134–135
        more helpful, 133
        unhelpful, 132–133
    solutions, 135–137
    training *vs.* reality, 124–125
FirearmsDespite, 226
Fisher, R, 100, 106
Fiske, Susan, 32
five dysfunctions of team, 94
Five Elements of Emotional Intelligence (Goleman), 100, 109
Flourish (Seligman), 71
Floyd case, 7
fundamental attribution bias, 37–38

G
Garda Síochána Code of Ethics, 221
Garland, D, 166
'Generation Z' demographic, 56
Gibbs, G, 247
Gillham, PF, 170
Gittell, Jody Hoffer, 67, 247
GJP, *see* Good Judgement Project
GMP, *see* Greater Manchester Police
Goldstein, Herman, 200
Goleman, Daniel, 29, 32, 63, 65, 100, 107, 109, 189, 199, 213
    Five Elements of Emotional Intelligence, 109
'good judgement,' large-scale work on, 151
Good Judgement Project (GJP), 151
Gore-Tex, 187
Graham, Les, 193
Greater Manchester Police (GMP), 208, 211, 215
Green Bay police, 145
GROW model, 62, 248

H
Harrison Assessment, 91
Hartley, J, 238
Herriot, P, 16
high-level principles, 224, 227
HMIC, 100, 185, 188, 192, 194, 195, 197
Home Office, 10, 11, 13, 15, 211
Honey, P, 246
The Human Brand (Fiske), 32
Hungerford Massacre, 124

I
IARPA, *see* US Intelligence Advanced Research Projects Activity
ICT, 201–202
    in-house solutions, 202–203
    shaping commercial partnerships, 202
'identity' diversity, 9
inclusion, 16–17, 97
inclusivity, 8, 11, 17
Independent Advisory Groups, 20
Independent Commission on Policing, 224
independently investigated cases, 154
Independent Police Complaints Commission, 154
Initial Triage Assessment Form, 154
introversion, 86
intuition, 87
Investigating Officer's Log (IO Log), 154
involvement, 199
IO Log, *see* Investigating Officer's Log
IO Report, 154

J
judgement, 87
Jung, Carl Gustav, 37, 85
just triology, 69

K
Keeping the Peace, 172
Keller, Helen, 84

Kelly, George, 148
Kilmann, Ralph, 105
King, A., 170
Kolb, D, 246, 247

L
Labour-controlled Police Authority, 196
lack of demand, 202
laddering, 148
laddering downwards, 149, 150
laddering upwards, 149, 150
Lancashire, 200
Lancashire Constabulary, 188
L&D, see Learning and Development
Leadership 2030, 211
leadership styles, 64, 100, 202
Leadership Team Coaching (Hawkins), 75
Learning and Development (L&D), 238
learning culture and environment
   learning organisation, 235–237
     in police service, 238–239
       long-term benefits, 240
     in policing, 241–244
       challenges to organisational culture change, 244–245
       successful learner in police service, developing skills, 246–247
       experiential learning and reflective practice, 247–249
learning organisation, 235–237, 241, 250, 251
Livingstone, Iain, 53
Loader, Ian, 163
locally investigated cases, 154
'losing their mojo,' 196

M
Machiavelli, N., 196
Manning, K P, 168
Marchington, M, 245
Marks, Michael, 167
Marr, B., 186
Mayor of London Office for Policing and Crime (MOPAC), 238
MBTI, see Myers-Briggs Type Inventory
McPhail, C, 170
media coverage, 176
mentoring, 61
Monchuk, Leanne, 151
MOPAC, see Mayor of London Office for Policing and Crime
Moriarty Fallacy, 192
Mumford, A, 246
Murrow, E R, 185
Myers-Briggs theory, 85
   four dichotomies, 86
     extraversion and introversion, 86
     judgement and perception, 87
     sensing and intuition, 87
     thinking and feeling, 87
Myers-Briggs Type Inventory (MBTI), 107

N
National Crime Agency (NCA), 48, 51
   Child Exploitation and Online Protection (CEOP) command, 51, 52

National Crime Recording Standard, 152
National Decision Model (NDM), 124, 125, 174, 227–228
National Intelligence Model (NIM), 192, 200
National Police Chiefs Council, 237
National Standard for Incident Recording (NPIA), 152
'national statistics' badge, 152
Navarro, Joe, 33
NCA, see National Crime Agency
NDM, see National Decision Model
negotiated management, 170, 171
neuro-diversity, 11
neuro-linguistic programming (NLP), 28
NFA, see no further action
NIM, see National Intelligence Model
NLP, see neuro-linguistic programming
Noakes, JA, 170
no further action (NFA), 155
novelty value, 9
NPIA, see National Standard for Incident Recording

O
objectivity, 174
OCGM, see Organised Crime Group Mapping
OCGs, see Organised Crime Groups
Open University Centre for Policing Research and Learning, 238
Operation Comfort, 20–23
'order,' 169
organisational focus
   crime, 191–192
     context, 192–193
     results, 193
   ICT, 189–190
     in-house solutions, 190–191
     shaping commercial partnerships, 190
   inspection and empowerment, 194–195
   opportunities from austerity, 196–197
   promotion processes, 197–199
Organised Crime Group Mapping (OCGM), 192
Organised Crime Groups (OCGs), 127, 192
OSPRE, 19
'out-of-car experience' (Bill), 145

P
pace setters, 213
pace-setting and commanding, 189
Page, Scott, 11
Parsloe, E., 62
Patten Commission, 49, 224
Patten Report, 48, 49
Patterson, K, 103, 111
PCSO, see Police Community Support Officers
pedagogical learning, 246
Peelian principle 1, 152, 153
Peelian principles, 9, 162, 163, 200
Pemberton, C, 16
Pendleton Police Station, 211
'people person,' 1
perception, 87
persistence, 214
personal and organisational transformation

organisational background, 188–189
organisational focus
  crime, 191–193
  ICT, 189–191
  inspection and empowerment, 194–195
  opportunities from austerity, 196–197
  promotion processes, 197–199
personal focus
  learning leader, 199–201
strategy and its delivery, 186
  long-term strategy, 187–188
Personal Construct Theory, 148
personal cost, 231–232
perverse instantiation, 147, 148, 153
Peters, Steve, 29, 30, 130
plan, 186
planning cycle, 187
plan-on-a-page, 186
Plato, 148
Police and Fire Reform (Scotland) Act 2012, 55
police budgets, 196
Police Community Support Officers (PCSO), 144, 218
Police Constable Degree Apprenticeship, 76
Police Scotland, 48
  establishing single national police service, 53–55
Police Service of Northern Ireland (PSNI), 48, 221, 222, 226
  transition from RUC GC, 48–50
Police Support Units (PSUs), 161
'policing by consent,' 8, 54, 170, 176
policing purpose
  crime control, 163–164
    case study, 164–165
  moral order, 168–169
  social control, 166–167
    theory to practice, 167–168
Policing Vision 2025, 238, 241, 250
political capital, 23
POP, *see* problem-oriented policing
Porras, G., 186, 187
The Power of Now (Tolle), 31
problem-oriented policing (POP), 146, 200
professionalising service, 76–77
Professional Standards Department (PSD), 154
  Centurion System, 154
Progress Report, 154
protective equipment (PPE), 170
proximity, 65
PSD, *see* Professional Standards Department
PSNI, *see* Police Service of Northern Ireland
PSUs, *see* Police Support Units
psychological development, 138
public order
  negotiated management *vs.* escalated force, 170–171
  policy perspective, 172
    case study, 172–173
    command perception, 173–174
    theory to practice, 172
  risk, 175
    case study, 174
    command perception, 176–177
    officer perception, 177

role of policing, 162
  historical context, 162–163
  policing purpose, *see* policing purpose
  training approaches, 171
Public Prosecution Service, 232
push-pull analogy, 62

Q
quorum sensing, 157

R
Race Relations Act, 12
radical Islamic groups, 21
'rainbow' police service, 9
Randel, Amy E, 11
The Red Head, 139
Reflective Cycle (Gibbs), 247
Regulation 15/16 Notice, 154
Regulation 36 Notice, 154
'representative' population, 9
Restorative Justice (RJ), 200, 201
Roach, Jason, 153
Rogers, C, 246
Royal Ulster Constabulary officers, 157

S
Scarman Report, 13
Schein, E, 209
Scott, S., 100, 145
SCP, *see* Situational crime prevention
Select Committee on Home Affairs, 208
self-awareness and values, 100–101
Seligman, Martin, 71
sense of abandonment, 155
sensing, 87
Sergeant role, 19
Serious Crime Division, 216
The 7 Habits of Highly Effective People (Covey), 100, 110
Sex Discrimination Act, 1975, 12
SFC, *see* Strategic Firearms Commander
Silver Control Room, 22
Sinek, S., 59, 195
Situational crime prevention (SCP), 146
situational glasses, 38
Snape, E, 246
snoopervising, 197
sods law, 127
soft skills, 141–142
state of 'flow,' 29
Strategic Firearms Commander (SFC), 123
strategy, 186
'street-craft' skills, 161
struggle, 109, 224
superforecasters, 152
Super Injunction, 231
Surrounded by Idiots (Erikson), 36
Syed, M., 200

T
TacMed, *see* Tactical Medical Support
Tactical Firearms Commander (TFC), 124, 127

Tactical Medical Support (TacMed), 127
team coaching, 75–76
Tetlock, Philip, 151
Tetlock approach, 151
TFC, see Tactical Firearms Commander
Theory Y, 197
'Thin Blue Line,' 8
thinking, 87
Thomas, Kenneth, 105
  conflict modes, 105
Thomas-Kilmann model of approaches to conflict, 117
Thompson, Simon, 144, 149
Tolle, Eckhart, 31
Tomlinson, Ian, 172
tone-deaf officers, 150
traditional training, 66
Tuckman, Bruce, 89
  model of group development, 89
    forming stage, 89–90
    norming stage, 90
    performing stage, 90
    storming stage, 90

U
UK policing
  access all areas, 20
  belongingness and uniqueness, 11
    assimilation, 13–15
    differentiation, 15
    exclusion, 12–13
    inclusion, 16–17
    futile quest, 8–9
      emotional connection, 9–10
    hire for attitude, 10–11
    personal reflections, 23–24
unconscious bias, 36, 37, 61
uniform carriers, 156
uniqueness, 11
Ury, W, 100, 106

US Intelligence Advanced Research Projects Activity (IARPA), 151

V
victim satisfaction, criminal justice process, 201
vision, 186
voluntary severance, 196, 230
Vulnerable Persons Division, 216

W
Waddington, PAJ, 2, 163, 170
Whitmore, J, 62
Whyte, WF, 167
'Wicked Thinkers,' 11
Wilkinson, A, 245
wise policing
  Bill Bongle, 145
  expressions of appreciation, 142–143
  extra mile, 144–147
  goals, 147–150
  obstacles, 152
    charity begins at home, 153–155
    failing attitude test, 156–157
    killing cubs, 156
    outcomes, 152–153
  prediction, 150–152
  soft skills, 141–142
Wray, M., 62

Z
zone 3 listening skills, achieving rapport, 30–31
  asking right questions, 34
  authenticity, 34
  being present, 31
  body language, 33–34
  eye contact, building trust, 32–33
  matching mood, 33
  reflection, 35
  warmth and competence, 32
Zydziunaite, V, 107